A
DANGEROUS
GRACE

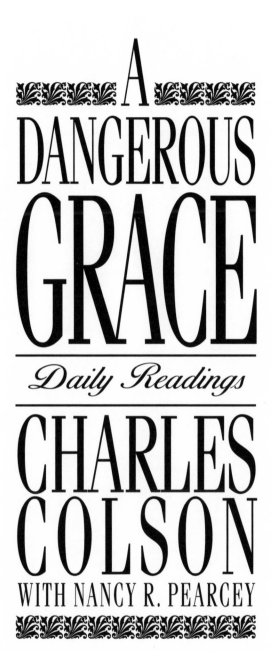

A
DANGEROUS
GRACE

Daily Readings

CHARLES
COLSON

WITH NANCY R. PEARCEY

WORD PUBLISHING
Dallas·London·Vancouver·Melbourne

Library of Congress Cataloging-in-Publication Data

Colson, Charles W.
A dangerous grace: daily readings by Charles Colson
     p. cm.
    ISBN 0-8499-1171-0
    1. Christian life. 2. Devotional calendars. I. Title.
  BV4501.2.C6445 1994
242'.2—dc20   94-33467
                                                        CIP

Printed in the United States of America.

4 5 6 7 8 9 RRD 9 8 7 6 5 4 3 2 1

ACKNOWLEDGMENTS

Heartfelt thanks to the various people who helped bring this book together. Free-lance editors Beth Spring and Evelyn Bence assisted with the initial selection and editing of the entries. At Prison Fellowship, Anne Morse selected *BreakPoint* commentaries; Cathy Nolan and Bonnie Burt typed and retyped entries at each stage, while Karen Scantlin coordinated the process. Thanks, finally, to Alyse Lounsberry, editor at Word Publishing, for guiding the book through production.

INTRODUCTION

ABOUT FOUR YEARS AGO, WHEN I first began to work with Chuck Colson, I told a close relative—I'll call him Barry—the news of my new job and my new boss.

Immediately he broke into derisive laughter.

Barry was a student radical in the 1960s and 70s, and for him Chuck Colson was indelibly stamped as a Watergate felon, a political scoundrel.

As an ardent secularist, Barry had no conception of the transforming power of God's grace. He simply assumed that Mr. Colson's much-publicized religious conversion was a farce, a deceptive gloss. But for the hundreds of thousands who have read Colson's books, there emerges a very different picture of the man. Reading the story of his conversion, and of his ministry through Prison Fellowship, we are struck by how *thoroughly* he was converted. What stands out vividly is the power of God to radically change the human heart.

And not only the heart but also the will, the mind—the whole person. The body of Colson's work reveals a person transformed in every area of his life, every part of his thinking. When God gets a grip on our lives, nothing is left untouched.

That's what makes His grace dangerous. It unsettles our preconceived ideas, uproots our ingrained habits, redirects our deepest desires. When we give ourselves to God, He becomes our security—but He is never "safe." He is determined to make us the very best we can be, and He will never let us rest comfortably in our weaknesses and sins. He works ceaselessly to remake us into the image and character of Christ.

Modern Christians often limp along with a truncated understanding of divine grace. We think of faith in therapeutic terms, as a way of meeting emotional needs, a means for coping with the stresses of life. But God wants to give us a whole *new* life. He wants to tear down the mental grids that limit our thinking and give us a fresh perspective—one that transforms every area of life.

This is what the Scripture means when it teaches the Lordship of Christ: that He rules not only over our own lives but also over all creation. As His people, we are called to view all of creation from a biblical point of view—politics, science, social life, economics, the arts and culture. In short, we are called to develop a full-orbed Christian world-view.

And nothing less is capable of meeting the challenge of living in the modern secular world. The great Dutch Calvinist Abraham Kuyper said the battle facing Christians today is between comprehensive "life systems"—in which "principle must bear witness against principle, world-view against world-view, spirit against spirit."

This is the burden of Chuck Colson's life and writings: to develop a biblically-grounded world-view. I pray that this selection of his work, arranged in daily readings, will convey a sense of God's unsettling yet exhilarating power to remake us in both heart and mind.

A sense of God's dangerous grace.

Nancy R. Pearcey
Executive Editor, *BreakPoint*
Washington, D. C., 1994

TABLE OF CONTENTS

CONTENTS

CONTENTS

CONTENTS

CONTENTS

Monday

GOD—OR A LUNATIC?

THE ESSENCE OF CHRISTIANITY is summed up in one mind-boggling sentence: *Jesus Christ is God* (John 10:30).

Not just part of God . . . or sent by God . . . or related to God. *He is God.*

The more I grappled with those words, the more they exploded a lot of comfortable old notions I had floated through life with. C. S. Lewis put it bluntly: For Christ to have talked as He talked, lived as He lived, died as He died, He was either God or a raving lunatic.

There was my choice, as simple, stark, and frightening as that. No one had ever thrust this truth at me in such a direct way. I'd been content to think of Christ as an inspired prophet and teacher who had walked the sands of the Holy Land. If one thinks of Christ as no more than that, I reasoned, then Christianity is like taking a sugar-coated placebo once a week on Sunday morning.

But even atheists concede that Christ's coming changed the course of history. He was a man without power in any worldly sense, no money, no armies, no weapons, and yet His coming altered the political alignments of nations. Millions have followed His promises and words.

No work of literature has even begun to approach the endurance of the Scriptures which record Christ's life and have the same vitality today as they did nearly two thousand years ago. Magnificent churches, in which are invested centuries of labor and treasure, have been built as altars to Him.

Could all this be the result of a lunatic's work, or even the result of one man's work?

No. The weight of evidence became more and more overwhelming to me. 🔳

PIERCING
THE ARMOR

Tuesday

O NE GRAY, OVERCAST EVENING, I sought out my friend, Tom
Phillips. He read aloud the chapter on pride from C. S. Lewis's
Mere Christianity. That one chapter ripped through the protective armor in which I had unknowingly encased myself for
forty-two years. Of course, I had not known God. *How could I?*
I had been concerned with myself. *I* had done this and that, *I*
had achieved, *I* had succeeded. In those brief moments while
Tom read, I saw myself as I never had before. And the picture
was ugly.

"Would you like to pray together, Chuck?" Tom asked, closing his Bible.

Startled, I emerged from my deep thoughts. "Sure—I guess I
would—fine." I'd never prayed with anyone before except when
someone said grace before a meal. Tom bowed his head. "Lord,"
he began, "we pray for Chuck and his family, that You might open
his heart and show him the light and the way."

As Tom prayed, something began to flow into me—a kind of
energy. Then came a wave of emotion which nearly brought tears.
I fought them back. It sounded as if Tom were speaking directly
and personally to God, almost as if He were sitting beside us. Later,
outside in the darkness, the iron grip I'd kept on my emotions
began to relax. Tears welled up in my eyes as I groped in the
darkness for the right key to start my car. Angrily I brushed them
away and started the engine.

As I drove out of Tom's driveway, the tears flowed uncontrollably. I was crying so hard I pulled to the side of the road.

I forgot about machismo, about pretenses, about fears of being
weak. And as I did, I began to experience a wonderful feeling of
release. Then came the strange sensation that water was not only
running down my cheeks, but surging through my whole body as
well, cleansing and cooling as it went. They weren't tears of sad-
ness and remorse, nor of joy—but tears of relief.

And then I prayed my first real prayer. "God, I don't know
how to find You, but I'm going to try! I'm not much the way I am

now, but I want to give myself to You." I didn't know how to say more, so I repeated over and over the words: *Take me.*

 ## OPENING THE GATE

Wednesday

THE CURIOUS PHRASE "ACCEPT Jesus Christ" at first had sounded to me both pious and mystical, language of the zealot, maybe black-magic stuff. But I knew I could not sidestep the central question placed squarely before me.

Was I to accept, without reservations, Jesus Christ as Lord of my life? It was like a gate before me. There was no way to walk around it. I would step through, or I would remain outside.

"To accept" means no more than "to believe." Did I believe what Jesus said? If I did, then I accepted.

Not mystical or weird at all, and with no in-between ground left. Either I would believe or I would not—and believe it all or none of it.

It was Friday, at the end of a week spent in Maine searching for God and truth. As I pondered the week, my quest was not quite as important as I had thought. It simply returned me to where I had been when I asked God to "take me" in a moment of surrender on a little country road. What I studied so intently all week opened wider the new world into which I had already taken my first halting, shaky steps.

And so early that Friday morning, while I sat alone staring at the sea I love, words I had not been certain I could understand or say fell naturally from my lips: "Lord Jesus, I believe You. I accept You. Please come into my life. I commit it to You."

With these few words came a sureness of mind that matched the depth of feeling in my heart. God filled the barren void I'd known for so many months, filling it to its brim with a whole new kind of awareness.

A CHANGE
OF MIND

Thursday

FOR MOST OF US, THE WORD *repentance* conjures up images of medieval monks in sackcloth or Old Testament prophets rending their garments in anguish. But repentance is much more than self-flagellation, more than regret, more than deep sorrow for past sins. The biblical word for repentance is *metanoia* in the Greek. *Meta* means "change" and *noia* means "mind," so literally it means "a change of mind."

Repentance is replete with radical implications, for a fundamental change of mind not only turns us from the sinful past, but also transforms our life plan, ethics, and actions as we begin to see the world through God's eyes rather than ours. That kind of transformation requires the ultimate surrender of self.

The call to repentance—individual and corporate—is one of the most consistent themes of Scripture. The Old Testament contains vivid accounts of kings and prophets, priests and people falling before God to plead for mercy and promising to change. The demand for repentance is clear in God's commands to Moses, and its broken-hearted passion flows through David's eloquent prayer of contrition in Psalm 51.

Repentance is the keynote of the New Testament as well. It is John the Baptist's single message. According to Mark 1:14, "Repent and believe the good news," were among Jesus' first public words. And His last instructions to His disciples included the directive that "repentance and forgiveness of sins will be preached in his name to all nations" (Luke 24:47).

Repentance is an inescapable consequence of regeneration, an indispensable part of the conversion process that takes place under the convicting power of the Holy Spirit. But repentance is also a continuing state of mind. We are warned, for example, to repent before partaking of communion. Also, believers "prove their repentance by their deeds" (Acts 26:20). Without a continuing repentant attitude—a persistent desire to turn away from our own nature and seek God's nature—Christian growth is impossible. 🌑

SUMMONED TO
THE BENCH

Friday

IT WAS MY DAY IN COURT. I would be charged as a conspirator, guilty of crimes against the federal government.

Judge John Sirica summoned the seven Watergate defendants to walk forward, stand at the rail beneath his bench, and answer as the accusations were read against us. The words were chilling: "The United States of America charges John Mitchell . . . Charles W. Colson . . ."

All my life the mere words *The United States* had set my spine tingling like martial music. I have deeply loved my country, worn the Marine uniform with a sense of honor, felt pride every time I saw the flag.

Now those beloved words were accusing me, striking at me, filling me with shame. It wasn't the United States against me, I wanted to cry out, it was a group of politicized individuals. My own country was not accusing me—but of course it was.

That frightful realization, which until this very moment I resisted, brought a feeling of nausea. Nothing that could be done to me—trials, prison, ruin—nothing would match the dreadful knowledge that the country I loved was charging me with a breach of my trust and duty.

Of course, there would be trials and a chance to prove my innocence, but no vindication could erase the ugly stain of this day. I stared up at Judge Sirica's scolding eyes, his grim face silhouetted against the cold, black marble wall behind him. My mouth was so parched I wasn't certain my words could be heard: "Not guilty to all counts."

I lowered my eyes. "Neither death, nor life, nor angels, nor principalities, nor powers can separate us from Jesus," Paul wrote to the Christians in Rome (Rom. 8:38-39).

Never had those words been more important to me than at that moment in the courtroom. In that instant when I felt the full wrath of the principality I had worshiped now accusing me, I felt His presence too—utterly dependable, utterly caring.

BEHIND BARS

Weekend

M Y FIRST DAY AS PRISONER NO. 23226 at Maxwell Federal Prison Camp was sultry and hot. When night fell, the full weight of what it really means to be imprisoned settled upon me. I felt closed in and fearfully alone, even though surrounded by forty other men. I had known loneliness before—a brief stint in boarding school when I was twelve, long days and nights as a Marine in a far-away land. It was not homesickness which weighed on my heart, but the barrenness all around me, the empty shells of men, the pervasive feeling of despair that, like the stale air, filled the dusty, dimly lit dormitory.

Men lay on their bunks with glazed eyes, staring at nothing. There was some idle chatter, but unlike any group of men I had been with before there was no laughter, no jokes or good humor. Now and then, a harsh epithet or an angry outburst broke the steady whining of the fan.

One welcome break that first week was the regular Tuesday-night visit of Brother Edmon Blow, a local Southern Baptist preacher. Thirty of us gathered in the auditorium where a portable, red vinyl-covered altar was wheeled up to the front of the large barren room; on top of the altar was a lopsided steel cross with the words *U. S. Government* etched onto the crossbar. An old piano was moved alongside.

"Oh, how I love Jesus Christ," Brother Blow shouted at the top of his lungs, thrusting his arms upward, his jacket drawn tight across his chest. "He is *my* Savior—our Savior." *This man actually seems to be talking to Jesus*, I thought to myself. I had never seen the dignified pastors of my church do this, but before that hour was over I found myself shouting *"Amen!"* right along with the others.

As I was leaving, Brother Blow caught my eye. To my astonishment he charged over and gave me a bear hug. "Hallelujah, of all the men to be here," Blow exclaimed. "Hallelujah and praise the Lord." His protruding cheekbones highlighted his leathery face, the weathered look of rural Alabama, but his eyes were filled with warmth and love. I found a brother when I needed him most. 🔲

SECRET PLACE OF THE SOUL

Monday

NEW LIFE IN THE SPIRIT IS conceived in the secret place of the soul, hidden from human eyes.

Many evangelicals believe that a person must know the precise moment he or she prayed "the sinner's prayer," must be able to recount that dramatic experience of "accepting Christ." In my life, God intervened powerfully, in a moment I will never forget. Witnessed to by faithful friends and humbled by the Spirit, in a flood of tears I surrendered my life to Jesus Christ.

For others, it's not that way. After my much-publicized conversion, Christian brothers and sisters used to swarm around Patty whenever she accompanied me to public events. "And when were you born again, Mrs. Colson?" they would ask, eager for another gripping conversion story.

At first this drove Patty to tears. "I don't know," she would reply. "All I know is I believe deeply."

Her pursuers would shrink away, and more than once were heard to say, "Poor Mr. Colson. His wife isn't born again." But Patty, like millions of others, cannot pinpoint a precise moment or sudden awakening. She grew up in a Christian home, always attended worship services, can never remember a moment when she didn't believe, and in recent years she has experienced an ever-deepening relationship with Christ.

The wind of the Spirit blows where He wills. We hear the sound, we see the evidence, but we know not how this mysterious breath of God touches human hearts.

God builds His church in the most unlikely ways and places, stirring the convictions of the heart, bringing men and women to the knowledge of sin, to repentance, to the Savior Himself—and knitting them together in His body.

LOSING
YOUR LIFE

Tuesday

URING A VISIT TO AUSTRALIA, I was interviewed by a well-known radio host. As the program drew to a close, he posed one last question. "Mr. Colson, you are an unusual person. You have conquered the pinnacles of secular success. The goals most people strive their whole lives for, you have achieved—only to see it all collapse as you fell from the White House to prison. But now you're out, leading a new life as a Christian. It's like having lived two lives. How would you sum up the meaning of those two lives?"

I glanced at the clock. Only twenty seconds remained in the live broadcast. Then in a flash the "short" answer came. "If my life stands for anything," I said quickly, "it is the truth of the teaching of Jesus Christ, '. . . whoever wants to save his life will lose it, but whoever loses his life for me will find it. What good will it be for a man if he gains the whole world, yet forfeits his soul?'" (Matt. 16:25-26).

With that we went off the air, my questioner looking totally bewildered. And certainly those words do embody a staggering paradox. But in my life I've experienced the truth of those words.

I had spent my first forty years seeking the whole world, to the neglect of my soul. But what I couldn't find in my quest for power and success—true security and meaning—I discovered in prison where all worldly props had been stripped away. And by God's grace, I lost my life that I might find true life in Christ. ✿

WHAT KIND
OF KING?

Wednesday

NE BRISK DECEMBER NIGHT as I accompanied the president from the Oval Office in the West Wing of the White House to the Residence, Mr. Nixon was musing about what people wanted in their leaders. He slowed a moment, looking into the distance across the South Lawn, and said, "The people really want a leader a little bigger than themselves, don't they, Chuck? There's a certain aloofness, a power that's exuded by great men that people feel and want to follow."

But Jesus Christ exhibited none of this self-conscious aloofness. He served others first; He spoke to those to whom no one spoke; He dined with the lowest members of society; He touched the untouchables; He washed His servants' feet. He had no throne, no crown, no bevy of servants or armored guards. A borrowed manger and a borrowed tomb framed His earthly life.

Kings and presidents and prime ministers surround themselves with minions who rush ahead, swing the doors wide, and stand at attention as they wait for the great to pass. Jesus said that He Himself stands at the door and knocks, patiently waiting to enter our lives. 🔳

A LAWYER'S SKEPTICISM

Thursday

C AN WE RELY ON BIBLICAL ACCOUNTS? When I first became a Christian, I began to study the Bible with a lawyer's skepticism. I suspected it was a compilation of ancient fables that had endured through the centuries because of its wisdom.

But I made some startling discoveries. The original documents from which the Scriptures derive were rigorously examined for authenticity by early canonical councils. They demanded eyewitness accounts or apostolic authorship.

Today a growing body of historical evidence affirms the accuracy of the Scriptures. For example, the prophecy recorded in Psalm 22 explicitly details a crucifixion, with its piercing of the hands and feet, disjointing of the bones, dehydration. Yet crucifixion was a means of execution unknown to Palestine until the Romans introduced it—several hundred years *after* the Psalms were written. As a result, modern critics concluded the Psalms were written later, such "prophecies" perhaps even recorded after the fact. But then came the discovery of the Dead Sea Scrolls, which make it possible to date portions of the Psalms back to hundreds of years before Christ.

No wonder historian Paul Johnson writes, " A Christian with faith has nothing to fear from the facts." ✺

HOW DO
WE KNOW?

Friday

I F JESUS IS GOD, AS HE CLAIMS, He cannot be mistaken in what He teaches and He cannot lie. An infallible God cannot err; a holy God cannot deceive. So He is either telling the truth, or He is *not* who He says He is.

Therefore, if Christ's divinity and perfect humanity are established, we know that His view of the Scriptures as infallible and authoritative is true. The real proof of the Scriptures' authenticity turns on the proof of Christ's authenticity.

But what proves Christ's authenticity?

It is the fact that He was bodily raised from the grave. The historical truth of His victory over death and His consequent eternal kingship over the world affirms Jesus' claim to be God. The Resurrection establishes Christ's authority and thus validates His teachings about the Bible and Himself. Paul minces no words about this: "If Christ has not been raised, your faith is futile."

Some might think Paul rash for staking the case for Christianity on the bodily resurrection. But Paul was absolutely certain about Christ's resurrection. He had encountered Jesus face to face on the road to Damascus and had talked both with the apostles who were with Jesus and with many of the five hundred eyewitnesses who saw the resurrected Lord. The Resurrection resolves Christ's authenticity. ✺

CAN WE TRUST
THE BIBLE?

Weekend

W E DEPEND ON SCRIPTURE FOR the fact that Jesus said certain things; but how do we know He really said them? How do

we know His words and the events of His life are accurately recorded in the Bible?

Because this is so crucial, no question has been more ex-
haustively and critically examined through the centuries. My own
study brought me to these basic conclusions. The men who penned
the New Testament were Hebrews, and scholars agree that the
Hebrews were meticulous in precise and literal transcriptions.
What was said or done had to be recorded in painstaking and
faithful detail; if there was any doubt on a particular event or
detail, it was not included.

Moreover, the gospel accounts were written by contemporaries of Jesus who had firsthand knowledge of His life and the
events of the early church (unlike, for example, Buddhist literature which was developed two centuries after Buddha's death).
"We proclaim to you what we have seen and heard,' said the apostles.

And external evidence continues to add historical verifica-
tion. New archaeological discoveries in the field of biblical studies
have added weight to the evidence that the Gospels were written
by contemporaries of Jesus. For example, at one point critics at-
tributed the Gospel of John to the late second century and
considered it possibly a romanticized fable about a simple Galilean
peasant "deified" long after his death. However, a recently discovered early papyrus on which John 18 was written was scientifically
determined to have been written *no later than* 125 A.D.

The more evidence is uncovered, the more scholars agree
that the New Testament is a reliable accounting of what the writers saw and heard.

FAITH BASED ON FACTS

Monday

GOD'S DEFINITIVE REVELATION in Jesus Christ is given authoritative witness in the Bible. John Calvin argued that "We owe to Scripture the same reverence which we owe to God." Pope Leo XIII insisted that "Divine inspiration not only is essentially incompatible with error but excludes and rejects it absolutely and necessarily."

Earlier in this century biblical criticism and theological speculation seemed to have turned against orthodoxy. Most of the Old Testament was seen as ancient fables, and some scholars denied that Jesus lived at all.

But today the situation is quite different. As British historian Paul Johnson says, "Christianity, like the Judaism from which it sprang, is a historical religion, or it is nothing. It does not deal in myths and metaphors and symbols, or in states of being and cycles. It deals in facts." Johnson cites archaeological evidence supporting the historical claims of the Old Testament, as well as overwhelming textual support for the early dating and reliability of New Testament documents.

Johnson concludes: "It is not now the man of faith, it is the skeptic, who has reason to fear the course of discovery."

DID MAN CREATE GOD?

Tuesday

THE INFLUENTIAL GERMAN philosopher Ludwig Feuerbach believed that God was made in the image of man, a creation of the human mind. So did Sigmund Freud. "A theological dogma might be refuted [to a person] a thousand times," he wrote, "provided, however, he had need of it, he again and again accepts it as true."

Is religion just a psychological prop? Consider the nature and character of the God revealed in the Bible. If we were making up our own god, would we create one with such harsh demands for justice, righteousness, service, and self-sacrifice as we find in the biblical texts?

Would the pious New Testament religious establishment have created a God who condemned them for their own hypocrisy? Would even a zealous disciple have invented a Messiah who called His followers to sell all, give their possessions to the poor, and follow Him to their deaths? The skeptic who believes the Bible's human authors manufactured their God out of psychological need has not read the Scriptures carefully.

WAS JESUS REAL?

Wednesday

SKEPTICS USED TO SAY the New Testament wasn't written until hundreds of years after Jesus lived—after a jungle of myth and legend had grown up and distorted the original events. But we now know the New Testament books were originally written a mere twenty to forty years after Christ's crucifixion.

That's within a single generation—less than the time separating us from the end of World War II. Far too brief a span for myths and legends to take hold.

In fact, if we compare the historical evidence for Jesus to the evidence for other figures who lived in ancient times, there's just no comparison. Consider: Though we don't have the original documents of the New Testament, we do have several thousand copies—some of them written only a hundred years after Jesus lived.

Compare that to the Roman writer Tacitus. He's considered a first-rate historical source. Yet we have only twenty copies of his work, and the earliest manuscript is dated a thousand years after he lived.

And no one doubts the authenticity of the Greek philosopher Aristotle. Yet the earliest manuscript of his work that we have is dated fourteen hundred years after he lived.

We all know about Caesar. Yet the earliest copy of his *Gallic Wars* is dated a thousand years after the original.

There can simply be no doubt any longer that the New Testament is an authentic document—that it describes real events. Jesus is better authenticated than any other figure from ancient times.

So if people ask you how you know Jesus was a real person, respond with your own question: Was Caesar a real person? Was Aristotle? If they say yes, tell them the evidence for Jesus is much stronger.

Or you can turn the question around: If people doubt that Jesus was real, tell them they'll also have to throw out everyone else we know from ancient history—Tacitus, Aristotle, Caesar. The evidence for their lives is much weaker than the evidence for Jesus' life.

There's just no middle ground: Either you believe the New Testament account of Jesus is authentic—or you become a complete skeptic about all of ancient history. ❧

Thursday

COLOR-CODING THE GOSPELS

A GROUP OF SCHOLARS MET a few years ago to discuss and determine the authenticity of Christ's statements in the Gospels. One by one Jesus' words were considered; then the scholars solemnly raised slips of colored paper. A red slip meant the statement under consideration was "authentic"; pink meant "probably authentic"; black meant "not authentic."

The Beatitudes and the Sermon on the Mount took a beating in the balloting. "Blessed are the peacemakers" was swiftly voted down. "Blessed are the meek" got only six timid red and pink votes out of thirty cast. In all, only three out of twelve assorted blessings and woes from Matthew were deemed authentic.

We might dismiss this exercise as merely a party game of liberal scholars—except that it represents an attitude that has subtly invaded the personal lives of many even in the evangelical church today. Namely, the tendency to put Scripture on our terms rather than God's, applying the parts we like and ignoring those we find too hard to handle.

If we are to be Christians whose hearts beat and break with the rhythm of the heart of God, we must accept His whole Word wholeheartedly. That means reading the Bible, studying it, committing it to memory, allowing His words to dwell richly in our minds. It means understanding Scripture in its historic, classical context. It means accepting Christ as Savior and allowing His rule to permeate our thoughts, decisions, and actions. ▨

Friday

CONTEMPORARY CHRISTS

THERE'S A GROWING TREND to recast Jesus to fit a modern secular perspective. And theologians are leading the pack. Just listen to some of the titles hitting the bookshelves.

Anglican Bishop John Spong wrote *Born of a Woman*, offering the preposterous suggestion that Mary was raped—and that the virgin birth was concocted by the church as a cover-up.

Divinity professor Barbara Thiering authored *Jesus: The Man*, in which she says Jesus didn't die on the cross, He was just poisoned. He was revived and went on to marry and raise three children.

In *The Historical Jesus*, Catholic theologian John Crossan argues that Jesus didn't rise from the dead. Instead His body was buried in a shallow grave, Crossan says, where it was dug up and devoured by dogs.

Taken together, books like these can create a widespread climate of opinion that the Bible is simply a collection of myths and errors. Even evangelical Christians may gradually accept the same principle and begin to separate faith from facts. The Bible is true in its *spiritual* message, they say, but full of errors in its *history*.

But Scripture never separates faith from facts. In 1 Corinthians 15 Paul explicitly argues that if Christ was not physically raised from the dead, our faith is worthless. Besides, once you accept *in principle* that Scripture can be wrong, you start performing surgery on the text. You sort out certain historical details and stack them in a pile marked "believable," label the rest "unbelievable" and dump them out.

But surely this is illogical. It's all the same text. If the Bible is reliable on *some* facts, why does it suddenly become unreliable on others?

No, the Bible must be accepted in its total message. Otherwise, all we're doing is remaking Jesus to fit our own personal prejudices. 🅦

DIGGING
UP DIRT

Weekend

I N 1993, ARCHAEOLOGISTS DIGGING in the Near East made a remarkable discovery about King David. They uncovered a rock fragment inscribed with an ancient text referring to "the House of David," a phrase used for the ruling dynasty founded by King David. The rock appears to be a victory monument erected by a Syrian king nearly three thousand years after a battle described in 1 Kings.

What makes the finding so significant is that it's the first reference to King David or his royal family found outside the pages of the Bible—providing new external evidence for the historical reliability of the Bible.

This is by no means the first time archaeology has supported the Bible. Time and time again, critics have flatly stated that some portion of the Bible could not be true. Time and time again, archaeologists chipping away with their hammers have uncovered stunning support for the biblical text.

For example: Critics once said that the first five books of the Bible could not have been written by Moses, because the text mentions rituals and sacrifices not developed until much later. But clay tablets have now been discovered that describe many of the same rituals—tablets that date from even *before* Moses. There's no longer any reason to doubt that Moses wrote the Pentateuch, just as the Bible claims.

Critics used to dismiss as legend the stories about the patriarchs—Abraham, Isaac, and Jacob. But then cuneiform tablets were discovered containing references to several biblical names, such as Abraham and his brothers Nahor and Haran. Suddenly the passages in Genesis were transferred from the realm of myth into the realm of real history—where the Bible had put them all along.

With a record like this, Christians don't ever need to be intimidated. Some of us are too ready to give in: There are some Christians who say the Bible is not always true in its history, only in its religious message. But there's no need to retreat to this defensive position.

From the late nineteenth century, when archaeology first became a science, the Bible has been proved reliable on all levels—religious *and* historical.

The God of faith is also the God of history. 🕮

JUST ANOTHER BOOK?

Monday

THE BIBLE—BANNED, BURNED, beloved. More widely read, more frequently attacked than any other book in history. Generations of intellectuals have attempted to discredit it; dictators of every age have outlawed it and executed those who read it.

Yet fragments of the Bible smuggled into solitary prison cells have transformed ruthless killers into gentle saints. Pieced-together scraps of Scripture have converted whole villages of Indians.

Yearly, the Bible outsells every best-seller. Portions have been translated into more than eighteen hundred languages and even carried to the moon.

Literary classics endure the centuries. Philosophers mold the thoughts of generations unborn. Modern media shapes current culture. Yet nothing has affected the rise and fall of civilization, the character of cultures, the structure of governments, and the lives of the inhabitants of this planet as profoundly as the words of the Bible.

"My word that goes out from my mouth . . . will not return to me empty, but will accomplish what I desire and achieve the purpose for which I sent it," said the Lord through the prophet, Isaiah, in Isaiah 55:11.

Just another book? Hardly.

The Bible's power rests upon the fact that it is the reliable, errorless, and infallible Word of God.

And if that is true, then it has authority over the life of every believer. On this assertion the Christian faith stands or falls, for if the Bible is faulty, so is our faith. 🔲

Tuesday

NO GRAVEN IMAGES

Neil Postman's devastating critique of television, *Amusing Ourselves to Death*, was welcomed by critics, reviewed in all the right magazines—but not once did we learn where Postman got his ideas.

It turns out, he got them from the Bible.

Postman's thesis is that different types of media encourage different ways of thinking. The printed word requires sustained attention, logical analysis, and an active imagination. But television, with its fast-moving images, encourages a short attention span, disjointed thinking, and purely emotional responses.

Postman says he first discovered this connection in the Bible. As a young man, he read the Ten Commandments and was struck by the words: "You shall not make for yourself a graven image." Postman says he realized that the idea of a universal deity cannot be expressed in images but only in words. As he writes, "The God of the Jews was to exist in the Word and through the Word, an unprecedented conception requiring the highest order of abstract thinking."

This is the God Christians worship today—a God known principally through His Word.

Many religions have a scripture, of course. Yet most teach that the way to contact the divine is through mystical visions, emotional experiences, or Eastern-style meditation. Judaic Christianity alone insists on the primacy of language.

Gene Edward Veith, in *Reading Between the Lines*, explains why: The heart of our religion is a relationship with God—and relationships thrive on communication. We can't know people intimately by merely being in their presence, Veith says. It takes conversation to share thoughts and personalities. Christians are meant to have an ongoing conversation with God. We address Him in the language of prayer, and He addresses us in the language of Scripture.

Historically, this emphasis on the Word has had a deep impact on Western culture. In earlier societies, reading was confined to an elite. It was the Reformation that first aimed at universal literacy, so that the Bible could be put into the hands of every believer. Today, missionaries are still doing the same thing.

Yet we are in danger of coming full circle: The visual media created by modern science may ultimately *undermine* literacy, turning us back into an image-based culture. In the Old Testament, God's people were tempted by graven images.

Today, the images are graven by electrons on cathode-ray tubes. Christians need to learn when to flip the switch—to remain true to our historical reputation as the "people of the book." ▓

FREE
AGENTS

Wednesday

I F GOD IS GOOD, WHY does He preside over such an evil world? My legal training suggested a useful parallel. In the beginning, God gave to mankind dominion over the earth He created (see Gen. 1:26-30). He made us, in lawyers' parlance, His agents.

In the field of law, the theory of *agency* suggests that someone acts on behalf of someone else with some freedom, something beyond being a servant or mechanical robot. The agent is given the power to act within the *scope*, lawyers say, of authority—within certain set limits. The limits of this authority—the *delegation* as we call it in the law—God also laid out in Scripture.

But at the same time, He gave us free will. Give someone less and he is no agent; the giver ends up doing it all himself. But with a free will we can also defy God's limits and His instructions to us as readily as any agent exceeds the scope of his authority in civil law. That happens each day; there are hundreds of lawsuits going on to prove it.

As with the failure of agency in the law, so man often fails in discharging our Creator's agency. As C. S. Lewis put it, "The moment you have a self at all, there is a possibility of putting yourself first—wanting to be the center—wanting to be God."

Down through the years it has been man's *abuse* of God's authority that has created the preponderance of human grief. ▓

CHARACTER WITNESS

Thursday

NOVELIST EVELYN WAUGH HAD a gift for making sharp comments that wounded even his friends. A woman once asked him, "Mr. Waugh, how can you behave as you do, and still call yourself a Christian?"

Waugh replied, "Madam, I may be as bad as you say. But believe me, were it not for my religion, I would scarcely be a human being."

Christianity doesn't make people perfect. But it does make us better than we would have been without it. Remove the restraint of God's law, and the worst barbarism breaks forth.

C. S. Lewis put it this way. A crotchety old lady may be considered a poor witness for Christian faith. But who is to say how much *more* cantankerous she might be if she were not a Christian? And a nonbeliever who is a gentle, pleasant fellow—who is to say how much better he might be if he *were* a Christian?

I'm sometimes accused of being a hard-driving man. But I know what I was like before I became a Christian. When I worked in the White House, it was said I would run over my own grandmother to get what I wanted.

Despite our human faults, Christianity has made the world and the people in it—not perfect—but far better than they would have been without it. ▧

WHAT DO YOU THINK ABOUT HELL?

Friday

DURING A VISIT TO ENGLAND, I gave an address at a meeting attended by the eminent historian Paul Johnson, author of *Modern Times*. At the end of my talk, Johnson looked at me with his ruddy Irish face, and said, "I think the biggest problem facing the modern age is what to do about the doctrine of hell. What do you think?"

I was taken aback; the question had nothing to do with my talk. But as Johnson explained, I realized how right he was. When the Church does not clearly teach the doctrine of hell, society loses an important anchor. In a sense, hell gives meaning to our lives. It tells us that the moral choices we make day by day have eternal significance; that our behavior has consequences lasting to eternity; that God Himself takes our choices seriously.

When people don't believe in a final judgement, they don't feel ultimately accountable for their actions. There is no firm leash holding back sinful impulses. As the book of Judges puts it, there is "no fear of God" in their hearts, and everyone does what is right in his own eyes.

The doctrine of hell is not just some dusty theological hold-over from the Middle Ages. It has significant social consequences. Without a conviction of ultimate justice, people's sense of moral obligation dissolves; social bonds are broken.

People who have no fear of God soon have no fear of man— no respect for human laws and authorities. ※

Weekend

THE
SCARLET "F"

FUNDAMENTALISTS HAVE RECEIVED a lot of bad press lately. In the 1970s, many Christians came out of their spiritual enclaves and entered the political arena. They began to fight publicly for their convictions about abortion, homosexuality, education, and family issues.

And they scared a lot of liberals—who had complacently pronounced America a secular society.

Now liberals are fighting back. One of the sharpest weapons in their arsenal is that handy label "Fundamentalist." In current lingo, a Fundamentalist is a reactionary, unthinking, anti-intellectual thug. Call someone a Fundamentalist and the argument is over: Your victim is hung without trial.

But what does the word *Fundamentalist* really mean? The term started out as a perfectly good description of someone who holds to the fundamental doctrines of the Christian faith.

During the nineteenth century, various scholars began to question Christianity.

The philosopher Georg W. F. Hegel said that everything is in process of historical change—even our ideas about God; so how can the Bible be true for all times? Charles Darwin said living things evolve; so why invoke God to create life? Sigmund Freud said belief in God is simply a neurotic illusion—a father figure in the sky. Taken together, it was a massive assault upon the Christian faith.

Christian leaders reacted in one of two ways. Some abandoned the classic doctrines of miracles, revelation, and the divinity of Christ. This is what we call liberal theology.

But other theologians stood strong for the historic doctrines of the faith. In 1910, they published a series of books entitled *The Fundamentals*, which argued for certain fundamental biblical doctrines: that the Bible is without error, that Christ is God, that He died to pay the penalty for our sins, that He rose from the grave.

These were the fundamental doctrines of Christianity in 1910—and they still are today. Believing them makes you a Fundamentalist, whether you are Lutheran, Baptist, Presbyterian, Catholic, or Eastern Orthodox. Once we understand the real meaning and history of the term, it's a label we should be proud to wear.

The world may scoff, but you can call me a Fundamentalist any time.

PROPHETS
OF MTV

Monday

NOT LONG AGO MTV DECIDED to tackle the subject of sin. It was a special MTV news report called "The Seven Deadly Sins" featuring interviews with pop celebrities and ordinary teens. They were asked to talk about the seven sins condemned by Christian tradition as the most dangerous: lust, pride, anger, envy, sloth, greed, and gluttony.

The program was intended to show that people still grapple with the same sins that have plagued human nature for millennia. But what it really showed is that modern young people are woefully ignorant of even the basic moral categories.

Take lust. Rap star Ice-T glared into the MTV camera and said, "Lust isn't a sin. . . . These are all dumb." One young man on the street seemed to think sloth was a work break. "Sloth. . . . Sometimes it's good to sit back and give yourself personal time." Anger didn't fare much better. "Kaboom! That's anger," said one not-so-articulate young woman.

The hardest sin for the MTV generation to grasp was pride. Actress Kirstie Alley would have none of it. "I don't think pride is a sin, and I think some idiot made that up," she snapped. "Who made these up anyway?"

When told that the seven deadly sins are a heritage of medieval theology, Alley showed a slight spark of contrition. She didn't mean "to knock monks or anything," she said. But really—the anti-ego thing didn't work for her.

That just about captures the tone of the whole program: No one seemed concerned about whether the seven deadly sins represented moral *truth*; the only standard was whether something "works" for them.

It's amazing that even in the context of talking about sin, there was not a word about moral responsibility, repentance, or objective standards of right and wrong.

And this failure of moral insight is not limited to the entertainment industry. If you listen closely, you'll hear the same language in serious news shows, best-seller books, and even Sunday morning sermons.

MTV might just be giving us a clue about our own moral confusion. And our own need for serious moral reformation. 🔳

THE AGE
OF AQUARIUS

Tuesday

THE CATHOLIC CHURCH HAS suspended one of its most colorful priests: best-selling author Matthew Fox. The *New York Times* responded with a sympathetic profile, portraying Fox as a religious celebrity who fills empty churches with his user-friendly spirituality.

Why would the Catholic church risk ridicule by defrocking such a popular priest? The answer is that Matthew Fox's theology looks a lot more like New Age mysticism than orthodox Christianity.

There is hardly a New Age cause that Fox has not embraced: astrology, environmentalism, goddess worship. At his teaching center he has hired a well-known witch, or "Wiccan priestess." Other faculty members include a Zen Buddhist and a North American shaman.

At the heart of Fox's theology is the teaching that we are all divine. Hatred, strife, environmental disaster—it all stems, he says, from forgetting our true divinity. What the human race really needs is not so much redemption from sin, Fox says, but "deification"—a mystical awakening to our divine nature.

Fox calls this pan*en*theism, but it's hardly any different from Hindu pantheism, where enlightenment means realizing we are all part of God. In fact, all mystical religions boil down to the same thing: a spiritual experience in which we sense our unity with the divine. As Fox puts it, "Mysticism is . . . a common language uttering a common experience."

This is why Fox teaches that no spiritual tradition gives absolute truth—that they're all relative. Mysticism renounces absolute truth claims because what is ultimate is the *experience* itself—the mystical insight into our divine nature. In Fox's view Christianity is merely one of several routes to that "common experience."

We should applaud the Catholic church for its courage in taking an unpopular stand by defrocking a popular priest. But the real solution is for all Christians to ground their faith in the objective Word of God in Scripture. For if we ground our faith in experience, we open ourselves to every wind of mysticism. 🕮

IS FEMINISM A CRUTCH?

Wednesday

"W E CANNOT HAVE ONE SAVIOR" for the whole world, said a Chinese theologian. That would be "imperialistic."

Her words were spoken at a conference of feminists who claim, at least, to be Christian. The title of the conference was "RE-Imagining," and it called on women to dig deep into their imaginations to create new images for God.

Apparently the biblical images of Father, Son, and Holy Spirit aren't good enough anymore. Instead, conference leaders asked, "Who is *your* God? What does *your* God . . . look like?"

Aruna Gnanadason, of the World Council of Churches, said *her* god has nothing to do with the crucifixion. The "cruel and violent death of Christ on the cross, sanction[s] violence against the powerless in society," she charged.

Delores Williams of Union Theological Seminary chimed in: "I don't think we need folks hanging on crosses and blood dripping and weird stuff . . . we don't need atonement, we just need to listen to the god within."

That, it appears, is exactly what these feminist theologians were doing. The god they talked about was based firmly "within"— in their own psychological needs.

Though the RE-Imagining conference was supposedly Christian, the biblical God was repeatedly denounced as patriarchal. Instead, conference leaders spoke about God in terms of Sophia, the Greek word for Wisdom, personified in the book of Proverbs.

Conference participants prayed to Sophia, sang a liturgy to Sophia, and even held a mock communion service featuring milk and honey.

"Our mother, Sophia, we are women in your image," they chanted. "Sophia Creator God, let your milk and honey flow."

I must say, the whole conference would have tickled Sigmund Freud, the father of psychoanalysis. Freud argued that religion is a neurosis, where people project their own psychological needs into the divine realm. Modern feminists are playing right into Freud's hands. The Father image doesn't meet my psychological needs, they say; the crucifixion doesn't meet my needs; so I'll simply create my own feminist image of God.

Religion is reduced to therapy. God becomes a symbol of psychological need.

As Christians, we need to stand against any attempt to reduce God to a cosmic crutch. As Francis Schaeffer put it, Christianity is about the God Who Is There. We aren't interested in reducing religion to a form of therapy. We want to respond to the God who exists objectively.

Feminist theologians may complain that Christianity is "imperialistic"—but they themselves place religion under the imperialism of their own therapeutic needs. ▨

FROM SITCOM TO SPIRITUAL GURU

Thursday

NORMAN LEAR HAS A REPUTATION for producing television programs that break down social conventions and mock moral traditions—from "All in the Family" to "The Powers That Be." So it came as a bit of a jolt to read a newspaper article by the same Norman Lear entitled "A Call for Spiritual Renewal," urging Americans to a dialogue over "our common spiritual life in this desolate modern age."

And Norman Lear is not the only voice crying in the Hollywood wilderness. Actress Shirley MacLaine published an article in the *Wall Street Journal* urging "an open recognition of the spiritual dimension."

Phrases like "spiritual dimension" may seem like streams of water in a barren land to Christians who have battled against the pervasive secularism of modern society. But today we're facing a *post*-modern society, and it promises to present a whole new set of challenges for Christians. The "spirituality" we are hearing so much about has little to do with biblical religion.

If you read carefully what Norman Lear says, he talks about vague things like searching for "ultimate meaning" and honoring "the unquantifiable and eternal." But there's nothing there about Jesus, sin, or salvation. Shirley MacLaine is more specific about what her version of spirituality is—but, alas, it is completely New Age: channeling, reincarnation, crystals.

Clearly Christians need to be more discerning today than ever. Secularism has been tried and found wanting. Americans are groping for something more—some sense of transcendent meaning to life. But many are settling for empty, religious-sounding phrases in the place of solid, biblically based religion.

Centuries ago the great French scientist Blaise Pascal wrote that there is a God-shaped vacuum in every human heart, which can only be filled by God Himself. Norman Lear has correctly diagnosed the hole in America's heart. But only the gospel prescribes the heart surgery that will mend it. 🔹

RETURN OF
THE MUMMY

Friday

THERE'S A NEW AMERICAN FAD that comes from ancient Egypt: People are signing up to have their bodies turned into mummies when they die.

So far about 140 mummy-wannabes have put money down with a Utah-based company. The owner of the mummy company says his clients don't want to be "covered with dirt and forgotten." They want to be remembered after death—to live on in some way.

Apparently even thoroughly modern Americans still experience longings for eternity.

The longing is being expressed in other ways too. The hottest topic in health circles these days is longevity. Two of

The New York Times best-selling advice books are both called *The Longevity Factor*, filled with advice on how to eat right and live longer. Another best seller is *Ageless Body, Timeless Mind*. It's written by a Hindu, who informs us that our bodies are creations of our own minds—that we can control our health and live longer by controlling our consciousness.

The irony is that modern secular culture has tried so hard to be, well, *secular*—to rid itself of all the trappings of Christianity, including its doctrine of the afterlife. But the waning of Christianity has created a spiritual vacuum that has attracted all sorts of modern mystery religions: mummification, Hinduism, mind control—all touted as the true path to immortality.

Let's face it: The hunger for everlasting life has been around since long before the Pharaohs, and it's not going to go away now—just because secular intellectuals find it unbelievable. Most people sense that if death is really the end, then all our achievements in this life are ultimately meaningless. The grave makes a mockery of all our hopes and ideals.

As a result, people will always search for something more than this life. God has set eternity in our hearts. The only question is whether we turn to mummies and mind control . . . or to the resurrection of Jesus Christ.

In rising from the grave, Jesus conquered death. This is no mythical religion. It happened in real history. And it's the only path to eternal life. 🖾

THE REAL RHETT

Weekend

THEY SAY TRUTH IS STRANGER THAN fiction. A case in point is the book *Scarlett*, a sequel to the classic novel *Gone With the Wind*. For decades, readers have dreamed about what might have happened next. Now one reader has written her dreams down in a book.

What many people don't know is that the original novel *wasn't* just dreams. It was based on real people.

Yes, there was a Rhett Butler, though his real name was Rhett Turnipseed. And there was a Scarlett O'Hara, though *her* real name was Emelyn Louise Hannon. And yes, Rhett really did walk out on her and join the Confederate army.

The history of what happened next has been kept by Rhett's family, the Turnipseeds, a fine old South Carolina family. It was recounted in a column by Wesley Pruden in the *Washington Times*.

After the Civil War, Rhett Turnipseed became a drifter and gambler, eventually ending up in Nashville. On Easter morning 1871, Rhett attended a Methodist revival meeting. He was moved by what he heard and converted to the Christian faith.

Soon after, Rhett attended divinity classes at Vanderbilt University. Eventually he became a Methodist preacher riding a circuit in rural Kentucky.

Did Rhett and Scarlett ever cross paths again? Yes, the Turnipseeds tell the following story. Reverend Rhett was worried about a young woman in his flock. She had run away, and rumor had it she was working in a house of prostitution in St. Louis. Reverend Rhett rode off to look for her.

He found the young woman, but he was told the madame of the house had no intention of letting her go. Asking to speak with the madame, Rhett discovered that she was none other than his former love, Scarlett. Excuse me—Emelyn Louise Hannon. Reverend Rhett challenged the madame to a game of cards. If he won, the young girl he had come to fetch would be free to leave. And win he did: with a royal straight flush—an ace, king, queen, jack, and ten of spades.

The story ends well for all concerned. The young girl married well. After her encounter with the reformed Rhett, Emelyn left prostitution, converted, and joined the Methodist church. Eventually she opened an orphanage for Cherokee children. She died in 1903, and her grave is marked to this day.

The true sequel of Scarlett and Rhett is more astonishing than any fictional account could be. It's a story of God moving in the lives and hearts of a man who was a drifter and a gambler and a woman who lived off the proceeds of prostitution. If God can save the likes of *these*, surely He can work to save people in our world today. ※

Monday

HOLY COMMUNITIES

THE CHURCH'S ROLE IN THE WORLD is not a series of independent items on an action checklist. Instead, the church's role (what it *does*) is dependent on its character (what it *is*) as a community of believers.

What we do flows from who we are.

The bold believers in Eastern Europe had no Moral Majorities, no carefully designed church-growth strategies. Their strength derived not from what they did, but from who they *were*—the church. Their very presence invoked a power that the most ruthless government could not repress.

The same was true of the early church. The first Christians worshiped God and lived as a holy community, conforming their character to the demands of Christ rather than Caesar. They didn't purpose to turn the first-century world upside down. They did so because of *who* they were.

This character-oriented perspective is totally foreign to our achievement-oriented society. And it goes against everything in our consumer-oriented religious culture, where we pick and choose churches on the basis of fellowship or outreach programs or music or location or convenient parking. Rarely do we hear believers say, "I decided to join this church because of its character as a holy community." Nor do most choose a church on the basis of its capacity to disciple and equip them for ministry.

Yet that should be our very first consideration. If the church is the Body, the holy presence of Christ in the world, its most fundamental task is to build communities of holy character. And the first priority of those communities is to disciple men and women to maturity in Christ and then equip them to live their faith in every aspect of life and in every part of the world. 🔲

A ZONE OF TRUTH

Tuesday

G. K. CHESTERTON OBSERVED that the doctrine of original sin is the one philosophy empirically validated by 3,500 years of human history. Certainly the violence that plagues the Middle East, South Africa, Central America, Northern Ireland, and the streets of America testifies to that fact. Perhaps that's why repentance is, as J. Edwin Orr has put it, "the first word of the gospel."

The Greek word for repentance is *metanoia*, which means a "change of mind." Repentance is the process by which we see ourselves, day by day, as we really are: sinful, needy, dependent people. It is the process by which we see God as He is: awesome, majestic, and holy.

"The Christian needs the church to be a repenting community," proclaims Richard Neuhaus. "The Christian needs the church to be a zone of truth in a world of mendacity, to be a community in which our sin need not be disguised, but can be honestly faced and plainly confessed."

It was not by accident, I suspect, that the first of the ninety-five theses Martin Luther nailed to the Wittenberg church door read, "When our Lord and Master Jesus Christ said 'repent,' He willed that the entire life of believers be one of repentance."

WHEN GOD PITCHES HIS TENT

Wednesday

THE REMARKABLE PROMISE that God made to Moses—that He would *pitch His tent* and dwell in the midst of His people—is a central theme throughout Scripture. In the familiar passage of John 1, "The Word became flesh, and *dwelt* among us," the Greek word for *dwelt* literally means to "pitch a tent." Through Christ, God comes to "pitch His tent" among His people. And to carry the theme to its conclusion, John, in describing his apocalyptic vision of the new heaven and new earth, writes, "The tabernacle of God is among men, and He shall dwell among them, and they shall be His people" (Rev. 21:3, NASB). Again the word *dwell* is literally translated "to pitch a tent."

From Exodus to Revelation we find the identical imagery: a holy God "pitching His tent" among His people. First in the tabernacle, then in Christ, and ultimately in His kingdom. By pitching His tent in our midst, God identified with His people through His very presence. The reality of a "God who is here"—personal and in our midst—is an extraordinary assurance, one that distinguishes the Judeo-Christian faith from all other religions. 🔲

HOW THE CHURCH SURVIVED STALINISM

Thursday

FIFTY YEARS AGO, JOSEPH STALIN decided to destroy the Lutheran church in Russia. The Lutherans were to be a case study in how all the Christian denominations might eventually be liquidated.

First, Stalin had the pastors killed or imprisoned. Then the church buildings were confiscated. Bibles, hymnbooks, and religious writings were destroyed. Lutheran families were broken up. Men were forced into the army. Women and children were loaded into boxcars like cattle and scattered throughout the remote regions of the Soviet Union—some to the deserts of the Islamic republics, others to the arctic wastelands of Siberia. In a shockingly brief time, the Lutheran Church of the Soviet Union was wiped off the face of the earth.

But that's not the end of the story. Not by any means.

Though scattered, the Lutheran women worked stubbornly, painfully, to keep their church alive. They had no pastors, no church buildings, no Bibles or hymnbooks. But that didn't stop them. They sought each other out across miles of desolate countryside. They met in one another's homes to pray and minister to each other. They wrote down all the religious instruction they had learned by heart: Bible verses, Luther's catechism, hymns, liturgies. They held religious services. And, at the risk of imprisonment, they passed on the faith to their children.

Over time, some of the husbands managed to rejoin their families. Some of the surrounding people converted. A community of believers was formed that appointed elders and deacons.

The Lutheran church was reborn.

It now meets in more than five hundred house churches. Western Christians have sent them Bibles. And they have recently established a seminary. Soon they will have trained pastors again. The church has outlasted Communism.

How many Western churches would survive a deliberate attempt to exterminate them? Could your own church live on without a pastor, a building, even a Bible?

Jesus promised that the gates of hell would not prevail against His Church. We in the West believe that by faith; the Church in Russia knows it by bitter experience.

Will we have to learn it the hard way too? I pray not. ※

THE CHURCH
IS US

Friday

PLANNED IN THE LATE 1940s and constructed in the 1950s as a living monument to Communist utopianism, Nowa Huta, or "New Town," was originally designed as a center for the workers who would make up the backbone of the new Poland. Early in the town's construction, an open square attracted the workers' attention. "We need a church," the workers said. "A place to worship."

What was the problem with these troublesome Poles? the authorities wondered. After all, their new housing was the best planners could design. And now they even had hot and cold water. Why in the world did they need a church?

The Communists bought time, however, by nodding agreeably. "Fine," they said. "No problem."

So several young Christians and a Polish priest nailed together two rugged beams and pounded the rough timber cross straight and solid into Polish soil to mark the site where their chapel would be built.

Soon, however, the authorities returned with a different verdict. "We are sorry," they told the workers. "This space is needed for something else."

But the people wanted their church. Night after night they gathered around the cross. Priests offered mass, and the people sang and celebrated communion with one another and their Lord.

The authorities retaliated with water cannons, but this forceful baptism didn't faze the faithful. Then the Communists tore down the cross, but in the morning the cross was once again stretching toward heaven for all to see.

This went on for years—the authorities tearing down the cross and the people restoring it. And in the midst of the struggle the people came to a realization that would steel their faith in a way that Communism could never steal their souls.

"The church is not a building," they said to one another. "The church is us, celebrating the presence of our Lord among us! Praise be to God!" ▨

RELIGION WITHOUT THE CHURCH?

Weekend

AMERICANS TODAY HOLD A paradoxical attitude toward religion: Polls show a rise in interest in religion—but at the same time a decline in church membership.

The explanation is simple: A lot of people think they can have religion without the church. Many Christians—especially evangelicals—have come to see their faith primarily in individualistic terms, as the gospel of "Jesus and me."

It's true, of course, that the gospel begins by restoring our relationship with God. But that's only the beginning. In Matthew 16, Jesus asked His disciples, "Who do you think I am?" Peter burst out, "You are the Christ, the Son of the living God." It was a confession of faith inspired directly by the Holy Spirit.

Jesus' response was not, "Peter, that's wonderful. Go your way and have an abundant life." No, Jesus immediately announced that He would establish His church—a new society of people who share Peter's confession.

When we become Christians, we first become part of what theologians call the church universal: the whole body of believers, throughout the ages and across the globe, of every nation and color. This universal body is broken down, however, into smaller units—the church particular. This is where the work of the church is done: preaching the Word, making disciples, and administering the sacraments.

Once we see this bigger picture, it becomes obvious that membership in a local church is not optional for a Christian. It's the very essence of what it means to live out our faith. 🔳

DOCTRINE AND DANCING

Monday

K EFA SEMPANGI, A UGANDAN PASTOR, came to the United States for training at Westminster Seminary, where he was not only well educated with orthodox theology but also with conservative, Western evangelical culture. When Sempangi returned to his own country after several years, he was horrified to see Ugandan Christians dancing in the streets, hands upraised, chanting in unknown tongues. At Westminster the young pastor had learned that worship was solemn and reverent. Charismatic expression was distrusted.

As he sat in his room one night watching his exuberant countrymen dancing in the streets, it suddenly struck him: *These people could never identify with what I learned at Westminster. There's nothing unorthodox here. This is simply their natural means of expression, and they can use it to worship God just as I do.*

Cultures may differ and individual expressions may vary, but the intent of the heart is the same. Ecuadorians may present in drama or dance the same biblical truth that conservative Scottish preachers exposit from the pulpit.

I have beloved friends who, whenever they attend my church, feel uncomfortable over the hand-clapping informality. That's fine; they love the Lord no less because they choose a more somber mode of worship. Some individuals are drawn to liturgical services, others to those which emphasize teaching, still others to music. Pluralism about the form of worship, as distinguished from who we worship, is healthy; it broadens the outreach of the church. ▩

OF ONE MIND

Tuesday

I N 1978 MICHAEL ALISON, SENIOR member of the British Parliament, invited me to England to explore the possible formation of Prison Fellowship there. As the meetings began, spirits seemed high. But one by one the critics raised objections. I was relieved when Michael Alison announced late in the day that there would be a vote. "All those in favor," Michael said, and hands went up everywhere. Only about a dozen hands were raised in opposition.

I breathed a sigh of relief. I could return home satisfied. Prison Fellowship England would be under way—and I knew that eventually the critics would come around.

Suddenly Michael banged the gavel and announced, "In view of the fact that the decision is not unanimous, we will delay any action until we can meet again."

I couldn't believe it. *What's wrong with him?* I thought. *He's just thrown the whole thing away.*

"If this be of the Holy Spirit," Michael explained, "He will say the same thing to all of us. And if it is not God's doing, we want no part of it."

I left discouraged, feeling the trip had been wasted. But six months later the group assembled again. This time the vote was unanimous, and Prison Fellowship England has been one of the strongest ministries of the fifty now operating around the world.

For me, the lesson couldn't have been plainer, just as it is in the Book of Acts. There we read that the believers assembled in the Upper Room in obedience to the Lord's command, waited in continuous prayer, and were of one mind. Then the Spirit came and gave life to the church, which thereafter transformed the world.

The Holy Spirit, who empowers the church, can never lead believers into disunity. 🕸

Wednesday

THE FIGHTING FAITHFUL

INTERDENOMINATIONAL STRIFE can mar the witness of the Body. A few years ago an international group of evangelical leaders met to prepare for a conference in a country which happened to be predominantly Catholic. Since the conference was on a universal subject—evangelism—I urged that Catholic evangelicals be invited.

"Never," one of the participants shouted, slamming his fist on the table. "We fought that battle four hundred years ago, and we're not going to surrender now." Apparently he wanted to continue the Reformation warfare. A cease-fire would spoil his fun.

He prevailed, and as a result the political leaders in the country snubbed the conference; the local Catholic bishop led a separate evangelistic rally. All of this, of course, was widely reported by the press.

In view of all this, it is not difficult to understand the two most frequent reasons people give for avoiding church: "All Christians are hypocrites," and "Christians are always fighting with each other."

To the first I invariably reply, "Sure, probably so. Come on and join us. You'll feel right at home." But I haven't come up with a good answer to the second.

Holding the church to its historic faith, both in its practices and institutions, is a necessary corrective. But shouldn't it be done in love and with understanding, showing grace instead of rancor? The more confident people are of the truth, the more grace they exhibit to those who don't agree. "Tolerance is the natural endowment of true convictions," wrote Paul Tournier.

T IN HIS NAME

Thursday

IF WE ARE TRULY CONCERNED about our witness, the church at large must protect its unity. I recently heard a tremendous illustration of that oneness—from a group of kids in Louisville, Kentucky.

Several years ago a young minister named Dave Stone pastored the youth at Shively Christian Church. During the summer the kids focused on two things: the church softball league and rivalry with a neighboring church, Shively Baptist; and Dave's Bible study on the life of Christ.

One evening Dave taught about Jesus washing His disciples' feet. Then he said, "I want you to be Jesus. If Jesus came to Louisville, what would He do?" Dave divided the kids up into carpools and shoved them out of his apartment.

Two hours later they returned. The first group reported that they had bought ice cream cones and taken them to six widows. Another group bought a get-well card and took it to a church member in the hospital. A third team went to a nursing home and sang Christmas carols.

"In August?" asked Dave.

"Oh, yes," said one of the kids. "And one lady told us that it was the warmest Christmas she could remember!"

Then another group spoke up. We drove over to Shively Baptist!"

"Oh, no!" said the others.

"The pastor sent us to the home of an old lady. We mowed her lawn, trimmed her hedges, raked her grass. She told us, 'I just want to thank you all so much. You kids at Shively Baptist Church are always coming to my rescue.'"

"Wait!" interrupted Dave. "You told her you were from Shively *Christian* Church, didn't you?"

"No, Dave," one boy said. "We really didn't think it mattered."

No, it didn't. When we arrive in heaven, the Lord will not ask if we offered a cup of cold water in the name of our particular church or ministry. He will ask if we served others in the only name that matters: *His.*

COSTLY FELLOWSHIP

Friday

THE WORD FOR FELLOWSHIP in the New Testament Greek, *koinonia*, means "a communion," a participation of people together in God's grace. It describes a new community in which individuals willingly covenant to share in common, to be in submission to each other, and to "bear one another's burdens." Biblical fellowship involves serious commitment and obligation.

In the second century a pagan actor was converted to Christ. Since most drama of that day encouraged immorality, and since young boys were often seduced into homosexuality in order to play the parts of women, this new believer soon realized he would have to leave the theater.

All he knew was acting, however, so he decided to support himself by teaching drama to non-Christians. He went to his church elders and explained his predicament and his plan. The elders immediately objected. "If it is wrong to be in the theater, then it is wrong to teach others to be in the theater," they said. The logic seemed clear, but since it was a unique situation and the young man had no other means of support, the elders decided to seek the wisdom of Cyprian, the respected bishop of the church in Carthage.

Cyprian told the elders, "You are correct. What is wrong to do is wrong to teach."

"But," Cyprian added, "if the young man cannot find other employment, it is also the church's duty to care for him. And if your church is financially unable to do this, he can move over to us in Carthage and we will provide whatever he needs for food and clothing."

No wonder much of the known world came to Christ in the early centuries. They could see how believers loved one another in true fellowship.

HOT-TUB RELIGION

Weekend

TWO YEARS AGO *NEWSWEEK* HERALDED the dramatic resurgence of religion among baby boomers. But the trend is not so much a return to that old-time religion as a reshaping of it.

The goal of this religious revival is not salvation but support; not holiness but self-help; not spiritual authority but therapy. People don't want redemption; they want inner healing. They don't convert; they choose—as if religion were just one more product on the market.

Some churches have been quick to cater to the trend. They are like malls, offering everything under a single roof, from Overeaters Anonymous to Joggers for Christ. Church leaders research the latest marketing strategies; pastors feel pressure to act like businessmen whose goal is to attract the most customers.

Often unconsciously many pastors repackage the church's message to draw more people in. A little rationalizing here, a little rounding off there, and the church is transformed from a worshiping community into a comforting haven from life's pressures.

J. I. Packer calls it "hot-tub religion."

This all adds up to a massive identity crisis within the church. When Jesus talks about the church, He isn't talking about buildings or programs or therapy groups. He's talking about His people, purchased with His blood—the new community called to bring redemption to mankind and to give the world a foretaste of the coming kingdom.

The church has to pull the plug on the hot tub. Its real task is not to make people happy but to make them holy. Its goal is not growth in numbers but spiritual growth. Its true measure is not slick marketing techniques but biblical faithfulness.

So gimme that old-time religion. I'll take it anytime. ▓

UNJUST RULERS, UNJUST HEARTS

Monday

OVER THE YEARS, JAIME CARDINAL SIN, Archbishop of Manila in the Philippines, watched with growing dismay the corruption of Ferdinand Marcos' dictatorial regime. He prayed long over the plight of his nation.

After the assassination of Benigno Aquino, the archbishop knew he had to act. But what should he do?

As he studied his Bible, he saw in the Old Testament a pattern he felt applied to his own nation. *When God wants to punish a people*, he reasoned, *he gives them unjust rulers.*

What the people of the Philippines needed was not a call to revolt against their unjust ruler but a call to repent of their own unjust hearts.

Archbishop Sin spent months crisscrossing his homeland, preaching repentance, conversion, and obedience. He called the Filipinos to prayer and fasting; the people responded by organizing Bible studies and prayer groups.

A wave of revival—of holiness and renewal—swept through the Philippines. According to some reports, hundreds of thousands began to meet in small groups to fast and pray for their nation.

These Christian citizens became the foot soldiers for a nonviolent revolution, and the eventual result was the peaceful ousting of Marcos and the restoration of a democratic government.

I'm not suggesting that God blessed the Philippines because the people repented; it would be presumptuous to assume we could so neatly understand the mysteries of God's dealings with modern nations.

My point is simply that Jaime Cardinal Sin understood that the church's fundamental responsibility is to renew its own integrity and to be a repentant community. ▨

BARBARIANS
IN PINSTRIPES

Tuesday

AFTER THE ROMAN EMPIRE FELL, chaos ruled Europe.
Warring bands of illiterate Germanic tribes opposed and
deposed one another. People were scattered across the land in
crude huts and rough towns.

Early medieval Europe seemed destined for complete barbarism.

One force prevented this. The church.

Instead of conforming to the barbarian culture of the Dark
Ages, the medieval church modeled a counterculture to a world
engulfed by destruction and confusion. Thousands of monastic
orders spread across Europe, characterized by discipline, creativity, and a moral order lacking in the world around them.

In France, the monasteries ran schools and sheltered orphans,
widows, paupers, and slaves. They opened hospitals, constructed
aqueducts, banned witchcraft.

In Ireland, the monks cleared forests, plowed fields, fasted,
prayed, and lived lives of vigorous discipline.

In England, the religious orders fought illiteracy, violence,
lechery, and greed. They drained swamps, bridged creeks, cut
roads; they copied manuscripts, organized industrial centers and
schools.

By holding on to such vestiges of civilization—faith, learning, and civility—the monks and nuns held back the night, and
eventually the West emerged from the Dark Ages into a renewed
period of cultural creativity, education, and art.

Though the world now appears far more sophisticated than
when Visigoths overran Rome, it's only because today's barbarians wear pinstripes instead of animal skins and wield briefcases
rather than spears.

Like the monastic communities of the Middle Ages, the
church today can serve as outposts of truth, decency, and civilization in the darkening culture around us. ▩

NO SHADES
OF GRAY

Wednesday

URING A RIOT AT WASHINGTON, D. C.'s Lorton prison complex, inmates torched several buildings; armed, menacing gangs roamed the grounds. But in the main prison yard a group of Christian inmates stood in a huge circle, arms linked, singing hymns. Their circle surrounded a group of guards and prisoners who had sought protection from the rioting inmates. These Christians were a community of light, and lives were saved.

In prison, the contrast is sharp between dark and light. Choices for Christian inmates are usually clearcut. Yet most of us in the mainstream of Western culture live in shades of gray. It's comfortable to adopt the surrounding cultural values. Yet stand apart we must.

The monks and nuns of the Dark Ages acted out of obedience to God, and God used their faithfulness to preserve culture and to restore Western civilization. As Christopher Dawson has said: "The culture-forming energies of Christianity depended upon the Church's ability to resist the temptation to become completely identified with, or absorbed into, the culture."

The church cannot model the kingdom of God if it is conformed to the kingdoms of man.

COMMUNITY
OF LIGHT

Thursday

THE CHURCH IS TO BE A COMMUNITY of light, reflecting God's passion for righteousness, justice, and mercy. My most vivid impressions of the church shining forth have come from some of the darkest places on earth—from prisons around the world.

One prison in Zambia is an old colonial-era stockade. Emaciated inmates, wearing only loincloths, are crowded into primitive, filthy cells where they have to take turns sleeping, since there is not room for them all to lie on the floor at the same time. At night the prisoners are given a bucket of water; after they drink the water, the same bucket is used to carry off their waste in the morning.

I visited the prison with a Christian brother and former inmate at that prison, later chairman of Prison Fellowship Zambia. He led me to a maximum-security compound within the main block. "Listen," he whispered as we got closer. "They're singing."

Guards unlocked a pair of heavy gates, and we stepped into a dusty courtyard ringed by tiny cells. There to welcome us were sixty or seventy radiantly smiling inmates; they stood at the end of the yard before a whitewashed wall, singing praises to God in beautiful harmony. Behind them on the wall was a huge charcoal drawing of Christ on the cross: Jesus the prisoner who shared their suffering and gave them hope and joy in this awful place.

How can we be communities of light in our own dark neighborhoods? &

FLOCKED DOORS

Friday

WHEN I GOT OUT OF PRISON the last time," an inmate told me, "I really wanted to go straight. I went for help to the minister of my church, but he only lectured me on how terrible my life had been. Then I found that none of the people in the church would even talk to me."

I think of this tragedy whenever I visit a city and its downtown streets. Often I'll stop by to visit old historic churches in the center of the city. More often than not, I can't get in; the doors are locked. I know the reason, of course—vandalism is a tremendous problem in many cities. Yet it still bothers me to find a house of worship closed to passersby.

I wonder what Jesus would do if He walked our cities' streets today and found the doors to His church locked to those in dire need. When He was castigated by the religious authorities of His time for associating with—and even seeking out—notorious sinners, Jesus replied, "It is not the healthy who need a doctor, but the sick. I have not come to call the righteous, but sinners" (Matt. 9:12).

We Christians need to ask ourselves whether our churches have become "too good" to deal with the sick and the sinful, too heavenly bound to be of much earthly use to the thieves and harlots with whom our Lord spent so much time in prayer and ministry.

Of course, to do what Jesus commands requires us to take risks. But that's why Jesus also commands us to count the cost of discipleship to Him.

The church is the visible presence on earth of the living although invisible Christ. But it's hard to tell prisoners about the living Christ when they find themselves confronted with locked doors, or rebuke and rejection by Christ's people. 📷

CHARITY AT ITS GUTSIEST

Weekend

DURING AN EASTER VISIT TO an Ohio prison, I saw the director of the inmate choir suddenly turn toward the packed chapel. "I just want to thank Prison Fellowship for sending friends to me who have stood by me for ten years," he said.

Ovidio had been matched with two PF volunteer pen pals, Dennis and Betty Nagy, through our Mail Call program. Through four prison transfers, the couple had faithfully written to Ovidio, called him, and visited him.

"When I'm released in September," Ovidio grinned, "the Nagys are going to find a place for me to live until I get on my feet. And I'm going to make it!"

Plenty of inmates claim they're going to make it when they're released. But over the years we have seen that those prisoners who are "adopted," mentored, and embraced with real Christian love are most likely to succeed.

Tough, deep-rooted *agape*—charity—expresses itself not in poetry but in action. That's the kind of long-term love the Nagys expressed for Ovidio. Did they feel like driving three hours to his prison every few months to encourage him? Probably not. But their charity manifested itself in a long-term commitment that has made the vital difference in this man's life.

What would happen if the church at large made that kind of investment in individual lives? For an answer, we can look to the not-too-distant past.

Historian Marvin Olasky has profiled the church in turn-of-the-century America, when local charitable agencies and religious groups made it their business to be intimately involved in the lives of the poor. They took needy men and women into their homes, prayed with them, and trained them to work.

In Boston alone, Olasky writes, five hundred families each year took five hundred alcoholic or drug-addicted women into their homes—often with their infants—to help them to begin a new life. Instead of a handout, the poor were given tools to free themselves from their poverty.

Government welfare programs are merely dispensing life preservers to those drowning in dependence, when what they need are life boats and paddles—real help that will get them out of the swamp.

That help can come from only one place: the church—the people of God—exercising charity at its gutsiest. ▓

BODY AND SOUL

Monday

THEY'RE SO MUCH A PART of the urban scenery that we don't even notice them anymore. I'm talking about the names carved above the doors of sprawling hospitals in so many neighborhoods: St. Jude, St. Elizabeth, Holy Cross, Good Samaritan. The names speak eloquently of a rich Christian heritage in the field of health care.

Historically, Christians have taken seriously the social commands of Jesus, who came up with the original comprehensive health package: Feed the hungry, care for the sick, look after the widow and orphan.

He commanded *us* to do these things, not the government. And historically, we did: Over the past two centuries, American Christians covered the landscape with hospitals, orphanages, maternity homes, soup kitchens. These were places that treated the whole person, dispensing spiritual care along with physical and material care—something no government bureaucrat can do.

But as with so many other institutions founded by visionary Christians, the secularists moved in and the Christian vision was shoved out. Today hospitals with names like Holy Family Medical Center routinely abort babies in the same wards that once echoed with the cries of newborns. In geriatric wards, residents now urge families to fill out forms for Grandma that read "do not resuscitate."

Is there a way back to the Christian vision of health care? Yes, the vision is still alive in overseas missions. Medical missionaries in Africa and Asia still treat the whole person, diagnosing diseases of the body *and* the soul.

The same model is being revived in our own country in the inner cities. For example, the Esperanza Health Center in Philadelphia is staffed by Christian doctors, nurses, and social workers. It ministers to thousands of impoverished inner-city patients every year, many suffering from substance abuse or AIDS. Volunteers visit patients in their homes, pray with them, and take them to Bible studies.

As we enter the twenty-first century, Christians need to re-capture the vision of earlier centuries: ministering to the whole person. For if we neglect the social commands of Jesus, I guarantee that the government will step in to do it. And when it does, it will crowd out Christian missions—just as government welfare threatens to crowd out Christian charity and government schools compete with Christian education. ※

OUTCOME-BASED OBEDIENCE?

Tuesday

FROM HIS PEOPLE GOD WANTS obedience, no matter what the circumstances, no matter how unknown the outcome.

Most of the great figures of the Old Testament died without ever seeing the fulfillment of the promises they relied upon. Paul expended himself building the early church, but as his life drew to a close he could see only a string of tiny outposts along the Mediterranean, many weakened by fleshly indulgence or divided over doctrinal disputes.

In more recent times, the great colonial pastor Cotton Mather prayed for revival several hours each day for twenty years; the Great Awakening began the year he died. The British Empire finally abolished slavery as the Christian parliamentarian and abolition-ist leader William Wilberforce lay on his deathbed, exhausted from his nearly fifty-year campaign against the practice of human bond-age. Few were the converts during Hudson Taylor's lifelong mission work in the Orient; today millions of Chinese embrace the faith he so patiently planted and tended.

I am convinced there is a sovereign wisdom to this divine pattern. Knowing how susceptible we are to success's siren call, God does not allow us to see, and therefore glory in, what is done through us.

A scriptural analogy of unquestioning obedience is found in Jesus' healing of the centurion's servant. Matthew and Luke tell how the officer came to Christ on behalf of his paralyzed servant.

When Jesus offered to come to the home, the centurion quickly replied that Christ need only give the command and the man would be healed. The centurion understood such things because when he ordered his troops to go, they went; in the same way he perceived Jesus' authority as that of a military commander to whom one gives unquestioning allegiance.

Joyful to discover such faith, Jesus not only healed the servant, but used the centurion as an example of faith in His comments to the crowd. The unquestioning acceptance of and obedience to Jesus' authority is the foundation of the Christian life. 🕮

NO MAGIC WAND

Wednesday

I RECEIVED A TROUBLED LETTER from a Prison Fellowship volunteer— let's call her Susan. Her letter began with a report on several of the men she was helping. First was Jim, who had been doing well in his walk with Christ but had slipped back into his old lifestyle of homosexuality. Then there was Harry, back on drugs; Bill, dabbling in alcohol again; Barry, continuing to lose control of his violent temper.

Susan was worried. "We're supposed to get hold of the same resurrection power that brought Jesus back to life . . . what's wrong?" she asked.

The frustration of even mature believers like Susan is not hard to understand. Everything in our society is measured by the "bottom line": the results. Success is all that counts. That secular mentality has insidiously infiltrated and influenced our theology. Much of today's teaching and preaching communicates Christianity as an instant fix to all of our pains and struggles. Consequently, we begin to think of our faith as a sparkling magic wand: We wave it, and presto, our problems are gone in a puff of smoke.

But this is, bluntly put, heresy. Like most subtle heresies, it tickles our ears. It sounds so easy, and its appeal, particularly in the egocentric age, is also that it tells us what we want to hear: how to get what we want.

But at the same time it takes an awful toll. It not only makes Christians incredibly naive in approaching complex problems, but it can also shatter the fragile faith of the believer who expects the magic wand to work every time. When problems don't disappear, when ministry isn't just a snap of the fingers, he questions whether his spirituality is faulty. The result is guilt—and that clouds the believer's vision and withers the spirit.

We carry not a magic wand, but the cross. And we must understand what that cross signifies: suffering, persecutions, seeming failures. Not the success of the world—but the ultimate and far greater reward of God's approval. His "well done, good and faithful servant" depends not on our successes but on our obedient faithfulness.

FAITHFULNESS, NOT SUCCESS

Thursday

SHORTLY BEFORE I VISITED San Quentin prison, officials discovered hidden weapons in some cells. As a result, the prison was locked down, the inmates confined to their cells twenty-four hours a day. The few who showed up to hear me speak were mostly Christian: PF volunteers and honor camp inmates. I was glad to see them, but I was also disheartened. This had been my opportunity to preach the gospel to hardened offenders. Now I felt I was preaching to the choir.

I struggled with my lack of enthusiasm until I noticed a video camera in the far end of the room. *Perhaps this is being recorded for the chapel library. Maybe I'd better give it my all.* And as I started to speak, I suddenly felt the Holy Spirit's conviction. I remembered I was called by God to preach His Word, no matter if one inmate or a thousand were listening.

Afterwards, I noted my disappointment to the chaplain. He looked surprised. "Didn't you know?" he said. "Because of the lockdown, the administration agreed to videotape your sermon. They'll be showing it to all the inmates tomorrow on closed-circuit TV."

I was overwhelmed. Because of the lockdown, 2,200 prisoners would hear the gospel instead of the 300 who had signed up.

God had arranged a way for far more inmates to hear His Word. Yet if I had not been faithful to preach it, the opportunity would have been missed.

I am reminded of Mother Teresa's simple truth: God calls us to faithfulness, not success. He will work His will through our efforts.

NO SPIRITUAL BEAUTY CONTEST

Friday

MANY CHRISTIANS ASSOCIATE HOLINESS with a long string of "do's and don'ts." But seeing holiness only as rule-keeping breeds serious problems.

First, it limits the scope of true biblical holiness, which must affect every aspect of our lives.

Second, even though the rules may be biblically based, we often end up obeying the rules rather than obeying God; concern with the letter of the law can cause us to lose its spirit.

Third, emphasis on rule-keeping deludes us into thinking *we* can be holy through our efforts. But there can be no holiness apart from the work of the Holy Spirit—in quickening us through the conviction of sin and bringing us by grace to Christ, and in sanctifying us—for it is grace that causes us even to *want* to be holy.

And finally, our pious efforts can become ego-gratifying, as if holy living were some kind of spiritual beauty contest. Such self-centered spirituality in turn leads to self-righteousness—the very opposite of the selflessness of true holiness.

No, holiness is much more than a set of rules. It is the opposite of sin. Sin, as the Westminster Confession defines it, is "any want of conformity to, or transgression of, the law of God." Holiness, then, is the opposite: *conformity* to the law of God. Separating ourselves from sin and cleaving to Him is the essence of biblical holiness.

HOLINESS
IN ACTION

Weekend

O N A QUIET DECEMBER EVENING in the oncology unit at
Georgetown University Hospital, a man lay critically ill. The
patient was Jack Swigert, who had piloted the Apollo 13 lunar
mission in 1970 and was now congressman-elect from Colorado's
6th Congressional District. Cancer, the great leveler, waged its
deadly assault on his body.

With the dying man was a tall, quiet visitor, sitting in the
spot he had occupied almost every night since Swigert had been
admitted. Bill Armstrong, U. S. Senator from Colorado and chairman of the Senate subcommittee handling Washington's hottest
issue, Social Security, was one of the busiest and most powerful
men in Washington. But he was not visiting this room as a politician. He was here as a deeply committed Christian and as Jack
Swigert's friend, fulfilling a responsibility he would not delegate
or shirk.

This night Bill leaned over the bed and spoke quietly to his
friend. "Jack, God loves you. I love you. You're surrounded by
friends who are praying for you. You're going to be all right." The
only response was Jack's tortured and uneven breathing.

Bill pulled his chair close to the bed and opened his Bible.
"Psalm 23," he began to read in a steady voice. "The Lord is my
shepherd, I shall not want. . . ."

Time passed. "Psalm 150," Bill began, then his skin prickled.
Jack's ragged breath had stopped. Bill leaned over the bed, then
called for help. As he watched the nurse examining Jack, Bill knew
his friend was dead.

Politicians are busy people, especially Senate committee chair-
men. Yet it never occurred to Bill Armstrong that he was too busy
to be at the hospital. Nothing dramatic or heroic about his decision—just a friend doing what he could.

Holiness is obeying God—loving one another as He loved
us. ⚜

PEANUT BUTTER AND OBEDIENCE

Monday

WHEN JOYCE PAGE ARRIVES at the prison gate each weekday at noon, the guards wave her through. Prison officials ask how her kids are doing. After all, Joyce has been spending her lunch hour at the St. Louis County Correctional Institution just about every weekday since 1979.

Joyce began going to the prison with her supervisor, also a Christian. When the supervisor was transferred, Joyce continued by herself, leaving her office carrying a peanut butter sandwich while other secretaries bustled off in clusters for the cafeteria.

Each day Joyce meets with a different group of inmates, from the men in isolation to a small group of women prisoners. "Sometimes we have a worship service," she says, "or a time of testimony and singing, or in-depth Bible study and discussion."

When Joyce slips back to her desk at one o'clock, one of her coworkers is usually already bemoaning her lunchtime excesses and loudly proclaiming that she really will have the diet plate tomorrow. Joyce laughs to herself. She knows exactly what she'll have for lunch tomorrow—another peanut butter sandwich at the wheel of her car on the way to prison.

For many, meeting with inmates every day in the middle of a hectic work schedule would be an unthinkable chore. Joyce, in her matter-of-fact way, sees it differently. "For me it's a real answer to prayer," she says. "You see, I don't have time to go *after* work—I have six kids of my own that I'm raising by myself."

Holiness is obeying God—sharing His love, even when it is inconvenient.

BELIEVE AND
BE HAPPY

Tuesday

W HEN FILM DIRECTOR MARTIN SCORSESE updated the 1962 thriller *Cape Fear*, he made one significant change: He turned the crazed villain into a Bible-quoting, Pentecostal Christian, with a cross tattooed across his back. In a scene where he tries to rape a woman he shouts, "Are you ready to be born again?"

The film's message is clear: People who believe the Bible are deranged—and even dangerous.

Scorsese was giving expression to an assumption common in the secular media and in academia today: that religion is harmful to mental health. The idea goes back to Sigmund Freud, who regarded belief in God as a neurosis.

But in *Christianity Today*, Christian psychiatrist David Larson exposes that assumption as sheer myth. When he examined the empirical data, Larson says, he found exactly the opposite: religious people are actually healthier than the general population, both mentally and physically.

For example, in a literature review, Larson discovered that nineteen out of twenty studies showed religion plays a positive role in preventing alcoholism. Sixteen out of seventeen studies showed a positive role in reducing suicide. Religious commitment was associated with lower rates of mental disorder, drug use, and premarital sex. People who attend church regularly even show much lower blood-pressure levels.

The standard view that associates religion with psychological problems does have one small kernel of truth, however. Larson found that people who *believe* in Christianity but don't *practice* it do experience greater stress. People who believe in God but who neglect church attendance and Bible-reading, who are divorced or abuse alcohol, show higher rates of anxiety than the general population.

In short, the inconsistent Christian suffers greater stress than the consistent atheist. The empirical evidence shows that committed Christians are actually happier and suffer less mental illness than the general population. But the most miserable person of all is the one who knows the truth—and yet doesn't obey it. ※

THE PEDESTAL COMPLEX

Wednesday

THE ANCIENT ISRAELITES WERE NOT satisfied with Yahweh as their king; instead they demanded a human leader. Today this mentality translates into the pedestal complex—and it is rampant throughout the church. Too many clergy and parachurch organizers see themselves as leaders, not servants, and their followers eagerly reinforce that attitude.

But the pedestal complex can have disastrous consequences.

First, exalting leaders encourages spiritual Lone Rangers. The celebrity syndrome destroys accountability. "God told me to build this," announces the visionary leader. Who can argue with that?

Second, the pedestal complex leads to burnout. We expect the pastor to be a shrink in the pulpit, a CEO in the office, and flawless in every area of his life, says Os Guinness. The conscientious pastor who tries to live up to such unrealistic expectations can be swallowed up in his own frustrations and threatened by exhaustion, burnout, and even secret immorality.

Third, the celebrity syndrome leads to a distorted view of people's worth. We go after the rich or the influential, thinking if we can just bag this one or that one, we'll have a real catch for the Kingdom. We forget that it was an ordinary Sunday school teacher who effectively witnessed to Dwight L. Moody, who went on to evangelize two continents and shake nineteenth-century America to its roots.

Fourth, the celebrity syndrome skews the theology of the church. The Christian leader who is constantly the object of adoring crowds soon can't live without it and, often unconsciously, begins to shape his message to assure continued adulation.

Fifth, the pedestal complex lets everyone else off the hook. When we sit passively in our pews, paying some leader to do our job for us, we do much more than miss the task of the church. When we mimic the world with our pedestal complex, we offend a holy, all-powerful God—the most grievous consequence of all. 🔲

REMOTE-CONTROL CHRISTIANITY

Thursday

T HE ILLUSIONS OF OUR CULTURE have us believing that only big names or big organizations can accomplish anything. And so we send our checks off to worldwide Christian ministries and settle back in the easy chair. We serve God by remote control.

In truth, the most important work of the gospel is done directly by citizens living out their biblical responsibility in their everyday circumstances. This is one reason I look forward to visiting Third World countries. In most there are no evangelical superstars, no big organizations, and so those "poor" Christians simply go out and obey the gospel themselves.

In Madagascar, I found that the diligent efforts of one man kept alive several hundred inmates. I was so moved I asked if there was anything I could do to help, expecting him to say, "send money." "Oh, no," came his astonishing reply, "our God is sufficient for all things."

Those simple words and solid examples are a sobering message for today's evangelicals: We must forsake the worship of Christian megamen—and get on with our duty to the gospel. Our faith belongs not in corruptible media icons but in our God who is sufficient for all things. ※

THE FALL OF CHAINS

Friday

D URING A VISIT TO LONDON I asked a friend to take me to Clapham, the village where William Wilberforce lived almost two centuries ago. Wilberforce was the Christian member of Parliament who led the fight against the slave trade. He was joined by a small band of like-minded Christians who lived, worked, and prayed together in the home of Henry Thornton.

"There it is," my host exclaimed. "That's where Thornton's

home used to be!" "Used to be?" I replied in disbelief. "Surely it has been preserved as a historic site!"

"No," my friend responded, "leveled long ago."

I was stunned. In the U. S., there are markers at the site of even obscure battles. But here there was nothing. A nearby church where Wilberforce once preached featured a painting, a small plaque, and a pile of booklets. That was it.

We left the church and walked across Clapham Green. "After all these men accomplished," I mumbled, "Surely more could have been done to honor them." But suddenly I stopped and stared across the soft grass. In my mind's eye, I could see row upon row of men and women, freed from the slave ships; I could hear the clanging chains falling from their arms and legs.

Of course, I thought. Clapham is just what Wilberforce and his colleagues would want. No spires of granite or marble, no cold statues and lifeless buildings. Rather, the monument to Wilberforce is the legacy of countless millions, once enslaved, who today live in freedom.

Like the God-ordained work of Wilberforce and his friends, our success is measured not by a collection of handsome monuments but rather by living monuments around the world—men and women set free from the chains of sin. 🕮

MORE THAN EVANGELISM

Weekend

THE MOST FAMILIAR OF OUR mandates is the Great Commission: ". . . All authority has been given to Me in heaven and on earth," Jesus said. "Go therefore and *make disciples* of all the nations, baptizing them in the name of the Father and the Son and the Holy Spirit, teaching them to observe all that I commanded you. . . ." (Matt. 28:18-20, NASB).

Note that this is not a charge to individuals. It is a commission to the church. Baptism is the public witness of faith in Christ and the visible sign of entry into the church, and it can only be carried out by the church. Only the church can truly teach all that Christ has commanded, equipping believers to grow in maturity and to be the people of God.

And note also that "making disciples" involves more than evangelism. Though the church must be passionate in its duty to introduce people to Jesus Christ (who came into the world to save the lost), that is only the beginning, only a part of God's commission to us. Evangelism must be fully integrated with discipleship for the church to be truly obedient to Scripture.

I vividly remember hearing a visiting missionary use his entire message one Sunday morning to berate the congregation for failing to win souls. "The *only* purpose of the church is soul winning," he charged, pounding the pulpit and glaring at the worshipers before him. "Each and every one of you are failing if you are not out there winning souls for Christ."

But conversion is a process. The process of growth in holiness: sanctification. The nurturing and maturing of character, of putting off the old habits and putting on the new, takes a lifetime. And it takes place in the context of the community of saints, the church, through discipleship. ※

WHEN THERE'S WAR

Monday

CHRIST GAVE THE CHURCH A COMMISSION: the Great Commission. It was a call to make disciples—to baptize men and women and teach them to observe all that Christ commanded. To equip the saints, as Paul's letter to the Ephesians says.

The process of being equipped is like military training. I can't help but remember my own experience in the Marines. Intense physical training. Death-defying obstacle courses. Nerve-racking field exercises.

It was no game. The Korean War was at its bloodiest back then; many young men were coming home in pine boxes. We practiced our maneuvers until we could do them perfectly.

Shouldn't it be the same for the soldiers of the cross? Yet rather than being well-trained, well-disciplined troops for Christ, many believers act more like reserve units: weekend warriors who are occupied with other things during the week and who just turn out for occasional drills or to hang out in officers' clubs on Sunday.

If you're looking for a church, find one that realizes that it is the basic school of discipline and training for Christians. Pick a church where you will be best equipped for the spiritual battle raging around us. This isn't a battle for flesh and blood—like the Korean war was. It's a battle for eternal souls. And no Christian can afford to be just a weekend warrior. ▧

THE ORDINARINESS OF EVIL

Tuesday

ADOLF EICHMANN WAS ONE OF THE worst of the Holocaust masterminds. When he stood trial, prosecutors called a string of former concentration camp prisoners as witnesses. One was a small haggard man named Yehiel Dinur, who had miraculously escaped death in Auschwitz.

On his day to testify, Dinur entered the courtroom and stared at the man behind the bulletproof glass—the man who had presided over the slaughter of millions. As the eyes of the two men met—victim and murderous tyrant—the courtroom fell silent, filled with the tension of the confrontation.

Then suddenly, Yehiel Dinur began to sob, collapsing to the floor. Was he overcome by hatred . . . by the horrifying memories . . . by the evil incarnate in Eichmann's face?

No. As he later explained in an interview, it was because Eichmann was not the demonic personification of evil Dinur had expected. Rather, he was an ordinary man, just like anyone else. And in that one instant, Dinur came to the stunning realization that sin and evil are the human condition. "I was afraid about myself," Dinur said. "I saw that I am capable to do this . . . exactly like he."

Dinur's shocking conclusion? "Eichmann is in all of us."

Jesus said, "The things which proceed out of the man are what defile the man . . . these evil things proceed from within" (Mark 7:15, 23, NASB). This is where we really offend the modern mind; for this is a direct challenge to the dominant, secular, utopian view of men and women as innately good—whose bad actions result from corrupt social influences. Instead, Scripture teaches that men and women are independent moral agents who make moral choices and must accept responsibility for those choices.

For people to see their need for a Savior, they must first see this truth about themselves. ※

THE TRUTH ABOUT SIN

Wednesday

MR. ABERCROMBIE WAS A PILLAR of the community and hosted a weekly Bible study luncheon at his office. He had asked sinful nature—even speaking about "total depravity." After I finished, the first question was on sin.

"You don't really believe we are sinners, do you? I mean, you're too sophisticated to be one of those hellfire-and-brimstone fellows," one older gentleman said.

"Yes, sir," I replied. "I believe we are desperately sinful. What's inside of each of us is ugly. In fact we deserve hell and would get it, but for the sacrifice of Christ for our sins."

Mr. Abercrombie looked distressed. "Well, I don't know about that," he said. "I'm a good person. I go to church, and I get exhausted spending all my time doing good works."

The room fell quiet. "If you believe that, Mr. Abercrombie—and I hate to say this, for you certainly won't invite me back—you are, for all of your good works, further away from the Kingdom than the people I work with in prison who are aware of their own sins."

Later, when I was preparing to leave, Mr. Abercrombie led me down a corridor to an empty office. As soon as we were inside, he said bluntly, "I don't have what you have."

"But you can," I replied. Moments later we were both on our knees. Mr. Abercrombie asked forgiveness of his sins and turned his life over to Christ.

Martin Luther was right. "The ultimate proof of the sinner is that he doesn't know his own sin. Our job is to make him see it." ▨

TEARS AND TOILET PAPER

Thursday

GOSPEL SINGER STORMIE OMARTIAN was sharing her life story with the women at a California women's prison: a tale of childhood abuse and suffering. While she spoke, one inmate was walking up and down the center aisle, carrying a roll of toilet paper. I couldn't understand what she was doing. Toilet paper in a worship service?

But when I approached the front of the crowd to speak, I suddenly realized what the woman was doing. She was passing out sheets of toilet paper so the women who had no handkerchiefs could dry their eyes. They were crying tears of joy and repentance as they listened to Stormie's story of the God who had loved and restored her.

During the service a business man who had accompanied me sat next to an inmate who had told him the story of her fifteen-year sentence. My friend remarked that it must be tough to face such a long time in prison. "Oh, no. It is not," she said. "Because for me to live is Christ and to die is gain"—the very words the apostle Paul wrote almost two thousand years ago from another prison.

I believe if we want spiritual renewal to come to our communities, it will be when Christians are passing out toilet paper as people weep tears of repentance in our churches, and as Christians truly testify that "to live is Christ and to die is gain." ❦

EVANGELISM FOR THE 90s

Friday

W HAT WOULD YOU DO?" an ethics instructor asked a class of business majors. A man's car phone is stolen, and his employer has already paid for a new one when a check arrives from the insurance company. Do you refuse the money? Return the check? Give it to the employer?

Amazingly, nearly half the class said they'd keep the money and not say anything. The incident was described in a *Wall Street Journal* article, written by one of the students. "I was stunned," she wrote—not only by how many students said they'd keep the money but also by how few of the others tried to change their minds. Even students who would act ethically themselves treated it not as a matter of universal principle but only individual decision.

And no wonder: A favorite buzzword in moral education today is "responsible decision-making"—which sounds good until you realize it means teachers don't tell kids what's right and wrong any more; they only teach them a process for making their own decisions. They're not taught to practice respect, fairness, or honesty. Instead, they're told to decide for themselves whether these are their values.

This approach to moral education rests on the utopian assumption that people are innately good, and that if they're simply taught to reason clearly they will naturally choose what is good. But as we can see in the case of the ethics course described in the *Wall Street Journal,* it just doesn't work that way.

The Bible is more realistic: It teaches that human nature is fallen, and that all the reasoning in the world doesn't make us good. In fact, more often than not, we use our reason to rationalize *bad* choices.

In an earlier generation, effective Christian evangelism could begin with convicting people of sin and guilt. But today it's become much harder to convict anyone of anything. People are taught that *all* their choices are moral, so long as they can produce half-baked reasons for them.

In our post-Christian culture, evangelism needs to start at the very beginning: not with sin but with creation, and with God's right as Creator to set the moral standards for our lives. ▨

IRISH HEARTS CAN SMILE

Weekend

ST. PATRICK'S DAY

A S SHAMROCKS APPEAR IN SHOP WINDOWS, our thoughts turn to Ireland—that tiny country torn by centuries of bloody civil strife in the name of religion.

Yet the hidden story behind the headlines is that God is doing a remarkable work in Ireland. Every day, the volunteers in Prison Fellowship of Northern Ireland witness the power of God bringing reconciliation to that country.

Take the story of Mary and Joan (not their real names). Mary was once a member of a Marxist paramilitary organization—a group that even the IRA regarded as radical. Mary helped plant a bomb in a nightclub, setting off an explosion that killed eighteen people and injured sixty-six others—one of the worst atrocities in the history of the Irish conflict. Joan, on the other hand, was a soldier in the Ulster Defence Regiment, part of the British army stationed in Northern Ireland. She was sentenced to prison for murder.

stationed in Northern Ireland. She was sentenced to prison for murder.

In prison both women met Prison Fellowship volunteers; both converted to Christ. Today they have become fast friends, meeting frequently for prayer and fellowship. These two women, who once represented opposite sides in Ireland's armed conflict, now live in the peace of God.

Similar stories are happening all across Ireland. Peter, a Catholic, was hitchhiking to Belfast one day when he was picked up by a man named David. With alarm, Peter noticed that David's arms were decorated with loyalist tattoos—slogans and symbols used by Protestant terrorist groups.

Peter knew his life could be in danger. But David, it turned out, was a Christian, converted in prison and now working for Prison Fellowship. Before Peter climbed out of the car that day, he had given his life to Jesus Christ. Today the two men are inseparable friends, their lives a vivid message of the reconciliation that comes from God.

This is the message Christians should be bringing throughout the world as we commemorate the missionary work of St. Patrick so many years ago. The Bible teaches that our primary identity is that we are children of God—and that fundamental unity overrides all our differences. ☒

M AMBUSHED!

Monday

THE MOST COMMON PERSECUTION for American Christians takes a subtle form. Walking into a disbelieving world and announcing, "I believe," produces the inevitable snickers, the sideward, knowing glances, the eyes rolled upward. Syndicated Washington columnist Nicholas von Hoffman likened my conversion and others to "a socially approved way of having a nervous breakdown."

There is a cost to being born again. Arthur Taylor, named president of CBS before his thirty-eighth birthday, lived up to his "whiz kid" reputation and increased the profitability of this powerful network. He also committed his life to Jesus Christ one day during a quiet luncheon in his office.

Those of us who knew Taylor rejoiced; he was in a strategic position to reduce the amount of sex and violence being beamed through television into millions of homes. Taylor tried to do this, pioneering a "family viewing time" plan as one alternative.

But Taylor's ideas encountered brutal opposition. He was soon embroiled in law suits and was dismissed with a terse announcement by CBS which stunned the industry. Taylor's wholesome entertainment projects were quietly dropped.

The desire to tear down people who represent high moral character and spiritual values is evidence of an insidious sickness peculiar to times of moral decay.

"We wait in ambush," British journalist Henry Fairlie writes, "for the novel that fails, for the poet who commits suicide, for the financier who is a crook, for the politician who slips, for the priest who is discovered to be an adulterer. We live in ambush for them all so that we may gloat at their misfortunes . . . we feel cheated by our newspapers and magazines if no one is leveled in the dust in them."

Speaking our faith boldly is seldom easy. We may be ambushed!

BREAKING CULTURAL BARRIERS

Tuesday

ISN'T IT INTERESTING THAT Jesus didn't set up an office in the temple and wait for people to come to Him for counseling? Instead, He went to them—to the homes of the most notorious sinners, to the places where He would most likely encounter the handicapped and sick, the needy, the outcasts of society. He went out of His way to cross cultural barriers.

The cultural barriers in our American society are imposing. Millions live in conditions unimaginable to the typical white, middle-class American congregation. The family in the ghetto, for example, lives a day at a time, often one welfare check away from disaster; and odds are it's a one-parent family with one or more of its members a victim of one of the plagues epidemic in America's inner cities—child abuse, alcoholism, drug addiction, prostitution.

When the church fails to break the barriers separating classes and cultures, both sides lose. Those who need the gospel message of hope and the reality of love, don't get it; and the isolated church keeps evangelizing the same church-going people over and over.

The church cannot bridge the cultural chasms overnight. But we can come out of our safe sanctuaries and move alongside those in need and begin to demonstrate caring concern. Our presence in a place of need is more powerful than a thousand sermons. Being there is our witness. And until we are, our orthodoxy and doctrine are mere words; our liturgies and gospel choruses ring hollow. 🕮

GOD SPEAKS THROUGH A SPIDER

Wednesday

IN SHANGHAI, RED GUARDS CAME for the university professors and businessmen first. Some as young as fifteen, the guards paraded the accused through the streets in dunce caps to hastily arranged tribunals.

On September 27, 1966, Nien Cheng, a wealthy native of Shanghai, was brought before a tribunal as an imperialist spy. As her accusers read a long list of false charges, others shouted angrily, "Confess! Confess!"

"I have never done anything against the People's Government," Nien Cheng replied calmly.

She was taken to prison and locked into a small, damp cell. The bed and walls were caked with dirt. Weeks passed, while Nien Cheng dreamed of freedom. Then, one day encouragement came from an unlikely source.

As Nien Cheng gazed out her tiny window, a pea-sized spider crawled through the rusty bars and climbed toward the ceiling. Suddenly the spider swung out on a silken thread, attached the strand to the base of the bar, and spun another, then another, weaving a web of intricate beauty. "I had just watched an architectural feat by an extremely skilled artist," Nien Cheng wrote. "My mind was full of questions. Who had taught the spider to make a web? Could it have really acquired the skill through evolution, or did God create the spider and endow it with the ability to make a web so that it could catch food and perpetuate its species?

"I knew I had just witnessed something that was extraordinarily beautiful and uplifting. I thanked God for what I had just seen. It helped me to see that He was in control. Mao Zedong and his revolutionaries seemed much less menacing. I felt a renewal of hope and confidence."

That hope sustained Nien Cheng through six and a half years in prison. But this is not just a story about the human spirit; it is a story about God and His sovereign power—God who can speak even through a spider's handiwork. ▨

THE POWER
OF THE CROSS

Thursday

LIKE OTHER PRISONERS in the Soviet gulag, Alexander Solzhenitsyn worked in the fields, his days a pattern of backbreaking labor and slow starvation. One day the hopelessness became too much to bear. Solzhenitsyn felt no purpose in fighting on; his life would make no ultimate difference. Laying his shovel down, he walked slowly to a crude work-site bench. He knew that at any moment a guard would order him up and, when he failed to respond, bludgeon him to death, probably with his own shovel. He'd seen it happen many times.

As he sat waiting, head down, he felt a presence. Slowly he lifted his eyes. Next to him sat an old man with a wrinkled, utterly expressionless face. Hunched over, the man drew a stick through the sand at Solzhenitsyn's feet, deliberately tracing out the sign of the cross.

As Solzhenitsyn stared at that rough outline, his entire perspective shifted. He knew he was merely one man against the all-powerful Soviet empire. Yet in that moment, he also knew that the hope of all mankind was represented by that simple cross—and through its power, anything was possible. Solzhenitisyn slowly got up, picked up his shovel, and went back to work—not knowing that his writings on truth and freedom would one day enflame the whole world.

Such is the power God's truth affords one man willing to stand against seemingly hopeless odds. Such is the power of the cross. ▓

A CHILD'S LOGIC

Friday

A YOUNG MAN "ACCEPTED CHRIST" and enrolled at a fine evangelical institution. Yet he emerged embracing not faith but a renewed skepticism.

It's all a sham, he concluded. Sharing Christian faith is a matter of perfecting sales techniques. Blanket a neighborhood with enough tracts, he writes, and you're sure to "win" a soul or two.

Skeptics have long argued that Christianity is perpetuated solely by human techniques. But it is not up to evangelists to save souls. It is God who works in people's hearts—in often inexplicable ways—to quicken men and women dead in sin with new life in Christ.

Consider Irina Ratushinskaya, the Soviet dissident and poet. When Irina was a girl, she was drilled in atheism, told by her Communist teachers that there was no God. Irina had no reason to believe otherwise—no Sunday school, no Christian influences, no tracts or missionaries.

But through the processes of a child's clean logic, God made Himself manifest to her. "There must be a God," she thought. "Otherwise they wouldn't tell us over and over that there is no God."

Much later, in her twenties, Irina finally got hold of a Bible—and saw that the God of the Scriptures was the same God she had met in her childhood. "Then I realized," she says today, "that I was a Christian."

The breezes of the Holy Spirit blow where He chooses; we see the movement in human lives and the evidence that He has been there. Would that the skeptics could see in us not sales pitches and tract tossing but the reflections of this God who is. ▨

Weekend

JESUS,
THE PRISONER

ODESSA MOORE WAS VISITING A juvenile jail where she met a teenager waiting to be tried for first-degree murder. His eyes were full of hate and anger.

As they talked a familiar story emerged—father a drug user, mother an alcoholic, both parents abusive. They would beat the boy and tie him up in the closet for hours. All of his life he had been told he was nothing. No one cared about him. But that was all right, he said.

"I don't care about nobody."

"There is Someone who loves you," Odessa told him.

"No way," he responded. "Nobody."

"You're in here for murder, right?!" asked Odessa.

"Yes, and I'd do it again," he said.

"How would you like it if Someone came in here tonight and said, 'I know you committed the murder, and they are going to give you the death penalty, but I am going to take your place for you.' How would you like that?"

For the first time the boy showed a spark of life. "Are you kidding? That would be great!"

Odessa went on to tell him about Jesus, the Prisoner who did take his place, who had already paid the price for his wrong-doing. Using word pictures the young man could understand—he had obviously never heard the gospel—she walked him through the concepts of sin, repentance, forgiveness, and freedom—in Christ. By the end of the evening the stone-cold teenager had melted, weeping tears of repentance. He committed his life to Christ that night.

I have experienced the same thing on hundreds of occasions. Christianity seems remote to prisoners, but when I talk about the historic Jesus who was executed for a crime He didn't commit, on a cross between two thieves, their eyes light up. This they can relate to.

How can you proclaim the gospel creatively and sensitively to people God puts in your life? ▩

HANDS-ON EVANGELISM

Monday

ANYONE LISTENING WITH EYES CLOSED might think it was a group of excited school girls. "I'm going to try this one." "Oo, I like *this* one." "Let me see too."

But open your eyes and you'll find yourself inside the gray walls of a women's prison. The lively women are inmates, and they're clustered around magazine photos, picking out hair styles. They've come for a free haircut, courtesy of Prison Fellowship volunteer Barb McCabe.

Barb isn't the type to wear her religion on her sleeve. But when she heard of an opportunity to minister to inmates in a practical way, she knew that was for her. Every three months, after a busy day at the shop, she collects a small troupe of other hairdressers and they drive down to the correctional institution.

Barb and her assistants quickly find their way to a basement utility room, which they transform into a bare-bones beauty parlor. A single mirror is hung on the wall; a few straight-backed chairs are set up.

"'Why are you doing this?' is the first question they ask," Barb says. "We tell them because God loves them, and we love them too."

As the women wait their turn, they can pick up tracts and Christian literature Barb spreads on the table. By the time a woman climbs into the chair and puts herself into Barb's capable hands, she's been primed with questions about spiritual things.

After prisoners are released, Barb offers one last free hair appointment to give them a good start in their new life. She takes that opportunity to encourage them to get involved in a local church.

Barb was never the type of person who would just walk up to someone and present the gospel. But God is using her gifts to reach out to needy people with His love. What a metaphor for all of us. It doesn't matter if you're not a great Bible teacher or evangelist. God can use you for His service no matter what your gifts are.

Any talent, any trade—dedicate it to God, and He will use you in ways you never dreamed of. ※

AWOL FROM CHURCH

Tuesday

PASTOR, WHAT CAN WE DO ABOUT OUR son?" In a flood of tears, the story came out. This was a couple who had labored hard to raise their children within the Christian faith. But when their oldest son went to college, he cast it all aside. He told his parents he wanted nothing to do with God anymore.

It's a heart-wringing story, one that pastors hear all too often. Why do so many young people leave the faith? A team of social scientists decided to find out. They polled several hundred university students and published the results in the *Review of Religious Research*.

The number one reason cited for abandoning the faith was hypocrisy: 38 percent of the students said they saw behavior by church members that contradicted their professed beliefs. Reason number two—cited by 36 percent of the students—was a sense that Christianity was not successful in solving the problems of life. Reason number three—30 percent—was learning things in school that contradicted what they were taught in church. Reason number four was reading books that contradicted their religion.

What should our response be to this study?

First, it should drive us to our knees before God, to ask Him to show us where our own actions may be discrediting the gospel. Are we hypocrites?

Second, are we really teaching our congregations how to *apply* their faith? People who say the gospel doesn't answer the needs of real life often don't understand how to apply what they believe.

Third, what about apologetics? Are we giving church members reasons for their faith? The same study showed that the earlier a person begins to entertain doubts about his faith, the more likely he is to leave the church. Those who begin doubting at age thirteen are more likely to reject the faith than those who begin doubting at age fifteen.

That means children of eleven and twelve ought to be introduced to the evidence for the historical reliability of the Bible, the evidence against evolution, and the rationale for Christian ethics.

Ultimately, of course, each individual is responsible for his or her own response to God. But you and I are also responsible for presenting the gospel in an attractive and persuasive manner.

After all, what group did Jesus criticize most harshly?

The Pharisees—whose hypocrisy and lack of love drove others away from God. ▨

REACHING TODAY'S PAGANS

Wednesday

A S PAGANISM SPREADS ACROSS AMERICAN culture, our impulse could be to panic, to circle the wagons and keep strictly to our own kind. But is this the right response? Should Christians retreat into a new isolationism? Or should we go on the offensive, infiltrating increasingly hostile territory?

The latter, I submit, is the right strategy. We should seize opportunities to challenge pagans on their own ground.

Certainly this was the New Testament pattern. The clearest example is Paul on Mars Hill, disputing with the philosophers of Athens. Acts 17 says Paul was accosted by Stoics and Epicureans. The Stoics taught that virtue lies in an act of sheer will—not unlike modern existentialists. The Epicureans endorsed a philosophy of eat, drink, and be merry—not unlike today's consumption-driven pleasure seekers.

Standing before these pagan philosophers, Paul drew on literature familiar to them. In describing God as the architect of the universe, he echoed a reference to Plato. The line "in Him we live and move and have our being" was a direct quotation from a Greek poet.

Yet Paul never compromised his message. The climax of his speech was a bold proclamation of Christ's resurrection and the empty tomb—unarguable evidence for the truth of the gospel.

We must learn from Paul how to address the pagans of our own day, to engage them in their own frame of reference, to invade their intellectual strongholds. ▨

RELIGION AS FASHION

Thursday

I N THE EARLY 1990S, the fashion world discovered a chic new accessory: the cross. Top designers like Bill Blass draped crosses around models on Seventh Avenue. Jewelers offered crosses in every conceivable size and style.

And to go along with the crosses, designers came up with what they called the monastic look. Ralph Lauren introduced long black dresses with demure white collars that made the models look like convent novices. Calvin Klein showed long, dark coats and tunics, reminiscent of the Amish or Orthodox Jews.

What's going on here? A spiritual revival among designers?

No, what we're witnessing is religion reduced to a sort of ethnic curiosity. It's exactly like the southwestern fashion of wearing Indian jewelry or decorating your home with Indian rugs and pottery. Rugs may show the Rain God casting down thunderbolts, but for most Americans the religious dimension only makes these objects more "interesting," in an anthropological sense.

This is the same attitude the fashion industry has adopted toward Christian symbols. The cross is used for its ethnic and historical associations, not its religious meaning. The sacred is being reduced to an empty fad.

So empty that some people no longer even remember its original meaning. The story is told of a jeweler whose customer asked to see a cross. He replied, "Do you want an ordinary one or one with a little man on it?"

The jeweler apparently had no idea who the "little man" was.

This appalling spiritual ignorance is a reminder that as our nation grows more secular, our own communities are becoming mission fields. In fact, maybe you can turn the new fad into an advantage. If you see people wearing a cross, why not find out if they know what it means? It just might be the perfect conversation opener.

And they might hear for the first time who the Man is who was hung on the cross for our sins. ✠

BODY COUNT

Friday

I WAS RECENTLY INVITED TO APPEAR on a national talk show, where I discussed the role of values in public life. The host caught me afterward and said, "I don't understand why you religious people are such absolutists—why you want to impose your values on everyone else."

Many people assume that anyone who holds absolute moral principles must automatically be absolutist in mentality as well: rigid, inflexible, and hostile. But there are two completely different kinds of absolutes.

For Christians, God Himself is the only absolute; truth and ethics are rooted in His character. This keeps us from looking for absolutes anywhere in the created world. We should never deify any person, idea, or political system.

But nonbelievers *always* end up deifying some part of creation. People who deny God's existence still feel the need to base their lives on something bigger than themselves. As a result, they take some part of the created world and absolutize it. They turn it into an idol.

This explains why the modern world has become a battle-ground of ideologies. Bereft of religious faith, many people turn to a system of ideas—like communism or fascism—which becomes a secular absolute, taking the place of God. These secular absolutes are much more likely to produce an absolutist mentality than Christianity ever has. In fact, the twentieth century is witness to the worst slaughters ever committed in the name of absolutist ideas.

Take a simple body count. Christianity has on its record the Crusades and the Inquisition. But the crusading armies were tiny by modern standards, and medieval warfare consisted mostly of isolated battles between professional soldiers.

Compare that to World War II, when the Nazis plunged the whole world into war. Not to mention the millions they exterminated in concentration camps.

By modern standards the Inquisition was small potatoes too. It's estimated that three thousand people were killed over a period of three hundred years. Of course, that's three thousand too many—but compare it to the sixty million killed during seventy years of communist oppression.

Secular absolutes are often advanced by the power of the sword. But transcendent absolutes, when rightly understood, foster tolerance—because our ultimate allegiance is to the things above, not to any group or government deified here on earth. ▓

DOUBTING TOM

Weekend

A WELL-KNOWN MEDIA FIGURE once invited me to dinner. "Come talk to me about God," he said. Soon my friend (we'll call him Tom) was sitting across from me in a posh New York restaurant. But I had no clue to the tough intellectual battle that was brewing.

"I don't believe in God," Tom told me straight out. "But I'd like to hear what you have to say." He was trying to maintain his newsman's cultivated air of cynicism, but his eyes were eager. He was obviously searching.

I started telling my testimony, but Tom cut me off. "I know your story," he said. "Obviously Jesus worked for you."

So I switched gears. Tom had suffered health problems; surely he had wondered about death and the afterlife. But again he cut in. "Heaven is a myth invented in primitive times," he declared.

I quoted scripture, but Tom held up his hand. "I've studied the Bible," he said, "wonderful collection of ancient fables."

As I fumbled with my fork, finally a new idea popped to mind. "Have you seen Woody Allen's movie *Crimes and Misdemeanors?*"

Yes, he had. It's about a doctor who hires a killer to murder his mistress. Afterward he is haunted by guilt. His Jewish father had taught him that God sees all, and will surely bring justice. But the doctor's crime is never discovered. Eventually he quells conscience by deciding that in the "real world" there is no justice; that life is nothing but a Darwinian struggle where the ruthless come out on top.

For the first time, Tom was thoughtful, picking at his food. I went on to Tolstoy's *War and Peace*, where the central character, Pierre, wrestles with his conscience, crying out, "Why is it that I know what is right, but do what is wrong?"

That led to C. S. Lewis's argument for natural law. And then to Romans, which teaches that, try as we might, we cannot run from the voice of conscience.

I don't know what will happen to Tom; clearly the Hound of Heaven is after him. But I do know that without Woody Allen and Tolstoy and Lewis, I would never have found common ground with him to discuss spiritual matters.

Of course, God's Word alone can penetrate the hardest of hearts. But my experience with Tom is a sobering illustration of how resistant the modern mind has become to the Christian message. The spirit of the age is changing more quickly than many of us realize. 🔲

CHRIST AND COMMUNISM

Monday

EASTER

I T WAS MAY DAY, 1990. THE PLACE—Moscow's Red Square. "Is it straight, Father?" one Orthodox priest asked another, shifting the heavy, eight-foot crucifix on his shoulder.

"Yes," said the other. "It is straight."

Together the two priests, along with a group of parishioners holding ropes that steadied the beams of the huge cross, walked the parade route. Before them had passed the official might of the Union of Soviet Socialist Republics: the usual May Day procession of tanks, missiles, troops, and salutes to the Communist party elite. Behind the tanks surged a giant crowd of protestors, shouting up at Mikhail Gorbachev. "Bread! . . . Freedom! . . . Truth!"

As the throng passed directly in front of the Soviet leader standing in his place of honor, the priests hoisted their heavy burden toward the sky. The cross emerged from the crowd. As it did, the figure of Jesus Christ obscured the giant poster faces of Karl Marx, Friedrich Engels, and Vladimir Lenin that provided the backdrop for Gorbachev's reviewing stand.

"Mikhail Sergeyevich!" one of the priests shouted, his deep voice cleaving the clamor of the protestors and piercing straight toward the Soviet leader. "Mikhail Sergeyevich! Christ is risen!"

In a matter of months after that final May Day celebration, the Soviet Union was officially dissolved. Christ is risen indeed and is building His church, ". . . *and the gates of hell shall not prevail against it.*" ▨

A CONJURING TRICK WITH BONES?

Tuesday

EASTER

A NGLICAN BISHOP DAVID JENKINS CREATED a ruckus in England when he dismissed Christ's resurrection as a "conjuring trick with bones." The colorful phrase was widely reported by an amused secular Press.

Just how widely I discovered during a visit to Sri Lanka. I asked Desmond Goonasekera, an Anglican rector and chairman of Lanka Prison Fellowship, about the growth of the Christian church in his country. He shook his head. Aggressive Moslems were visiting Christian communities, he explained, and they were using Bishop Jenkins's quote as authoritative proof that Christians no longer need to believe in Christ's resurrection.

"They are killing us with our bishop's own words," Desmond concluded.

What I had dismissed as one man's heresy had become a stumbling-block to Christian faith halfway around the world—a sobering reminder of the grave consequences of trifling with the truth. If indeed Jesus was bodily raised, that is the most important fact of human history. It establishes the deity of Christ, validates what He taught, and demonstrates that He was and is the only true God.

The Resurrection is not just an event we celebrate at Easter. It is the heart of Christian evangelism—the message for all seasons to a needy world. 🕮

WATERGATE AND THE RESURRECTION

Wednesday   EASTER

BEFORE ALL THE FACTS WERE KNOWN to the public—in March 1973—it was becoming clear to Nixon's closest aides that someone had tried to cover up the Watergate break-in. There were no more than a dozen of us. Could we maintain the cover-up and save the president?

Consider that we were political zealots, among the most powerful men in the world. With all that at stake, you'd expect us to be capable of maintaining a lie to protect the president. But we couldn't do it.

The first to crack was John Dean. He went to the prosecutors and offered to testify against the president. After that, everyone started scrambling to protect himself. The great Watergate cover-up lasted only three weeks.

Some of the most powerful politicians in the world—and we couldn't keep a lie for more than three weeks.

What does this twentieth-century fiasco tell us about the first century? One of the most common arguments against Christianity is a conspiracy theory. Critics often try to explain the empty tomb by saying the disciples lied—that they stole Jesus' body and conspired together to pretend He had risen. The apostles then managed to recruit more than five hundred other people to lie for them as well, to say they saw Jesus after He rose from the dead.

But how plausible is this theory?

To support it, you'd have to be ready to believe that over the next fifty years the apostles were willing to be ostracized, beaten, persecuted, and (all but one of them) suffer a martyr's death—without ever renouncing their conviction that they had seen Jesus bodily resurrected. Does anyone really think they could have maintained a lie all that time?

No, someone would have cracked, just as we did so easily in Watergate. There would have been some kind of smoking-gun evidence or a deathbed confession. But these men had come face to face with the living God. They could not deny what they had seen.

The fact is that people will give their lives for what they believe is true, but they will never give their lives for what they *know* is a lie. The Watergate cover-up proves that twelve powerful men in modern America couldn't keep a lie—and that twelve powerless men two thousand years ago couldn't have been telling anything *but* the truth. 🕮

CURING MADNESS AND BADNESS

Thursday   EASTER

A FRUSTRATED PRISON PSYCHIATRIST was describing his day's cases to a Prison Fellowship volunteer. "I'll tell you, Reverend, I can cure somebody's madness, but I can't do anything about his badness," he moaned after describing an especially difficult encounter. "Psychiatry, properly administered, can turn a schizophrenic bank robber into a mentally healthy bank robber; a good teacher can turn an illiterate criminal into an educated criminal. But they are still bank robbers and criminals!"

Weary prison psychiatrists are not the only ones who cry out in despair over the human condition. The apostle Paul posed the eternal question: "What a wretched man I am! Who will rescue me from this body of death?" (Rom. 7:24). He saw that moral precepts could not free him; in fact, paradoxically, they made matters worse. "I would not have known what it was to covet if the law had not said, 'Do not covet.' But sin, seizing the opportunity afforded by the commandment, produced in me every kind of covetous desire."

What a desperate plight. Trapped in and by our own sin. Thankfully, there is an answer to the wrenching dilemma, described in the next chapter of Paul's letter to the Romans: "There is now no condemnation for those who are in Christ Jesus. . . . For what the law was powerless to do in that it was weakened by the sinful nature, God did by sending his own Son . . . to be a sin offering" (Rom. 8:1-3). That took place that momentous day on Golgotha nearly two thousand years ago. 🔅

YOU WERE THERE

Friday   EASTER

GOLGOTHA—WHAT A GRIM SET on which to play out the crucial act in the drama of redemption. The rocky hilltop was chosen as an execution site because of its location near the heavily traveled highway outside the walls of Jerusalem. This assured that people passing by would witness the terrible spectacle of crucifixion, for the authorities believed (as many vainly believe today) that public violence would discourage individual violence.

"Are you not the Christ? Save yourself and us," cried one of the thieves crucified alongside Jesus. Angry to the end, he might even have believed that the limp figure beside him was the Son of God. But so what? If He couldn't save Himself, He certainly couldn't save anyone else.

The other thief, convicted by the Holy Spirit, realized that he deserved to die. He understood that no matter what he had done or not done, no matter what the circumstances, "no punishment comes to us in this life on earth which is undeserved."

Therein lies the crucial distinction between the two thieves. It had nothing to do with their crimes, the relative goodness or badness of their lives. The distinction was that one recognized his sin. His reply to the other, "We are punished justly, for we are getting what our deeds deserve. But this man has done nothing wrong," is one of the purest expressions of repentance in all Scripture. And his words "Remember me" are the classic statement of faith. With such simplicity and power this man repented and believed and died trusting in Christ.

I am reminded of the old spiritual, "Were you there when they crucified my Lord?" I have always understood this refrain in the classic theological sense that we were all guilty of putting Jesus to death because of our need of atonements. But as I began looking more closely at the crucifixion scene, I felt cause to "tremble, tremble." For those two men who died alongside my Savior are representative of all mankind. Either we recognize our sinful selves, our sentence of death, and our deserving of that sentence, which leads us to repent and believe—or we curse God and die.

You were there. What was your response?

THE MEASURE
OF SUCCESS

Weekend

EASTER

ONE EASTER MORNING, AS I SAT in the chapel at the Delaware State Prison waiting to preach, my mind drifted back in time . . . to scholarships and honors earned, cases argued and won, great decisions made from lofty government offices. My life had been the perfect success story, the great American dream fulfilled.

But all at once I realized that it was *not* my success God had used to enable me to help those in this prison, or in hundreds of others like it. My life of success was not what made this morning so glorious—all my achievements meant nothing in God's economy. No, the real legacy of my life was my biggest failure— that I was an ex-convict. My greatest humiliation—being sent to prison—was the beginning of God's greatest use of my life; He chose the one experience in which I could not glory for *His* glory.

Confronted with this staggering truth, I understood with a jolt that I had been looking at life backward. But now I could see: Only when I lost everything that I thought made Chuck Colson a great guy had I found the true self God intended me to be and the true purpose of my life.

It is not what we do that matters, *but what a sovereign God chooses to do through us.* God doesn't want our success; He wants us. He doesn't demand our achievements; He demands our obedience. The kingdom of God is a kingdom of paradox, where through the ugly defeat of a cross, a holy God is utterly glorified. Victory comes through defeat; healing through brokenness; finding self through losing self.

THE SEEDS
OF FAITH

Monday

THE DAY OF CHRISTIAN MARTYRS IS not over. In 1994, more than two thousand people gathered in Iran to mourn the death of a great Christian leader, Bishop Haik Hovsepian-Mehr—apparently murdered by Iranian authorities.

But if the Muslim government in Iran thinks this is the way to wipe Christianity out of their country, they're making a serious mistake. The cross of Christ teaches us that when the church is persecuted, it only grows stronger. When the seeds of the gospel are buried, they blossom ever more brightly.

From the day Bishop Haik entered the ministry, he endured frequent persecution. His Assembly of God church was vandalized several times by radical Islamic groups. Bishop Haik himself was repeatedly arrested, threatened, and harassed. Yet his ministry thrived.

After the Iranian revolution in 1979, evangelical churches suffered even harsher persecution. Foreign missionaries were expelled from the country. Bible courses by correspondence were cut off. All publication of Bibles and Christian literature was stopped. The government even made it a capital crime to convert from Islam to any other religion. Becoming a Christian could mean the death penalty.

And still the Christian church in Iran thrived. The number of Muslim converts grew from only 300 in 1977 to more than 7,500 today—with many more Iranian Christians dispersed across the globe.

The bishop became a real thorn in the government's side when he protested the persecution of another Assembly of God pastor. The pastor's only crime was that he had become a Christian. Yet he had been imprisoned for ten years and was about to be executed. This time international outrage was so vehement that Iranian authorities set the pastor free.

But just days later, Bishop Haik disappeared.

When his family came to identify the body, they saw that he had been stabbed ten times. No one claimed responsibility, but Middle East human-rights groups are convinced that the Iranian government did away with the troublesome pastor.

Iranian Christians mourned deeply over the loss of their bishop. Yet the message of our faith is that the cross is always followed by resurrection. The seed that is buried will blossom a hundredfold. ▩

THE WIND AND WAVES OBEY

Tuesday

TALK ABOUT THE BIBLE BEING historically true, and the first thing you hear is, What about Jonah and the whale? Noah and the flood? The parting of the Red Sea? These stories are held up as so preposterous that no one could possibly take the Bible seriously.

But scientists who study these events say they are not as impossible as they might seem. Sometimes they are just special cases of perfectly normal laws of nature.

Take, for example, the parting of the Red Sea.

The biblical record says God used the east wind, blowing all night to push the waters back. Now, it's a well-known scientific fact that a steady wind blowing over a body of water can change the water level. So two oceanographers decided to see if the same thing could happen on the narrow sliver of the Red Sea reaching up into the Gulf of Suez where, many scholars believe, the Israelites crossed as they were escaping from Pharaoh's army.

Writing in the *Bulletin of the American Meteorological Society*, the scientists concluded that a moderate wind blowing constantly for about ten hours could very well have caused the sea to recede a mile or two. The water level would drop ten feet, leaving dry land for the Israelites to cross. "The Gulf of Suez provides an ideal body of water for such a process because of its unique geography," said one of the scientists.

Later, an abrupt *change* in the wind could cause the water to return rapidly—in a sudden, devastating wave. It could easily have trapped Pharaoh's troops, just as the Bible describes.

The study doesn't prove that the crossing of the Red Sea happened exactly this way, of course. It merely shows that there are perfectly normal forces that God could have used to perform His miraculous deliverance.

Now, a skeptic might argue that if there's a natural explanation, then it wasn't a miracle after all. But if it was only a natural event, isn't it strange that the sea parted *just* when Moses held out his staff? And that it fell back *just* when Pharaoh's soldiers were in hot pursuit?

No, God may use a natural process to accomplish His goals, but it's still a work of His hand, in His timing, and for His purposes. 🔅

FRIEND OR FOE?

Wednesday

ARE SCIENCE AND CHRISTIANITY mortal enemies? Many people think so. They point to the classic controversies: Did humans evolve? How old is the earth? Are there miracles? There are even people who think science disproves Christianity.

Well, there's a simple answer for these people: without Christianity, we wouldn't even *have* science.

Most of the early scientists were Christians: Copernicus, Kepler, Galileo, Newton, Pascal. They believed the world had an orderly structure that could be scientifically studied because it was created by an orderly God. In fact, science may never have developed were it not for Christianity.

For example, science writer Loren Eiseley says that many civilizations developed great technical expertise—Egypt with its pyramids, Rome with its aqueducts—but only one produced the experimental method we call science. That civilization was Europe at the end of the Middle Ages—a culture steeped in Christian faith. As Eiseley writes, "Experimental science began its discoveries . . . in the faith . . . that it was dealing with a rational universe controlled by a Creator who did not act upon whim."

The very idea that there are "laws" in nature is not found in any other culture. Science historian A. R. Hall says the idea came from "the Hebraic and Christian belief in a deity who was at once Creator and Lawgiver."

Sociologist R. K. Merton says modern science owes its existence to biblical moral obligation. Since God made the world, Christians have taught that we have an obligation to study it and use it to the glory of God and the benefit of mankind.

The scholars just quoted are not Christians. Yet they are expressing a consensus among historians that Christian faith actually propelled the development of modern science.

It's true that God Himself can't be put in a test tube or studied under a microscope. But it is God who created and sustains the natural laws that scientists appeal to in their theories. And scientists who reject Christian faith are actually cutting off the branch they're sitting on. ▧

PEPSI ADS— "UH UH!"

Thursday

PEPSI COLA FLOATED AN AD CAMPAIGN in Israel . . . which promptly sank. Orthodox rabbis were outraged over an ad featuring an ape slouching along an evolutionary path to become a Pepsi Kid. The rabbis denounced the ad as counter to the biblical teaching on creation and threatened a boycott.

A 1993 Gallup poll found that nearly half the American people would agree. In fact, only 9 percent believe in evolution by strictly natural law. Yet naturalistic evolution is what public schools are teaching young people.

But there's an argument against evolution that is simple to grasp, based on facts that have been known for centuries. Evolution assumes that change in the living world is unlimited. Obviously, anyone who wants to derive elephants and octopuses and butterflies all from an initial one-celled organism *has* to assume that biological change is virtually unlimited.

The trouble is, the only changes actually observed are limited. Farmers can breed for sweeter corn, bigger roses, or faster horses, but they still end up with corn, roses, and horses. No one has ever produced a new kind of organism. What evolutionists do is take these small-scale changes and extrapolate them: They speculate what might happen if minor changes are added up and extended millions of years into the misty past.

There's nothing wrong with extrapolation per se, but this particular one is unsound. The variation induced by breeding does not continue at a steady rate through each generation. Instead, it is rapid at first and then levels off. Eventually it reaches a ceiling that breeders cannot cross.

If they try, the organism grows weaker and more prone to disease—until it finally becomes sterile and dies out. So you can breed for bigger roses but you'll never get one as big as a sunflower.

Darwin believed nature could select among organisms the way a breeder does, which is why he called his theory natural *selection*. But whether it's done by breeders or nature, selection produces only limited change.

If scientists stick to actual observations, all they have ever seen is the modification of existing categories of living things, not the rise of new categories. As Genesis puts it, God created living things to reproduce "after their kind." In modern language, they were created to remain true to type—just as the breeders show. ✺

CRITICAL THINKING

Friday

PUBLIC SCHOOL OFFICIALS IN LOUISVILLE, Ohio, have decided that students will no longer be taught critical thinking in the classroom. At least not when the topic is evolution.

It was not always this way. Several years ago the Louisville School Board recommended teaching both the pros and cons of evolutionary theory. Teachers were directed to "contrast, compare, and discuss alternatives to the evolutionary theory."

This is excellent teaching methodology. Students learn better when they're taught to evaluate arguments on *both* sides of a controversy, instead of being force-fed a single, dogmatic view.

But when it comes to evolution, teaching "alternatives" means telling students that some scientists actually believe in divine creation. And that prospect apparently struck fear into the hearts of ACLU attorneys. They threatened to sue—and the Louisville School Board capitulated. Teachers are now forbidden to teach anything but a strictly naturalistic account of life's origin.

But when science is taught dogmatically, it is no longer scientific. Many scientists are so committed to naturalistic evolution that they see evidence for the theory in the most unlikely places. Take the famous example of the peppered moths in Britain. Peppered moths come in light and dark varieties. When factory smoke darkened the tree trunks, birds could see the light-colored moths better and ate more of them, leaving a predominance of dark-colored moths.

This is held up as a classic demonstration of natural selection.

But anyone who thinks about it knows that a shift in color is an extremely minor change. It tells us nothing about where moths came from in the first place. It certainly does not prove that they evolved from an original one-celled organism.

In fact, the change in color can be explained just as well in theistic terms: A wise Creator would surely endow organisms with the ability to adapt to a changing environment; otherwise they would soon die out.

You and I need to check what our own children are being taught in science courses. Naturalistic evolution is only one philosophy among many. The scientific evidence itself is equally compatible with divine creation. 🔳

DARWIN'S FINCHES

Weekend

W HEN CHARLES DARWIN MADE HIS famous voyage to the Galapagos Islands, he discovered finches and tortoises that differed slightly from island to island. He thought he had discovered evolution in action. But did he? After all, the finches stayed finches—they never evolved into a new kind of bird—and the tortoises stayed tortoises.

Scientists are apt to present any form of change as evolution. But evolution is not just any change; it is the emergence of new categories of living things. Darwin's finches don't represent new categories. They're just modifications of existing categories.

Creationists accept this kind of minor change. The same God who created living things "after their kind" must have built in a capacity for adaptation—otherwise those "kinds" wouldn't last very long.

Darwin set evolution off on the wrong foot more than a century ago when he listed adaptation as evidence of evolution. It was an error made in reaction to the rigid creationism of his day. Many creationists back then taught that living things never change. So in Darwin's mind, even minor adaptations counted as evidence for evolution.

Creationists back then also taught that living things never die out; so for Darwin, the fact that organisms become extinct counted as evidence for evolution.

Creationists back then taught that living things were created in the same location they are found today. Giraffes were created in Africa, buffalos in North America, llamas in South America. So for Darwin, migration counted as evidence for evolution.

Today, of course, none of these facts affect the evolution debate one way or the other. Genesis says God created "kinds," not species. The phrase "after its kind" suggests that the boundary between kinds is defined by reproduction: A kind is an interbreeding group.

The entire cat family—from domestic cats to leopards and tigers—forms a breeding chain and hence constitutes a single "kind." So does the dog family, from our familiar canine friends to wolves and jackals.

What Darwin's finches really show is that change always takes place within created kinds. Just as Genesis says. ※

JIGSAW PIECES FROM THE ROCKS

Monday

THERE'S BEEN A LOT OF CONTROVERSY in the scientific community in recent years over fossils. Darwin's theory of evolution assumes that life evolves gradually, by imperceptibly tiny steps—from the simplest one-celled organism to the most complex birds and beasts.

But, of course, this continuous chain is nowhere to be seen. In the world today, bears and beavers and bats are all quite distinct. There are clear gaps between major biological categories, with no blurring of the boundaries.

Darwin knew this, of course, so he appealed to the past. He suggested that the missing links have died out and would one day be found in the fossil record. The history of paleontology is largely a history of the search for the missing links. If Darwin was right, the fossil record should show literally millions of transitional forms.

But that's precisely what it does *not* show. Yes, the fossils do show that life was often very different from today. Some forms of elephants were once hairy: the woolly mammoths. Some forms of reptiles were once gigantic: the Tyrannosaurus Rex.

But—here's the important point—those strange forms still fit clearly within the same basic categories known today. Elephants were still elephants, reptiles were still reptiles. The same gaps exist in the fossil record that exist in the living world today.

Some paleontologists have faced the problem head on and come up with an alternative to Darwin's theory of slow, gradual change. Stephen J. Gould at Harvard suggests that evolution happened in sudden bursts—too fast to leave behind any fossil evidence.

This theory, called punctuated equilibrium, places scientists in a very awkward position. If you ask why we don't see evolution happening today, they tell us it happens too slowly to be observed. If you ask why we don't see evidence in the fossil record, they tell us it happens too quickly to leave a trace in the rocks.

So where's the evidence for evolution? It isn't there.

As Christians, we don't ever have to be apologetic about having faith. Everybody does. But we can show people that *our* faith fits the facts.

LIFE IN A TEST TUBE?

Tuesday

BACK IN THE 1960s WE BEGAN to read headlines claiming that scientists were about to conjure up life in a test tube. Biochemists discovered they could mix chemicals—ammonia, methane, and water—zap it with an electric spark, and create amino acids, the building blocks of proteins.

The scientific community was euphoric. But then things ground to a halt. The amino acids never did form proteins or evolve into a living cell. And critics charged that even the amino acids were obtained only by "cheating"—by rigging the experiment.

You see, origin-of-life experiments are supposed to be re-enactments of what could have happened in a warm pond on the early earth. The most realistic experiment would be pouring various chemicals into water and mixing them up. But no researcher ever does that, because it doesn't yield anything. Instead, scientists tinker with the experiment at several points.

For example, in a real pond, there would be all sorts of chemical reactions—many of them cancelling out the reactions the scientist needs. So what does he do? He starts with pure ingredients. That's strike number one: In a natural setting, there's no way to purify the starting materials to get the results you want.

Origin-of-life experiments often use ultraviolet light to simulate sunlight. But certain wave lengths of light destroy amino acids. So what does the researcher do? He screens them out. Strike number two: In a natural setting, you have to deal with real sunlight—in all its wavelengths.

The amino acids formed in these experiments are delicate, easily breaking back down into the chemicals that make them up. So what does the researcher do? He rigs a trap to remove them from the reaction site as soon as they form, to protect them from disintegration. Strike number three: Nature doesn't come equipped with protective traps. Any amino acids that form in nature quickly disintegrate.

The upshot is that even the most successful experiments tell us nothing about what can happen in nature. They only tell us what can happen when brilliant scientists direct and manipulate conditions.

So experiments *don't* prove life can arise spontaneously in nature. On the contrary, they give experimental evidence that life can only be created by an intelligent agent directing and controlling the process. ▨

POP GOES THE THEORY

Wednesday

SCIENTISTS THOUGHT THEY HAD LIFE ALL figured out. The origin of life, that is. The idea that life evolved from a primordial soup has been elaborated into a network of complex theories. But at the 1993 International Conference on the Origin of Life, the practicing chemists turned thumbs down on all the lovely theories.

What has chemists stymied is how to concentrate all the right ingredients in one place. You see, to make chemicals link up, you have to apply energy—heat or electricity. Most origin-of-life theories start with a chemical soup heated by volcanoes or zapped by lightning.

But there's a fly in this chemical soup. The chemical reactions that form DNA are reversible: The molecules that come together can separate again. In fact, as every chemist knows, it's actually *harder* to link molecules together and *easier* to break them apart.

What does that mean for origin-of-life theories? If you simulate the origin of life in a test tube, any organic compounds that form will quickly break up again. You never get enough of them concentrated in one place to form DNA. This one fact makes it impossible for life to have evolved on the early earth. As Charles Thaxton says in *The Mystery of Life's Origin,* the primordial soup would always be thin and diluted—as thin as the Atlantic Ocean is today.

We've all heard it said that evolution is like millions of monkeys pounding randomly at typewriters for millions of years. One of them, so the argument goes, will eventually type out a Shakespearean play. But since chemical processes are reversible, that analogy doesn't hold. Instead, it's as though each monkey has a partner nearby, and every time he bangs out a few letters, the second monkey grabs the paper and tears it up. The first monkey bangs out a few more letters; the second monkey tears it up; over and over again.

Obviously, these monkeys are never going to produce a Shakespearean play. And by the same token, a chemical soup will never form DNA.

For life to emerge, the right organic compounds need to be sorted out and protected so they don't break up. But nature doesn't come equipped with any sorting mechanisms. There's only one thing that can select and sort: an intelligent agent.

And when we're talking about the prehistoric world, that means a Creator. ※

WHISTLING IN THE DARK

Thursday

W HEN IT COMES TO THE ORIGIN OF LIFE, scientists don't have any good theories . . . and they seem determined to make up for it with a multitude of bad ones. For example, *Time* magazine gave a breathless account of all the theories currently on the market. Life may have formed near undersea thermal vents, *Time* said. Then again, maybe it began in sea foam. Or perhaps in clay, or pyrite. Or wherever.

But not a single one of these theories solves the crucial puzzle—what scientists call the sequence problem: If life evolved from a soup of chemicals, how did the components line up in the right sequence?

For example, many origin-of-life theories start with protein. A protein consists of a chain of amino acids. Scientists have discovered that you can mix amino acids in a flask, zap them with an electric spark, and they will link up into short chains. *Voilà!* scientists say. Rudimentary proteins.

But the dirty little secret of these experiments is that the amino acid chains don't resemble living proteins in the slightest. The sequence is all wrong.

Imagine that amino acids are Scrabble letters and that you want to spell the word *protein*. Amino acids come in two types, known as left-handed and right-handed. But living things use only one type. We can illustrate this by turning half the Scrabble letters over— the blank side representing the wrong type of amino acid. The word *protein*, P-R-O-T-E-I-N, now reads P-[blank]-O-T-[blank]-[blank]-N.

Problem number two is that amino acids are like Tinker Toys: They can hook together on different sides, with different chemical bonds. We can illustrate that by twisting the Scrabble letters around so we have, say, a sideways P and T and an upside-down N.

Of course, in a chemical soup we cannot even ensure that the letters are in the correct order. So let's scramble the letters until we end up with something like O-[blank]-upside-down N-[blank]-sideways P-[blank]-[blank]-sideways T.

The final product bears almost no relation to the word *protein*. This is about how close scientists come to creating a real protein in a test tube. There are no natural forces capable of organizing amino acids in the right sequence to produce a functional protein.

Of course, you or I could arrange Scrabble letters in the right sequence easily. But we do it by using something *beyond* natural forces. We use intelligence. The missing ingredient in standard theories of life's origin is an intelligent agent.

The idea of a Creator suddenly looks a lot more reasonable than any other theory on the market today. 🔲

CODE
OF LIFE

Friday

I N 1967 ASTRONOMERS WERE STARTLED to discover radio pulses coming from outer space. "Our first thought," they said, was that "this was another intelligent race" trying to communicate with us. They labelled the signals "LGM," standing for Little Green Men. But it turned out they had discovered a pulsar, a rotating star that mimics a radio beacon.

How can scientists tell whether something is coming from a natural or an intelligent source? When you think of it, this is the question at the heart of the creation/evolution debate. How can we tell whether life originated by natural causes or was created by an intelligent being?

Think of some common analogies. Imagine we are traveling and see a mountain with the faces of four presidents carved in it. Immediately we recognize the work of an intelligent agent. No one would mistake Mount Rushmore for a natural phenomenon.

Or imagine we're walking along a beach and see words written in the sand: "John Loves Mary." Immediately we recognize that this is not something produced by the waves.

Suppose we look up at the sky and see something that looks fluffy and white that spells out, "Drink Coca-Cola." Without a moment's doubt we conclude that this is no ordinary cloud, and we look around for an airplane pilot doing skywriting.

Common experience gives us a good idea of the things nature is capable of creating by itself—and the things that can only be created by an intelligent source.

What does this tell us about the origin of life?

At the core of life is the DNA code, which functions exactly like a language. In other words, when geneticists probed the nucleus of the cell they came across something analogous to "John Loves Mary" or "Drink Coca-Cola." So if these short phrases had to be written by an intelligent being, how much more the DNA code, which contains as much information as a city library.

You don't need sophisticated knowledge of chemistry and genetics to respond to challenges from evolution. Based on common experience, you can argue logically that life was created by an intelligent agent.

Which is exactly what Christians have always believed. ※

SCIENCE
BY DECREE

Weekend

A T SAN FRANCISCO STATE UNIVERSITY, the question of scientific truth was put to a vote. The biology department voted 27 to 5

that naturalistic evolution is the only theory admissible in biology—and that reference to an intelligent cause at the origin of life
is strictly unscientific.

With this resolution, quips science writer Paul Nelson, we
have witnessed nothing less than the birth of a new method in
science. Why run costly experiments? To do science today, all we
need is a ballot box.

The farce began when a prominent biologist named Dean
Kenyon was called on the carpet for teaching that the standard
Darwinian model of evolution is riddled with problems. Kenyon
himself was once a true believer in evolution, and even co-authored
a best-selling advanced textbook teaching that life originated from
a soup of chemicals.

But over the years Kenyon detected weaknesses in the theory.
Experiments designed to simulate the origin of life yielded dis-
couraging results: mostly a tarry sludge with only traces of the
simple building blocks of life, such as amino acids. When it comes
to highly complex molecules such as protein and DNA, no experiment gives the slightest evidence that they can form spontaneously
under realistic natural conditions.

In fact, the existence of DNA means that the core of life is a
code, a message—analogous to a book or a computer program.
Where did the messages come from? There are no natural causes
known to science that can create messages. The messages you
and I read come from the hand of intelligent beings—from book
authors and computer programmers. The DNA code is powerful
evidence that life itself came from the hand of an intelligent Being.

These are the ideas Dean Kenyon was teaching his biology
students—not religion, just scientific facts. Still his colleagues accused him of teaching religion and yanked him out of his classes.

Fortunately, the action was protested by the university's
Academic Freedom Committee, and Dr. Kenyon was reinstated.
That's when the faculty tried to muzzle him by decree—by sim-
ply voting his ideas unscientific.

But if anything qualifies as unscientific, it is putting theories
to a vote. Textbooks tell us science relies on evidence from experiments, not on pronouncements by authorities. Dean Kenyon is like
a modern Galileo, and the secular faculty members are like the
church officials who refused to look through Galileo's telescope. ▨

NATURAL EVILS

Monday

ONE SPECIES OF FIREFLY HAS PERFECTED the art of deception. Hungry males too lazy to go hunting have learned to mimic the distinctive flash of the female. When a would-be suitor is attracted and comes courting, the fake female gobbles him up.

Examples like this were the stock in trade at a symposium entitled, "The Evolution of Deception." Scientists concluded that deception can be a helpful evolutionary adaptation. Which raises a haunting question: If deceit is a normal part of nature, is it natural for *humans* as well?

A similar question was raised when scientists studied chimpanzees and monkeys that kill their infants. If evolution has selected the behavior, scientists argued, it must confer some kind of adaptive benefit. A *Newsweek* article entitled "Nature's Baby Killers" said, "Infanticide can no longer be considered 'abnormal.' It is, instead, as 'normal' as parenting instincts, sex drives, and self-defense."

This is horrifying—and yet perfectly logical once you accept the premise of evolution. If human beings are kin to the beasts, then whatever exists in nature must be normal.

The only way to avoid these ghastly conclusions is by accepting the biblical concept of a transcendent standard. The Bible teaches that the world as it exists today is far different from the world God originally created. The world was created good, a reflection of God's character.

But that reflection has been darkened by sin and evil. In Romans, Paul says even nature was affected by the fall into sin. The world we see around us today isn't normal, it's *abnormal*. It falls short of God's original plan. That means we don't take our standards from the world as it exists today. We have a higher standard in God's revelation.

But evolution doesn't recognize any higher standard. Whatever people do, whatever beetles do, whatever chimpanzees do, is normal. Things like deception and killing aren't sins, they're just part of the natural order. They may even be helpful evolutionary adaptations.

At stake in the evolution controversy are not just esoteric scientific details about genes and fossils—but the entire biblical system of ethics. Christianity teaches that we are governed by a law higher than natural law. For we are not animals in a state of nature. We are sinners in the hands of a holy God. ▓

DID VIOLENCE EVOLVE?

Tuesday

B OSNIA. THE PHOTOS SHOW FLEEING refugees with their ragged bundles and mournful eyes. But what really caught my eye was an article in the *Boston Globe* trying to explain *why* tragedies like this happen. The cause of the bloodbath in Bosnia, says the *Globe*, lies in our genes.

Ethnic conflict is merely part of our evolutionary inheritance, the article explains. Xenophobia—fear of foreigners—has its roots in conflict between animal groups in the jungles and savannahs.

This idea comes from a school of thought known as biopolitics: the attempt to explain politics by biology. Since aggression and conflict exist among primates, the theory says, they must serve a useful evolutionary function. Anthropologist Charles Southwick says aggression helps maintain social groupings. It's an evolutionary "adaptation," just like the tiger's claws or the eagle's feathers.

But isn't this carrying evolution too far? Biopolitics nearly makes ethnic conflict sound like a good thing. After all, if intergroup aggression has been preserved by natural selection, presumably it must confer some sort of evolutionary advantage.

This is the flaw that plagues any theory reducing human beings to biology: It eliminates the moral dimension. Men and women become pawns of their genes; no behavior is right or wrong, it is merely a natural phenomenon.

Is it wrong when the lion ambushes the gazelle? Or when the hawk swoops down on the rabbit? No, these things are just part of nature. In biopolitics, human actions are likewise just part of nature. Warfare and "ethnic cleansing" aren't immoral, any more than the food chain is.

What's worse, these things cannot be changed. You see, if violent patterns of behavior are coded into our genes through millions of years of evolution, you can bet no one is going to change that in a single lifetime.

But if violence is sin—a result of wrong moral choices—then what a wonderful freedom we have. If we have sinned, we can repent. If we've made a wrong moral choice, we can set it right.

So the choice is ours: When we see the wrenching photos of Serbs and Croats locked in bloody warfare we can attribute it to an irresistible biological imperative, as biopolitics does.

Or we can call it sin, and apply the message of redemption. ✷

ARMCHAIR
BIBLE CRITICS

Wednesday

WHEN AN ANCIENT BURIAL CAVE was excavated in Jerusalem in 1993, one casket had a name carved on it: "Joseph, son of Caiaphas." Biblical scholars immediately took notice. The high priest in Jesus' day was named Joseph, often called Caiaphas. Could these be the remains of the man who handed Jesus over to the Romans?

Many archaeologists think so. Which means that once again archaeology fits the biblical record and confounds the skeptics.

Most skeptical theories of Scripture were devised *before* archaeology had become a science. People became skeptics not because of any *facts* but because of their *philosophy*—the philosophy of evolution.

Long before Darwin developed evolution as a biological theory, it was already a philosophy. Nearly two hundred years ago, the philosopher Hegel argued that everything moves in stages from simple to complex—including societies and ideas. No idea is true in an absolute or timeless sense.

In theology Hegel's evolutionary philosophy led to what we call "higher criticism." If ideas evolve, theologians decided, then religious ideas must begin with crude, simple notions about God and move gradually to more sublime notions.

The trouble is, the Bible doesn't show any such progression. It doesn't begin with "primitive" ideas, like animism and polytheism, and then progress to more "advanced" ideas, like monotheism. Instead, it reflects a high ethical monotheism right from the opening words of Genesis.

But that didn't stop the modernist theologians. We'll just figure out the "correct" evolutionary sequence, they said, and rearrange the Bible to *make* it fit. Passages that theologians regarded as crude and anthropomorphic they dated earlier, while passages they regarded as more refined they dated later—no matter *where* those passages actually appear in the biblical text.

The very fact that the Bible *doesn't* fit the evolutionary sequence, critics said, proves that it is full of errors.

Here is the root of biblical skepticism. It didn't stem from any difficulty in fitting the Bible to the historical facts of archaeology. It was purely an armchair effort to force Christianity into an evolutionary philosophy.

So when you hear the word *evolution*, don't just think of Darwin. The most destructive part of evolution has been its philosophy—one that insists on forcing everything, even religion, into a preconceived evolutionary sequence.

And as archaeologists make new discoveries, it's a philosophy that is increasingly discredited. ▨

IS EVERYTHING IN FLUX?

Thursday

WE'RE OFTEN TOLD THAT EVOLUTION IS just a scientific theory, but it has become much more than that. It's become an entire philosophy of life, shaping every subject area.

Take, for example, sociology. The founder of sociology was August Comte, who proposed three stages of social evolution. All societies, Comte said, move upward until they reach a stage of scientific enlightenment.

In the field of law, most students today are trained in what is sometimes called "sociological law:" It rejects any transcendent standard of justice and bases law on the judge's perception of changing social norms. This is explicitly labeled an evolutionary approach to law.

In psychology virtually all the leaders in the field have been committed Darwinists, from Freud to Pavlov to B. F. Skinner. They began with the assumption that human beings are merely advanced animals and then sought to reduce human nature to animal functions—instincts and reflexes.

What about education? John Dewey, regarded as the "father" of American education, was an enthusiastic evolutionist. He argued that the human mind is a tool that has evolved by adaptation to the environment, just like a fin or a claw. The test of an idea is therefore not whether it is *true*, Dewey said, but merely whether it *works*—whether it helps us adapt to our circumstances.

Dewey's evolutionary philosophy led to a profound relativism that is everywhere evident in our schools today. Values courses teach children they can choose whatever values work for them.

So you see, evolution is not just a theory that tries to explain how fish grew legs and how birds developed feathers. It affects every subject area. It serves as scientific justification for a philosophy that treats human beings as merely evolving organisms. ※

DREAMS
OF SCIENCE

Friday

NEXT TIME YOU'RE IN A BOOKSTORE, BROWSE through the science section for some startling new titles: *Theories of Everything, The God Particle, The Mind of God.* The theme of these books is that physics may soon find a supertheory that explains everything in the universe.

Physics, it seems, is replacing theology as the "queen" of the sciences—with physicists playing the role of theologians.

Consider *Dreams of a Final Theory*, by Nobel-Prize winner Steven Weinberg. The final theory Weinberg dreams of would unify the four fundamental physical forces: the electromagnetic force, weak nuclear force, strong nuclear force, and gravity. This theory is often labeled the "holy grail" of physics, the "theory of everything."

But the idea that a theory of *physics* could also be a theory of *everything* assumes that everything is physical. The term for this is reductionism. Reductionists argue that human consciousness is nothing but chemical reactions in the brain; that life is nothing but the outworking of physical forces in the DNA molecule; that the universe itself is nothing but a collection of particles, traceable ultimately to the initial conditions of the Big Bang.

This is the dominant view in the scientific establishment today. And there's not much tolerance for alternative views. In *Dreams of a Final Theory*, Weinberg casts religion into the outer darkness of "wishful thinking." If we stick to science, Weinberg insists, what we see is a universe that is impersonal and without purpose. This may be a "bleak" and "chilling" view of the world, he writes, but it's the *only* one sanctioned by science.

Nonsense. Science doesn't require anyone to be a reductionist. Saying that a living organism is nothing but a collection of molecules is like saying that a house is nothing but a collection of bricks—or that a Dickens novel is nothing but a collection of words. No one believes that.

What people like Weinberg are really doing is equating science with their own personal philosophy. Science has been hijacked by reductionists who want to define for all the rest of us what qualifies as ultimate truth.

Christians need to insist on the distinction between science and philosophy. In our children's textbooks, in television nature programs, what goes under the rubric of "science" is not always a neutral search for knowledge. Often it is an expression of reductionist philosophy.

Where physics is taking over the role of theology. ▨

MY FATHER'S WORLD

Weekend

IF WE'RE LOOKING FOR THE REAL reason Western culture is polluting the air and water, it's "primarily the Judeo-Christian myth." So says actress Jane Fonda. What we need is a revival of "nature-based religions," said Fonda: to realize that "the earth, like us, is a living, breathing organism . . . and that we are all part of it."

We've all heard this before.

For years New Agers have blamed the ecological crisis on Christianity. But the Bible actually teaches a very *high* view of creation. When God put Adam in the garden to till and keep it, the Hebrew words mean "serve" and "take care of." Genesis teaches that humans have "dominion" over nature, but that doesn't mean arbitrary rule; it means stewardship. This is *God's* world, and we're accountable to Him for the way we treat it.

Granted, Westerners have often abused nature. But that didn't stem from Christianity, it came from humanism. As Western culture rejected the Bible, man was no longer regarded as God's servant but as the pinnacle of evolution, the victor in the Darwinian struggle for existence, who owes nothing to anyone.

Think back to the nineteenth century: The robber barons of industry didn't appeal to *Christianity* to justify their cutthroat tactics. They appealed to evolution. Listen to the words of William Graham Sumner, America's most influential Social Darwinist: "There can be no rights against Nature," he wrote, "except to get out of her whatever we can."

Today we are appalled at such a crass attitude, and rightly so. But the antidote to Western humanism is not Eastern pantheism—Fonda's "nature-based religions." Pantheism denies that humans are unique; it puts us on the same level as the trees and the grass.

But it's an obvious fact that humans do have unique powers that no other organism has. The only religion that can solve our ecological problems is one that *acknowledges* our uniqueness— and then gives ethical guidelines to *direct* our unique capabilities. Christianity does just that: It teaches that humans were made in the image of God to be stewards over His creation. ※

Monday

ARE ANIMALS EQUAL?

SOME PEOPLE THINK ANIMAL RIGHTS activists are just sensitive people who love animals. And no doubt some of them are. But the basic assumption behind much of the animal-rights movement is that nature is all there is, that there is no God.

The philosophical label for this is naturalism. In naturalism, humans are not unique: We are just another part of nature, along with birds and bears and polliwogs. As one animal-rights leader put it, "In the scheme of life, we're all equal."

But the biblical world view teaches that humans are unique, created in the image of God to be stewards over the rest of creation. This basic biblical insight is confirmed daily by common experience: Humans do have power over nature—for good or for ill—that no other creature has.

Our calling, of course, is to use it for good. The earth doesn't belong to us; it belongs to the Lord, who made it. We are stewards, accountable to God for everything we do.

Historically, Christians have often crusaded to treat animals humanely. Saint Francis of Assisi is the best-known example, living his simple life among the creatures he loved. In the 1800s, one of my own heroes in the faith, William Wilberforce, took a public stand against cruelty to animals. Not in the name of animal rights but in the name of stewardship.

That difference is crucial. The animal-rights movement is not just about being kind to animals. It's about a radically naturalistic world view that denies any special status to humans.

Animal rights may sound appealing because it promises a naturalistic utopia—a future when we will live in harmony with nature, when the lion will lie down with the lamb. But this is a secular substitute for heaven—a secular second coming: Not when Christ comes down to earth, but when humanity comes down to the level of the animals.

RAT TALES

Tuesday

A TROPICAL FISH OWNER LEFT HIS FISH alone for several days while he went on vacation—only to be summoned to court and charged with cruelty to animals.

Why are animal-rights activists sometimes so extremist? The answer is that they don't believe there is any fundamental difference between animals and humans. Ingrid Newkirk of People for the Ethical Treatment of Animals (PETA) even compares eating meat to the Nazi holocaust. "Six million Jews died in concentration camps," Newkirk says, "but six billion boiler chickens will die here in slaughterhouses."

Comparisons like this are meant to make us more sensitive to the plight of chickens and cows, but what they really do is trivialize evil committed against humans. And the haunting danger is that when humans are put on the same level as animals, we may begin *treating* them as animals. Charles Oliver of *Reason* magazine puts it well: "By placing chickens and Jews on the same ethical plane," he warns, "animal-rights activists may inadvertently make it easier for a future Hitler to herd millions of humans into gas chambers."

Oliver is right. As Christians, we have a moral duty to respect the animal world as God's handiwork. But *respect* for animals is completely different from *rights* for animals—and we should never confuse the two.

PETA's Ingrid Newkirk says openly that the animal rights movement is "at great odds" with Christianity. She denounces Christian teaching as "supremacist" because it confers special moral status on human life. In her view, humans are merely a part of nature—nothing more.

Ultimately, that is the question we all have to answer: Are we made in the image of God? Or is there really no difference between a child and a chicken? ✺

SICK MINDS

Wednesday

IN THE MAGAZINE *FREE INQUIRY*, BRITISH biologist Richard Dawkins calls religion a mental virus—a false belief that infects your mind the way a virus infects your body. Consider the symptoms, Dawkins writes. People don't adopt a religion after carefully weighing the evidence; faith is "caught" the way a cold is. It spreads from person to person like an infection, especially in families. For those who convert, Dawkins says, an evangelist may be the infectious agent. Revivals are virtual epidemics of faith.

Well, it's all a clever biological metaphor, but I say Dr. Dawkins is a bit too quick with his diagnosis. It's true, of course, that many of us learn our religious faith at our parents' knees. But the way we *learn* about religion is a separate question from whether or not it is *true*.

No matter what we learned as children, we all come to a point when we make our own commitment—when we believe because we are personally convinced by experience and evidence. Unlike some religions, the Bible does not preach a mystical experience that overrides reason. Instead, Scripture connects its message to historical events that could be seen and confirmed by anyone present at the time—from Elijah calling down fire from heaven on Mount Carmel to Jesus publicly crucified and raised from the dead.

When Dawkins calls religion a virus, he's ignoring the real character of Christianity. He's simply assuming that people accept it without any intelligent reasons—that they are driven by sheer emotional need.

But haven't we heard this somewhere before? It's nothing but the old argument that religion is a crutch for weak people. Karl Marx called religion the "opiate of the people." Sigmund Freud labeled it a neurosis.

But notice that neither Dawkins nor Marx nor Freud ever *proved* that religion is a mental sickness. They simply *assumed* that Christianity is false, and then set out to identify some aberration of the mind to explain why people still believe it.

The entire argument is hopelessly circular. First it assumes that Christianity is false, then it diagnoses faith as a sickness to *convince* people that it's false. This is question-begging of the worst kind.

Genuine Christian faith doesn't *infect* your mind, it *respects* your mind. Christians ought to be the most tough-minded of all, unafraid to face any question about our faith. ※

THE SERMON
AND THE SWORD

Thursday

AFTER LECTURING ON A COLLEGE campus I was asked, "Mr. Colson, how can you try to live by the Sermon on the Mount and at the same time support the use of military might?"

It's a fair question. Jesus teaches that we should love our enemies, return good for evil. But is this realistic in a world where evil so often triumphs?

When Jesus announced the Kingdom, He set forth radical standards by which its citizens are to live. He knew such a lifestyle would be both costly and complex, but it would witness the values of God's kingdom even in the midst of the evil of this world.

Christ was not suggesting that the obedient Christian would be able to usher in the kingdom of God on earth. Only Christ Himself would do that when He returns. But for this period between the two stages—the announcement of the Kingdom and its final consummation—God has provided structures to restrain the evil of this world. The state is even ordained to wield the sword when necessary; and the Christian is commanded to obey the state and to respect its authority as God's instrument.

The Christian, therefore, follows two commandments: to live by Christ's teaching in the Sermon on the Mount, modeling the values of God's kingdom—the one yet to come in its fullness— and at the same time to support government's role in preserving order as a witness to God's authority over the present kingdoms of this world. So while the Christian is not to return evil for evil (he must instead exercise forgiveness, breaking the cycle of evil), he may participate in the God-ordained structure that restrains the evil and chaos of the fallen world by the use of force. ▧

WHO WANTS TO BE FIRST?
Friday

JESUS CHRIST TURNED CONVENTIONAL VIEWS of power upside down. When His disciples argued over who was the greatest, Jesus rebuked them. "The greatest among you should be like the youngest, and the one who rules like the one who serves," He said. Imagine the impact His statement would make in the back rooms of American politicians or in the carpeted boardrooms of big business—or, sadly, in some religious councils.

Jesus was as good as His words. He washed His own followers' dusty feet, a chore reserved for the lowliest servant of first-century Palestine. A king serving the mundane physical needs of His subjects? Incomprehensible. Yet servant leadership is the heart of Christ's teaching, "Whoever wants to be first must be slave of all."

His was a revolutionary message to the class-conscious culture of the first-century, where position and privilege were entrenched, evidenced by the Pharisees with their reserved seats in the synagogue, by masters ruling slaves, and by men dominating women. It is no less revolutionary today in the class-conscious cultures of the East and West where power, money, fame, and influence are idolized in various forms. ▧

KINGDOM POWER
Weekend

NOTHING DISTINGUISHES THE KINGDOMS of man from the kingdom of God more than their diametrically opposed views of the exercise of power. One seeks to control people, the other to serve people; one promotes self, the other prostrates self; one seeks prestige and position, the other lifts up the lowly and despised. As citizens of the Kingdom today practice this view of power, they are setting an example for their neighbors by modeling servanthood.

This does not mean that the Christian can't use power. In positions of leadership, especially in government institutions to which God has specifically granted the power of the sword, the Christian can do so in good conscience. But the Christian uses power with a different motive and in different ways: not to impose his or her personal will over others but to preserve God's plan for order and justice for all.

Those who accept the biblical view of servant leadership treat power as a humbling delegation from God, not as a right to control others.

It is crucial for Christians to understand this difference. For through this upside-down view of power, the kingdom of God can play a special role in the affairs of the world. ※

STANDING ON A PEDESTAL

Monday

HAVING WITNESSED WATERGATE FROM THE inside, I can attest to the wisdom of Lord Acton's well-known adage: Power corrupts; absolute power corrupts absolutely.

It is crucial to note, however, that it is power that corrupts, not power that is corrupt. It is like electricity. When properly handled, electricity provides light and energy; when mishandled it destroys. God has given power to the state to be used to restrain evil and maintain order. It is the use of power, whether for personal gain or for the state's ordained function, that is at issue.

The problem of power is not limited to public officials. It affects all human relationships, from the domineering parent to the bullying boss to the manipulative spouse to the pastor who plays God. It is also wielded effectively by the seemingly weak who manipulate others to gain their own ends. The temptation to abuse power confronts everyone.

The lure of power can separate the most resolute of Christians from the true nature of Christian leadership, which is service to others. It's difficult to stand on a pedestal and wash the feet of those below. ▨

CHRISTIANS IN OFFICE

Tuesday

MANY CHRISTIANS BELIEVE THEY HAVE found the means for bringing needed social change: simply elect Christians to political office.

But history puts the lie to the notion that just because one is devout one will be a just and wise ruler. Take the nineteenth-century leader who forged a unified Germany from a cluster of minor states. Otto von Bismarck-Schonhausen was a committed Christian who regularly read the Bible, spoke openly of his devotion to God, and claimed divine guidance in response to prayer. "If I were no longer a Christian, I would not serve the king another hour," he once declared.

Yet Bismarck was also the ruthless architect of *Deutschland Über Alles* (Germany Over All), a chauvinistic world-view that laid the foundation for two world wars. Historians describe Bismarck as a Machiavellian master of political duplicity who specialized in blood and iron.

Politicians, like those in any other specialized field, should be selected on the basis of their qualifications and abilities *as well as* on their moral character. Even in Israel's theocracy, Jethro advised Moses to select "capable men . . . who fear God" to help in governing the Jewish nation.

Jethro's advice makes sense. If terrorists were to take control of an airport, would we want policemen who were merely devout Christians handling the negotiations or would we choose those who had specialized training in hostage negotiations? Luther had it right when he said he would rather be ruled by a competent Turk than an incompetent Christian.

THE WILL TO POWER

Wednesday

THE HISTORY OF THE LAST FIFTY YEARS has validated Nietzsche's argument that man's desire to control his own destiny and to impose his will on others is the most basic human motivation. Christian psychiatrist Paul Tournier wrote, "We are moved without knowing it by an imperious will to power, which brooks no obstacles."

Nietzsche's prophecy that the "will to power" would fill the twentieth-century's vacuum of values has been fulfilled. We see it on an individual level in the quest for autonomy and the shedding of all restraints. On a corporate level, it is dramatically evident in the rise of gangster leaders like Hitler and Stalin, and evident as well in the bloated growth of Western governments. The resultant illusion—that all power resides in large institutions—is the salient characteristic of modern politics.

America's Founding Fathers were influenced by the Judeo-Christian teaching about the human vulnerability to abuse power. Hence they adopted the principle of the separation of powers. Within the government, power was diffused through a system of checks and balances so that no one branch could dominate another. The Founders also assumed that the religious value system, evidenced through the separate institution of the church, would be the most powerful brake on the natural avarice of government.

As Tocqueville observed, "Religion in America takes no direct part in the government or society but it must, nevertheless, be regarded as the foremost of the political institutions of that country." 🔲

POLITICAL SUBVERSIVES

Thursday

THE TENSION BETWEEN THE KINGDOM of God and the kingdoms of man runs like an unbroken thread through the history of the past two thousand years. It began not long after Christ's birth. Herod, the Roman-appointed king over the Jews and as vicious a tyrant as ever lived, was gripped with fear when the Magi arrived seeking the "King of the Jews." Herod knew the ancient Jewish prophecies that a child would be born to reign over them, ushering in a kingdom of peace and might.

Herod called the Magi to his ornate throne room. In what has become common practice in the centuries since, he tried to manipulate the religious leaders for political advantage. He told them to go find this king in Bethlehem so he too could worship Him.

The rest of the story is familiar. The Magi found Jesus but were warned in a dream to avoid Herod and return to the East. Jesus's parents, similarly warned, escaped with their son to Egypt—just ahead of Herod's marauding soldiers who massacred all the male children of Jesus' age in and near Bethlehem.

Herod didn't fear Jesus because he thought He would become a religious or political leader. He had suppressed such opponents before. Herod feared Christ because He represented a kingdom greater than his own.

Jesus was later executed for this same reason. Though He told Pilate His kingdom was not of this world, the sign over His cross read "INRE"—King of the Jews. The executioner's sarcasm was double-edged.

His followers' faithfulness to Christ's kingdom led to their persecution as well. During the early centuries Christians were martyred not for religious reasons—Rome, after all, was a land of many gods—but because they refused to worship the emperor. Because they would not say, "We have no king but Caesar," the Roman government saw them as political subversives.

Must the church and the state inevitably be in conflict? To some extent the answer is yes. In a sinful world the struggle for power, which inevitably corrupts, is unavoidable. When the church isn't being persecuted, it is being corrupted.

But every generation has an obligation to seek anew a healthy relationship between church and state. Both are reflections of man's nature; both have a role to play. 🔳

TAXES AND TIBERIUS

Friday

JESUS WAS REMARKABLY INDIFFERENT to those who held political power. He had no desire to replace Caesar or Pilate with His apostles Peter or John. He gave civil authority its due, rebuking both the Zealots and Peter for using the sword. This infuriated the religious right of His day. Eager to discredit Jesus, the Pharisees and Herodians tried trapping Him over the question of allegiance to political authority.

"Tell us," they asked, "is it right to pay taxes to Caesar or not?"

The question put Jesus in the middle: If He said no, He would be a threat to the Roman government; if He said yes, He would lose the respect of the masses who hated the Romans.

Jesus asked them for a coin. It was a Roman denarius, the only coin that could be used to pay the hated yearly poll tax. On one side was the image of the Emperor Tiberius, around which were written the words *Tiberius Caesar Augustus, son of the divine Augustus.*

"Whose portrait is this?" He asked. "And whose inscription?"

"Caesar's," they replied impatiently.

"Give to Caesar what is Caesar's and to God what is God's," replied Jesus, handing the coin back to them. They stared at Him in stunned silence.

Not only had He eluded the trap, but He had also put Caesar in his place. Christ might simply have said, "Give to Caesar what is Caesar's." That's all that was at issue. It was Caesar's image on the coin, and Caesar had authority over the state.

What made Him add the second phrase, "Give . . . to God what is God's"?

The answer, I believe, is found on the reverse face of the coin, which showed Tiberius' mother represented as the goddess of peace, along with the words *highest priest*. The blasphemous words commanded the worship of Caesar; they thus exceeded the state's authority.

Jesus' lesson was not lost on the early church. Government is to be respected and its rule honored. "It is necessary to submit to the authorities," wrote the apostle Paul. "If you owe taxes, pay taxes." But worship is reserved solely for God. ▨

Weekend

A NEW STATUS SYMBOL?

MOTHER'S DAY

IT'S THE LATEST STATUS SYMBOL, announced the *Wall Street Journal*. No, not designer clothes in the closet. Not even a BMW in the garage.

It's Mother in the kitchen.

Yes, the article says, in many communities mothers who stay home to raise their children have become fashionable again. Even chic. The way the *Journal* tells it, having Mom at home has become a new kind of one-upmanship—"a luxury that few families can afford."

But notice the almost disdainful tone reflected in these articles: Staying home when your children are young is portrayed as a "luxury" open only to the upwardly mobile.

What we're seeing is a reverse snobbery that says, *If you can afford to stay home, you must have money to waste—not like us honest working folks*. Raising your own children is being treated as a form of conspicuous consumption.

The irony is that this picture bears no relationship to the facts; most families with one parent at home are not wealthy. The average two-parent, single-income family earns less than $26,000 a year. By comparison, dual-income families average $38,000 a year. Clearly most families with a mother in the kitchen are making painful sacrifices to keep her there. Many mothers give up careers in favor of part-time and home-based work, for substantially lower pay.

Radical feminist dogma has taught women to find their true fulfillment in paid employment. But today we're witnessing a gradual reversal. In 1989 about 38 percent of women surveyed said they would quit their jobs to care for their children if they didn't need the money. By 1991 that number had grown to 56 percent. More than ever, Americans are realizing that individual accomplishment can never take the place of close family relationships.

On Mother's Day, let us remember that in Christian teaching, both parents are to make their children their top priority. And that's not just a luxury for the rich. It's the norm for all of us. ※

THE EVERLASTING INDIVIDUAL

Monday

EVERYONE WHO SPENDS TIME IN government becomes to some degree a "statist," dedicated to preserving the institutions of the state, often at all costs. The paramount place of the individual in the scheme of things is gradually, unknowingly subordinated. Law-and-order legislation, for example, is aimed at maintaining the stability of the state—even if a few individuals have their rights trampled on in the process.

A new perception came to me from a C. S. Lewis passage, one that sent many of my cherished political ideals scattering like tenpins hit by a perfect strike:

> If individuals live only seventy years, then a state, or a nation, or a civilization, which may last for a thousand years, is more important than an individual. But if Christianity is true, then the individual is not only more important but incomparably more important, for he is everlasting and the life of a state or a civilization, compared with his, is only a moment.

A Christian understanding of politics must begin with the fundamental conviction that the lowliest individual is more important than a state or nation. ▨

THE BEST OF CITIZENS

Tuesday

WHEN I WAS SERVING TIME FOR MY PART in the Watergate conspiracy, Al Quie, a senior congressman, made an astonishing proposal: He offered to serve the remainder of my prison sentence if authorities would release me so I could be with my then-troubled family.

Al, who later became governor of Minnesota, was a respected political leader; I was a member of the disgraced Nixon staff and a convicted felon. Al and I had not even been friends until a few months earlier when we met in a prayer group. Why would a man like Al Quie make such an offer?

Al took seriously Jesus' words: "As I have loved you, so you must love one another."

This commandment is a central law of the Kingdom and is what motivates Christians to serve the good of society. Certainly it motivated Christians of the nineteenth century when they spear-headed most of our nation's significant works of mercy and moral betterment. They founded hospitals, colleges, and schools; they organized welfare assistance and fed the hungry; they campaigned to end abuses ranging from dueling to slavery. Though much of this work has now been taken over by government agencies, Christians provided the original impetus. Today Christians still contribute the bulk of resources for private charities of compassion.

It is, in fact, their dual citizenship in God's kingdom and an earthly kingdom that should, as Augustine believed, make Christians the best of citizens. Not because they are more patriotic or civic-minded, but because they do out of obedience to God that which others do only if they choose or if they are forced. ※

CHRISTIAN PATRIOTISM

Wednesday

CHRISTIANS WHO ARE FAITHFUL TO Scripture should be patriots in the best sense of that word. As Augustine put it, Christians are commanded to love the whole world, yet practically speaking we cannot do so. Since we are placed as if by "divine lot" in a particular nation state, it is God's calling that we "pay special re-gard" to those around us in that state. We love the world by loving the specific community in which we live.

C. S. Lewis likened love of country to our love for the home and community in which we were raised. It is a natural love of the place where we grew up, he said, "love of old acquaintances, of familiar sights, sounds, and smells." However, in love of country, as in love of family, we don't love our spouses only when they are good. A patriot sees the flaws of his country, acknowledges them, weeps for them, but remains faithful in love.

Dr. Martin Luther King, Jr., spoke of love for his country even as he attempted to change its laws. "Whom you would change, you must first love," he said.

That's the kind of tough love Christians must have for their country: to love the land faithfully, but not at the expense of suspending moral judgment. 🕮

QUEST FOR COMMUNITY

Thursday

S OCIOLOGIST ROBERT NISBET SAYS man is engaged in a continual "quest for community." It is important to remember, however, that the state is not itself that community. Anyone who has ever dealt with a government bureaucracy knows that it is rare enough to get a phone call through, let alone to cultivate warm fuzzy feelings for the mammoth machine of big government.

But the state can protect people's voluntary efforts to shape community by granting equal protection of the law, by upholding principles of justice so the weak and powerless are not exploited, and by guaranteeing liberty and providing security. In this way the government sustains a stable environment in which people can live, producing art, literature, music, and children.

Or as C. S. Lewis said, they can partake of one of the primary benefits of democracy: the simple freedom to enjoy a cup of tea by the fire with one's family.

Christianity teaches that the state serves a divinely appointed and divinely defined task, although it is not in itself divine. Its authority is legitimate, though limited.

The *church* is the community that administers and encourages the worship of God and meets the spiritual needs of God's people, including teaching, offering the sacraments, and bearing one another's burdens. The church is not the actual kingdom of

God, but is to reflect the love, justice, and righteousness of God's kingdom within society. ◈

NO UTOPIAS

Friday

THE CHURCH MUST RESIST THE tempting illusion that it can usher in the Kingdom through political means. Jesus provided the best example for the church in His wilderness confrontation with Satan. The devil tempted Jesus to worship him and thus take dominion over the kingdoms of this world.

It was no small temptation. With that kind of power, Christ could enforce the Sermon on the Mount; love and justice could reign. He might have reasoned that if He didn't accept, someone else would.

This rationalization is popular today, right up through the highest councils of government: compromise to stay in power because there you can do more for the common good. But Jesus understood His mission, and it could not be accomplished by taking over the kingdoms of the world in a political coup.

Yet the most consistent heresy of the church has been to succumb to the very temptation Christ explicitly denied. In the Middle Ages this produced bloody crusades and inquisitions; in modern times it has fostered a type of utopianism. This century's social-gospel movement dissolved Christian orthodoxy into a campaign to eliminate every social injustice through governmental means.

In contemporary Christian circles utopianism crosses political lines, from the liberation theologians to the New Right and to the mainline church leaders.

It is on this point that the church has most frequently stumbled in its understanding of the kingdom of God. Oscar Cullman writes: "In the course of history the church has always assumed a false attitude toward the state when it has forgotten that the present time is already fulfillment, but not yet consummation."

The church's principal function is to proclaim the Good News and witness the values of the kingdom of God. ◈

Weekend

SPIRITUAL
D-DAY

THE JEWS OF FIRST-CENTURY PALESTINE missed the full significance of Christ's message of the kingdom of God. Jesus spoke
about a Kingdom that had come and a Kingdom that was still to
come—one Kingdom in two stages. This still confuses people today.

Perhaps a contemporary analogy will make it clearer. Probably the most significant event in Europe during World War II
was D-Day, June 6, 1944. That attack guaranteed the eventual
destruction of the Axis powers in Europe. Though the war continued, the outcome was determined. But it wasn't until May 8,
1945—V-E Day—that the results of the forces set in motion eleven
months earlier were realized.

We can compare this two-stage process to the strategy of the
kingdom of God.

A holy God would not take dominion over a sinful world. So
He first sent His Son, Jesus Christ, to die on the cross to pay the
debt for sin and thereby provide for men and women to be made
holy and fit for God's rule. Christ's death and resurrection—the
D-Day of human history—assure His ultimate victory. But we are
still at war. The enemy has not yet been vanquished, and the
fighting is still ugly. Yet Christ's invasion has assured the ultimate
outcome—victory for God and His people.

The second stage, which will take place when Christ returns,
will assert God's rule over all the universe; His kingdom will be
visible without imperfection. At that time there will be a final
judgment of all people, peace on earth, and the restoration of
harmony unknown since Eden.

Many soldiers died to bring about the victory in Europe. But
in the kingdom of God, it was the death of the King that assured
the victory.

Monday

CHEAP SUBSTITUTES

SINCE GOVERNMENT HAS FOR SO LONG promised to solve all human problems, the citizen sees paying taxes as his sole civic duty. Americans have grown accustomed to believing that the amount withheld from their pay checks satisfies their moral obligations to their neighbors, particularly to the less fortunate.

That is why, though we may grumble over high taxes and welfare cheaters, down deep, I suspect, we like the system. After all, it spares us the pain of looking into the vacant eyes of a hungry person, or drying the tears of an abused child. Money is a cheap substitute for human caring.

The Christian church should be leading the way toward a different response. Our Lord commanded us to care for the widows and orphans, feed the hungry, visit the sick and imprisoned, and bear one another's burdens.

Up until this century, evangelicals pioneered schools, built the first hospitals, cleaned up work abuses in the coal mines, provided homes for the poor and orphans. This is our heritage at Prison Fellowship.

There is a consistent refrain I hear whenever I visit a prison where our volunteers have been at work: "We never knew anyone cared for us," the inmates say, "but now we know someone does. Jesus does and the Prison Fellowship volunteers do—they care—someone cares." Government programs can't do that, but people can.

Tuesday

POLITICS AND PROGRESS

LONG AGO ENLIGHTENMENT THINKERS argued that through education man could eradicate sin and eventually build a perfect society. This, the prevailing myth of the twentieth century, was neatly capsuled in the second Humanist Manifesto: "By using technology wisely, we can control our environment, conquer poverty . . . modify behavior, alter the course of human evolution and cultural development . . . and provide humankind with unparalleled opportunity for achieving an abundant and meaningful life."

This is the humanist doctrine of sanctification by the free gift of progress. Its seduction lies in its appeal to our pride: The obstacles are not in ourselves but in our stars—or in unemployment, racism, poverty, or mental illness. Alexander Solzhenitsyn called this myth "the benevolent concept according to which man—the master of the world—does not bear any evils within himself, and all the defects of life are caused by misguided social systems."

The record of gore and inhumanity of this century, from the ovens of the Holocaust to the killing fields of Cambodia to the nightly slaughter on America's streets, ought to jar us into sober reality. The truth is, the human race hasn't outgrown sin, nor can we. It lives within us. Jesus put it succinctly: "From within, out of men's hearts, come evil thoughts, sexual immorality, theft, murder, adultery, greed, malice, deceit . . . All these evils come from inside and make a man unclean" (Mark 7:21-23).

That message may seem out of date in light of all the high-tech wizardry and enlightened sophistry of the 90s. But real progress, the kind that goes beyond satellites, FAX machines, and fiber optics, comes from only one source: from the One who can cleanse the evil within us by creating clean hearts within us. That is the only hope for real progress in this last decade of a tumultuous century. ▧

THE POLITICAL ILLUSION

Wednesday

MOST OF US INSTINCTIVELY TURN TO government to solve our social problems. It's a habit reinforced from the time we're young.

Listen to these quotations from the teachers' edition of a fifth-grade social studies textbook. "Today, when people lose their jobs," the textbook says, "they can get some money from the government."

A few pages later the book says, "Today, families who do not have enough money for food can get money from the government." A few pages later we read, "Today families who cannot afford to pay their rent can get help from the government."

The message is obvious: Government is the solution to every social need.

Here's a remarkable quotation that sums it all up. Explaining why the national government has grown so large, a junior-high civics textbook says that over time, "people were no longer content to live as their forefathers had lived. They wanted richer, fuller lives. *They wanted the government to help make their lives rich and full."*

This goes far beyond the traditional philosophy of limited government, in which the state is given only certain specified tasks, such as operating a police force and regulating traffic. And it shows that Americans have fallen prey to what political writer Jacques Ellul calls "the political illusion": the idea that government is actually capable of creating the good life, the good society.

This is nothing short of idolatry, treating the state as a god.

But like all idols, the state inevitably disappoints those who worship at its shrine. A government that can't even manage the simple accounting task of balancing its budget is certainly not capable of making people's lives "rich and full."

And it was never meant to.

There's only one way to make life "rich and full"—not by turning to government but by turning to God. The kingdoms of this world rise and fall, but the kingdom of God will rule in human hearts for eternity. ※

THE ART OF
SELF-GOVERNMENT

Thursday

THE AMERICAN EXPERIMENT IS UNIQUE in the central role played by free associations. The founders believed that no government can create virtue in citizens; government attempts to make people good are inherently coercive. Instead, our Constitution rests on the premise that virtue comes from citizens themselves—

acting through smaller groups, such as the family, church, community, and voluntary associations.

These are what English political writer Edmund Burke called the "little platoons." They are the arena where virtue—both the disposition to *be* good and the impulse to *do* good—can be cultivated. The little platoons are the roots of social order—schools in citizenship, where the art of self-government is practiced.

In the nineteenth century, Alexis de Tocqueville was impressed by the distinctively American habit of volunteerism. Americans form associations for everything, he wrote—to start libraries, send out missionaries, build hospitals and schools, raise funds for the needy. By contrast, Tocqueville remarked, in his own France there were not ten men doing what ordinary Americans do routinely. America is not historically a country of rugged individualists; it is a country of communities.

Little platoons not only inspire republican virtues, they also check expanding government power. As Russell Kirk argues, most grandiose schemes for engineering society are based on the idea that individuals are "social atoms"—isolated, unconnected, interchangeable—like Lego blocks that can be moved around and plugged in wherever the state wishes.

In the words of historian Hannah Arendt, totalitarian leaders seek to create a mass of atomized, isolated individuals—people who can be totally dominated by the state because they have no competing loyalties to family, church, neighbors, or community associations. The little platoons stand in the way of the totalitarian impulse, preserving an arena of voluntary virtue. ▨

LITTLE PLATOONS

Friday

ONE OF AMERICA'S POOREST neighborhoods is Summervill in Atlanta, Georgia—the site of the 1996 Olympic Games.

Only a generation ago, Summerhill was a bustling neighborhood, alive with block parties, church socials, and local businesses. But in the 1960s and 1970s, the neighborhood was targeted for urban renewal. The government promised to transform the neighborhood into a modern mecca, with new homes, schools, and community centers. Federal agencies poured nearly $200 million into the project. Yet today Summerhill is a mere ghost of the vibrant community it once was, a place of boarded-up buildings, weed-infested vacant lots, and crack-cocaine dens. What went wrong?

Urban renewal was based on a political philosophy that looked to the state as the only instrument for meeting human needs. It ignored social groupings like family, church, and neighborhood—what the great British statesman Edmund Burke called the little platoons: the groups where we meet people face to face and form our most intimate relationships.

With total disregard for the little platoons, urban planners brought their bulldozers into Summerhill and razed houses and local businesses to the ground. They built a highway that cut right across the neighborhood. They built a stadium for the Atlanta Falcons that displaced some five thousand residents. Then they tried to build a new community from scratch.

It was an abject failure.

Cases like Summerhill should make government rethink its philosophy: to decentralize power and return it to Burke's little platoons. At the turn of the century Christian statesman Abraham Kuyper said that a biblically based political theory should recognize the distinctive task of each social structure: family, church, school, business. The state's role is to protect these little platoons so they can carry out their God-given tasks. But instead the modern state tries to *usurp* their tasks, leaving behind broken families and shattered neighborhoods—like Summerhill.

If we want to be a nation of vibrant, caring communities, we have to tend the smaller structures where real relationships and real love can grow. ※

SOCIETY'S
SCAFFOLDING

Weekend

A FEW YEARS AGO, THE FALL OF Communism was hailed as a great victory for freedom and democracy. But the decline of tyranny has not led automatically to the rise of democracy. And the reason is something we all ought to think about seriously: Societies cannot be strong unless *every sector* of society is strong and free.

Under Communism the government controlled all sectors of society: the marketplace, the academy, the arts, the family, and most tragically the church. Any independent source of moral authority was reckoned as a threat to centralized government authority—and was squashed.

As a result, when the government dissolved, there were no other social structures strong enough to pick up the pieces. The state had insisted on being the scaffolding for all society—and when that scaffolding broke, Russian society collapsed.

Totalitarian control had destroyed the economic infrastructure, denying the rights of property and exchange. It had muzzled Russia's intellectual leaders, suppressing any vigorous exchange of ideas. Most harmful, it had seriously weakened churches and families, denying the rights of worship and moral education.

As a result, social and spiritual chaos has spread through Russia. Organized crime is bleeding the economy. Citizens are buying guns for protection from street thugs. Pornography is sold openly from street-corner kiosks. Prostitution is burgeoning. Rebuilding a social order from scratch is a long and difficult task.

Here in America we ought to take the lesson to heart: Every time we grant government the power to take on new functions, it takes power *away* from other social structures—inevitably leaving them weaker. In Russia it happened all at once, during the Russian revolution. In America it is happening piecemeal, as the government expands its power outside the realm of politics proper and tries to run the economy or regulate social and moral issues.

The anarchy in Russia is a vivid lesson in what can happen when state regulation becomes so broad that it cripples the private sector.

Monday

SAINTS AND BUREAUCRATS

IF MOTHER TERESA CAME TO YOUR CITY, would it welcome her? Silly question, you say. Mother Teresa is a Nobel Prize winner, a world figure.

Well, New York City didn't. The city government decided Mother Teresa just didn't have what it takes to run a proper charity institution.

What it takes, you see, is an elevator.

Mother Teresa has a powerful ministry to the sick and dying in India, and she decided New York City needed her services as much as Calcutta. So her organization, Missionaries of Charity, bought two crumbling town houses in New York City. Their plan was to renovate the houses and use them to care for the sick and the homeless. They found private funds to support the project. This wasn't going to cost the government one cent.

These nuns were accustomed to facing the obstacles of disease and poverty. But they were completely unprepared for the obstacles that could be thrown in their way by New York City bureaucrats.

Buried deep in the fine print of some city ordinance is a regulation decreeing that facilities like the one proposed by Mother Teresa must have an elevator. The elevator in question costs about $50,000, a fortune to nuns who are as poor as the needy people whom they serve.

The nuns were bewildered. They didn't need an elevator. They promised to carry the sick to bed in their arms, just as they always had. No good, said the bureaucrats. Rules are rules. In the end, Mother Teresa's nuns had to give up the houses and return to India. There they can care for the sick and the poor without an elevator. New York City's homeless now enjoy neither the loving arms nor the elevator.

All of this says a great deal about the bureaucratic approach to compassion. Government programs are often administered by men and women who work with all the moral passion of a computer. As Mother Teresa found out, the overriding concern is not helping the poor but keeping the rules.

Government charity may feed the body, but it is powerless to feed the soul. That is the realm of the Church. The tragedy is when government fails to recognize its own inadequacy and jealously uses its power to drive out private and Christian charity.

If Mother Teresa came to your city, would it welcome her? Maybe not such a silly question after all. ▨

Tuesday

A CONSTITUTION FOR A RELIGIOUS PEOPLE

THE BASIS OF THE AMERICAN IDEAL OF church and state came from the convergence of two conflicting ideologies: the eighteenth-century Enlightenment belief that both public and private virtue are possible without religion, and a reaction against the excesses of the state church in Europe. Among America's founders, the first view was held by Deists, while the second motivated Christians.

Thus two mortal enemies, the Enlightenment and the Christian faith, found a patch of common ground on American soil. Both agreed (for different reasons) that the new government should neither establish nor interfere with the church. This reasoning led to the adoption of the First Amendment, in order to protect the individual's right to freedom of conscience and expression, and to prevent the establishment of a state church.

Contrary to the belief of many today, the separation of church and state did not mean that America was to be a nation free of religious influence. John Adams eloquently acknowledged the understanding of our constitutional framers when in 1798 he wrote: "We have no government armed in power capable of contending with human passions unbridled by morality and religion . . . Our constitution was made only for a moral and religious people. It is wholly inadequate for the government of any other." ▨

 NOT MERELY
PRIVATE

Wednesday

AMERICA'S FOUNDING FATHERS WERE well aware that limited
government could succeed only if there was an underlying
consensus of values shared by the populace.

I am always reminded of this when I visit the House of Rep-
resentatives. A beautiful fresco on the upper walls of the chamber
itself contains the portraits of history's great lawmakers. Standing
at the speaker's desk and looking straight ahead over the main
entrance, one's eyes meet the piercing eyes of the first figure in
the series: Moses, the one who recorded the Law from the original Lawgiver.

Many original American visionaries believed that Christian
citizens would actively bring their religious values to the public
forum. George Washington said, "Of all the dispositions and habits which lead to a political prosperity, religion and morality are
indispensable supports."

When laws were passed reflecting the consensus of Christian values in the land, no one panicked supposing that the
Christian religion was being "established" or that a sectarian morality was being imposed on an unwilling people. The point of
the First Amendment was that such convictions could become
the law of the land only if a majority of citizens could be per-
suaded (without coercion), whether they shared the religious
foundation or not, of the merits of a particular proposition.

Today's widespread relegation of religion to something people
do only in the privacy of their homes or churches would have
been unimaginable to the founders of the republic—even those
who personally repudiated orthodox Christian faith.

Though America has drifted far from the vision of its
founders, our church-state system continues to offer one of the
world's most hopeful models in an otherwise contentious history
of conflict. ▨

ENEMY OF
GODLINESS

Thursday

ONE OF MY ASSIGNMENTS IN THE Nixon White House was liaison with special interest groups, including religious groups. I arranged cruises on the presidential yacht for prominent clergymen, Oval Office sessions for evangelical leaders.

The religious leaders got the chance to make their points with the president, but most important, those meetings paid off handsomely on election day. Religious leaders, I discovered, were the most naive about politics.

It's easy to become enthralled with access to power. In time, however, our well-intentioned attempts to influence government can become so entangled with a particular political agenda that it becomes our focus; our goal becomes maintaining our political access. When that happens, the gospel is held hostage to a political agenda—and we become part of the very system we were seeking to change.

So do we retreat from the political arena? Of course not. John Calvin argued the "cultural imperative," the need for Christians to make an impact in all areas of life; that includes politics. The real question is how do we reconcile the corrupting nature of power with our cultural imperative?

First, there are not political solutions to all our ills. That is an illusion that will distract us from the real problems—which are at root spiritual.

Second, Christians involved in politics need to remember that to lead, we must serve; political leadership is not about self-advancement, it's about service to others.

Third, power and authority must not be confused. Power is the ability to affect one's ends or purposes in the world. Authority is having not only the power (might) but also the right to affect one's purpose. Power is often maintained by naked force; authority springs from a moral foundation.

If the evangelical movement gains power in American life, it should lead us to some sober soul-searching. Worldly power—whether measured by buildings, budgets, baptisms, or access to the White House—is more often the enemy than the ally of godliness. ⚜

MINISTERS
OF GOD

Friday

HOW SHOULD WE LIVE UNDER A GOVERNMENT whose policies we sharply disagree with?

If we turn to Scripture, the answer is surprisingly simple: We live the same way we do under a government we *agree* with.

In 1 Timothy 2, Christians are commanded to pray for those who exercise civil authority over us. Paul hammers his message home using four different terms: supplications, prayers, intercessions, and giving thanks.

Why is prayer so crucial? Because, as Paul says in Romans 13, government officials are "ministers of God" to preserve order and administer justice in the public arena. Notice that Paul doesn't limit his description to good rulers only; in fact, he penned these words during the reign of Nero, one of the bloodiest of the Roman emperors.

Whether our rulers are good or bad, whether we agree or disagree with their policies, our duty remains the same: to respect and pray for them. This doesn't preclude criticizing their policies, of course; but even critique should flow from an attitude of prayer. ⚜

CIVILITY
OR SILENCE?

Weekend

THE BIBLE COMMANDS US TO "fear God, honor the King" and to "pray for those in authority." But what do we do when we disagree with the "King"—when those in authority impose harmful policies?

Samuel Rutherford, a seventeenth-century Scottish cleric, wrote a passionate treatise entitled *Lex Rex,* challenging the divine right of kings—contending that the law stands above the king. Rutherford's analysis rested on the crucial distinction between the office of the magistrate and the person of the magistrate. Christians are commanded to respect the *office*, he wrote; but if the *person* acts contrary to God's law, Christians have a duty to challenge him.

More recently, theologian Reinhold Niebuhr drew a similar distinction. On one hand, Niebuhr says, Christians are called to honor the ruling authority as a reflection of divine authority. On the other hand, the Bible is replete with prophetic judgments on *particular* rulers for oppressing the poor and defying divine law.

A genuinely biblical understanding of government must retain both these elements in tension: what Niebuhr calls "priestly sanctification" of the *principle* of government coupled with "prophetic criticism" of any *particular* government.

Modern evangelicals ought to show unfailing civility to government officials out of respect for their office. But being civil does not mean being silent or forsaking politics. "Priestly sanctification" must always be balanced with "prophetic criticism."

BATTLE OF
THE CROSSES

Monday

W HEN THE COMMUNIST TYRANTS held power in Poland, they ordered all crosses removed from classroom walls, factories, hospitals—all public institutions. But the Polish people rose up in a great wave of protest, and all across the land government officials backed down.

Yet in one small town, officials were determined to prevail. They insisted on taking down the crosses hanging in school classrooms. Students responded by staging a sit-in. Heavily armed riot police chased them out.

Then the students—nearly three thousand of them—carried the crosses to a nearby church to pray. The police surrounded the church. Violence was averted only when photographs of the confrontation were flashed around the globe, sparking widespread protest.

Compare that story to events in our own country. In 1963, the Supreme Court banned prayer from public schools. Many people took the decision as a signal that religion was no longer welcome in public places.

One small town was enmeshed in lawsuits for years. Zion, Illinois, was founded at the turn of the century as a religious community. Streets still bear names like Ezekiel, Gideon, Galilee. The city seal bears a cross, along with other Christian symbols.

I should say, it *used* to bear a cross. The seal came under the scrutiny of a group called American Atheists. Their Illinois director took the city of Zion to court, demanding that the seal be purged of its cross. After years of court battles, the American Atheists finally won. The crosses are now being removed from city stationary and police cruisers.

But what is this resounding silence that I hear? Where is the outcry that greeted Polish authorities when they tried to remove crosses throughout *their* country?

The courts say the state must maintain strict neutrality toward religion. But removing religious symbols from public places is not neutrality. On the contrary, it sends a highly negative message—that religion is something shameful, embarrassing, or at best strictly private.

We've come a long way from the day of the American founders, who regarded religious freedom as the first liberty. What they meant was that without the liberty to express our most fundamental beliefs, all other liberties inevitably crumble.

Alas, today the people of Poland seem to understand that better than we do here in America. ▩

DON'T SAY THAT WORD!

Tuesday

I T WAS THE MONDAY AFTER EASTER, and during show and tell a first-grade boy stood up to tell his friends about the Easter pageant held at his church. But as soon as he mentioned the resurrection of Jesus, the teacher cut him off.

"Sit down right now!'" she said in angry tones. "And don't ever say *that word* in here again." She was referring to the word *Jesus*.

All across America, school children are coming home with similar stories. Teachers have become so overly sensitive about religion in the classroom that they suppress any mention of it.

In another incident, a fifth-grade Indiana student was wearing a watch inscribed with the words, "Jesus Loves Me." A teacher saw the watch, demanded that she take it off, and confiscated it until the end of the day.

In a St. Louis public school, children decorate Easter eggs in art class. But they are no longer allowed to call them Easter eggs—because that has religious connotations. Instead, they're called "spring ovals."

As Stephen Carter says in his book *The Culture of Disbelief*, to America's intellectual elites, religion is acceptable as long it's treated as a private hobby, like building model airplanes. But if religious believers bring their moral concerns into the public arena, that's ruled out-of-bounds. A Freedom Forum study on religion and the news media found that some TV reporters and producers define church-state separation to mean that "religious dealings in moral-political issues are inappropriate subjects in the news."

What an astonishing misconception of the First Amendment.

And frightening. Remember that Hitler didn't start his barbarism by hauling Jews straight off to concentration camps. Instead, he embarked on a slow and insidious process, lopping off a few rights here, suppressing a few freedoms there.

We don't have a man with a funny mustache pinning yellow stars on anyone. But let Christians challenge the status quo in the name of religious principle, and all sorts of labels are pinned on us. ※

EQUAL ACCESS FOR ALL

Wednesday

LAMB'S CHAPEL IS A TINY CONGREGATION that meets in a storage room in an industrial park. Yet this little congregation won a huge victory for the rights of Christians across America. In a case that went all the way to the U. S. Supreme Court, Lamb's Chapel won a decision protecting the right of Christians to equal access to the public arena.

The story began when Lamb's Chapel wanted to rent a high school auditorium to show a film series featuring Christian psychologist James Dobson. School officials said no. They argued that showing religiously based films in a public school violates a statewide policy on separation of church and state.

The little church took the case to court. Their lawyers argued that the high school had created an "open forum," which means, in legal terms, that once a government institution permits outside groups to use its facilities, it cannot discriminate among them. In this case, the school had rented its auditorium to all kinds of groups, from the Cub Scouts to a New Age psychologist lecturing on extra-sensory perception.

But when it came to a church with a religious program, the school barred the door. The school's lawyer admitted that the policy allowed in virtually anyone promoting any viewpoint—*except* a religious one.

The lawyer denied that the policy was discriminatory. After all, he argued, the school bars *all* religions, not just Christianity. But this argument rests on a misunderstanding of state neutrality. Neutrality does not apply just between different religions, it also applies between religion and secularism. The First Amendment means policies cannot *deprive* religion vis-a-vis secular viewpoints any more than they can *reward* religion.

Fortunately, the Supreme court ruled in favor of Lamb's Chapel—and equal access. Christians don't want special favors. We just want equal access to the marketplace of ideas. 🔳

GOOD WITHOUT GOD?

Thursday

A NEW TEENAGE TREND HAS BEEN spreading through the public schools—and it's enough to keep ACLU lawyers lying awake at night. Across the country millions of students are pushing the limits of school-prayer legislation—and both state and federal lawmakers are saying, "Amen." At least nine states have introduced legislation allowing voluntary, student-led prayer.

The school-prayer movement has attracted a surprisingly wide range of supporters—from white, rural conservatives to black, big-city liberals. What links this diverse group together is the conviction that our nation is suffering from moral decay—and that secularism in the public schools is one of the main culprits.

Bringing prayer back into the schools has come to symbolize bringing back a transcendent source of morals and meaning. As one Florida legislator put it, "We're bringing back to our children the recognition that there is a place for spiritual and moral enlightenment."

Until the 1960s, school prayer and Bible reading served as a public acknowledgment that the Christian religion is the source of our moral code. But secularists have been busy trying to break the connection between religion and morality. We can be good without God, they claimed.

But when cut loose from any transcendent basis, morality degenerates into individual choice. For the past several decades, public school values courses have taught students to choose for themselves what is right and wrong.

Today the consequences of teaching do-it-yourself morality have become painfully clear: schools with metal detectors, drug raids, armed guards, and a generation of unmarried teen mothers.

The truth is that you cannot separate morality from religion. Historian Will Durant who conducted a massive survey of Western civilization, concluded that no society has ever been known to maintain "a moral life without the aid of religion." ❦

AN INVISIBLE KINGDOM

Friday

JESUS DID NOT COME TO ESTABLISH a political kingdom, yet the announcement of the Kingdom had profound consequences for the political order.

When Jesus said to Pilate, "My kingdom is not of this earth," Pilate may have breathed a sigh of relief. He should have reconsidered. Which is more threatening to a ruler—an external foe with mighty but visible armies or an eternal king who rules the very souls of men and women? The latter can command the will and affections, demand absolute obedience, impart unlimited power to His subjects, and radically change their values and lives; His followers fear no earthly power and His kingdom has no end. In the face of such a potentate, any mere political leader must shudder.

This is why the kingdom of God has had such an astonishing effect upon the most powerful of human empires in every age. It is not a blueprint for some new social order; nor does it merely set the forces of radical cultural change in motion. Rather, God's kingdom promises radical change in human personalities.

This is the crucial point. While human politics is based on the premise that society must be changed in order to change people, in the politics of the Kingdom it is people who must be changed in order to change society.

Through men and women who recognize its authority and live by its ethical standards, the kingdom of God invades the stream of history. It breaks the vicious and otherwise irreversible cycles of violence, injustice, and self-interest. In this way the kingdom of God equips its citizens, as Augustine said, to be the best citizens in the kingdoms of man. 🔲

NATION WITH THE SOUL OF A CHURCH

Weekend

W ISE MEN AND WOMEN HAVE LONG recognized the need for the transcendent authority of religion to give society its legitimacy and essential cohesion. Cicero maintained that religion is "indispensable to private morals and public order." Augustine argued that the essence of public harmony could be found only in justice, the source of which is divine. "In the absence of justice," he asked, "what is sovereignty but organized brigandage?"

In the West the primary civilizing force was Christianity. According to historian Christopher Dawson, Christianity furnished the soul for Western civilization and provided its moral legitimization. The American experiment in limited government was founded on this essential premise. John Adams wrote, "Our constitution was made only for a moral and religious people. It is wholly inadequate for the government of any other." G. K. Chesterton called America a nation with "the soul of a church."

But men and women need more than a religious value system. They also need civic structures to prevent chaos and provide order. Religion is not intended or equipped to do this; when it has tried, it has brought grief on itself and the political institutions it has attempted to control.

Both the City of God and the city of man are vital to society—and they must remain in delicate balance. "All human history and culture," historian Vernon J. Bourke observed, "May be viewed as the interplay of the competing values of these . . . two cities"; and wherever they are out of balance, the public good suffers.

This is why the conflict between church and state is so dangerous. It would be a Pyrrhic victory indeed, should either side win unconditionally. Victory for either would mean defeat for both. 🔲

MORAL RESISTANCE

Monday

T HE PRESENCE OF THE KINGDOM of God in society means the presence of a community of people whose lives testify to the Law behind the law. They eschew relativism, believe that some things are right, some are wrong, and adhere to universal ethical norms. The presence of such people in society, therefore, is a powerful bulwark to legal sanity.

But the kingdom of God is more than just a model. It actually operates as a restraint on the kingdoms of man through its individuals and through its most visible manifestation, the church. For in our society the church is the chief institution with the moral authority to mediate between individuals and the government, to hold the state to account for its obligations to its citizens.

The American government was established with the understanding that such transcendent values would affect what otherwise is simply a social contract. When the state forgets or denies those values that were original conditions of the contract, in essence it abrogates its contract with its citizens. It is then that the church must take the initiative and call the state to account.

This is the point at which the conflict between the two kingdoms often becomes the greatest. Government by nature seeks power and will always attempt to generate its own moral legitimacy for its decisions. Inevitably, it resents any group that attempts to act as its conscience.

But as history demonstrates, the result of government attempting to impose its own moral vision upon society or acting without the restraint of an independent conscience is tyranny. The job of propagating moral vision belongs not to government but to other institutions of society, most notably the church. When the state oversteps the bounds of its authority, the church becomes the one effective source of moral resistance. The church does this not for its own ends as an earthly institution but for the common good.

THE THREAT OF FAITH

Tuesday

THE FIRST ATTACKS UPON THE CHURCH by the Roman empire were to ban the evangelization of prisons. Why? Because when Christians went into prisons, they not only were used of God to bring many to Christ, but they were also giving an outward demonstration of their obedience to the Christ who commanded them to make a difference in the world around them. By their actions they were saying Christ is Lord—and that was an offense against the emperor.

To assert that Jesus is Lord is a dangerous threat to any totalitarian regime.

The same has been true in modern times. During Stalin's reign of terror in the Soviet Union, the church came under brutal attack. But it was not its ceremonies that were assaulted; repression focused on its involvement in society.

The 1929 legislation controlling "religious cults" expressly forbade the church to collect funds for the poor, feed the hungry, or aid the old and infirm. Church-sponsored education was outlawed. The Soviets allowed regulated, controlled worship, but not those manifestations of the church which demonstrated that Christ is Lord in every area of life. That, and that only, threatened the supremacy of the state.

So it is in China today. The "official" church is allowed to worship, but home churches are persecuted. Why? Because home churches penetrate the culture, determine how people live, shape their values.

Perhaps the great irony in our world today is that what the power of the state is incapable of accomplishing in despotic governments, we in the "free world" are willingly adopting. This attack on the lordship of Christ is not obvious, it is subtle, insidious—as when people argue that religion should be private and personal without application to public life.

Can we proclaim that Jesus is Lord as the first-century Christians did, by being living demonstrations of that truth? Does Christ control and shape our lives?

W REVIVAL AND ITS RESULTS

Wednesday

CORRELATION BETWEEN RELIGIOUS VALUES and public order was dramatically evident during a religious revival early in this century. The revival began in small Methodist churches in Wales and quickly spilled out into society. Prayer meetings sprang up in coal mines; stores reported stocks of Bibles sold out; dockets were cleared in criminal courts; and many police were unemployed. Stolen goods were returned to shocked store owners.

As historian Edwin J. Orr reported, "Cursing and profanity were so diminished that . . . a strike was provoked in the coal mines . . . so many men had given up using foul language that the pit ponies dragging the coal trucks in the mine tunnels did not understand what was being said to them and stood still, confused."

During New Year's week in 1905, for the first time ever there was not a single arrest for drunkenness in Swansea County, the police announced. In Cardiff the authorities reported a 40 percent decrease in the jail population while the tavern trade fell off dramatically. The revival soon spread throughout the British Isles and much of the English-speaking world. Church attendance rose, and public morality was dramatically affected.

Men and women who profess allegiance to the kingdom of God become models for the rest of society. The role of the City of God, as Augustine said, is "to inspire men and women to organize their communities in the image and likeness of the heavenly city."

T SHOULD WE "IMPOSE" MORALITY?

Thursday

CHRISTIANS HAVE AN OBLIGATION TO BRING transcendent moral values into the public debate. All law implicitly involves morality; the popular idea that "you can't legislate morality" is a myth.

Morality is legislated every day from the vantage point of one value system or another. The question is not *whether* we will legislate morality but *whose* morality we will legislate.

Law is a body of rules regulating human behavior; it establishes, from the view of the state, the rightness or wrongness of human behavior. Most laws, therefore, have moral implications. Statutes prohibiting murder, mandates for seat belts, or regulations for industrial safety are all designed to protect human life—a reflection of the particular moral view that values the dignity and worth of human life. And efficacy doesn't affect morality. If in America we have more homicides per capita than in any other country, it's no reason to repeal the laws making murder a crime.

As a result, Christians, both individually and institutionally, have a duty, for the good of society as a whole, to bring the values of the kingdom of God to bear within the kingdoms of man. 🔲

GENERIC RELIGION

Friday

THOSE WHO FEAR THE ENCROACHMENT of religion in public life can relax. In many cases what we're seeing is a politicized civil religion that holds the gospel hostage to a particular political agenda, and as a result has nothing to impose.

The politicization of the church in the 60s was largely the work of liberal mainline denominations, whose bureaucracies issued weekly policy papers on social issues. They became so absorbed in social causes that they neglected the church's first mission and in the process suffered declining membership.

Just as their influence was waning, the political polarity was reversed, and the Christian New Right emerged as a potent force in American politics. They made the same mistake—equating the gospel with a particular partisan agenda. Many in the New Right appeared ready to make politics the ultimate goal, putting politics ahead of spirituality.

Politicized religion simply reinforces the tendency toward civil religion, which was perhaps best articulated by Dwight Eisenhower who once said that American government makes no sense "unless it is founded in a deeply felt religious faith—and I don't care what it is." What Eisenhower was referring to was nothing more than a generic religion—any brand will do, no-name is the best—to encourage civic duty.

Christian values are in retreat in the West today primarily because of the church itself. If Christianity has failed to stem the rising tides of relativism, it is because the church in many instances has lost the convicting force of the gospel message. ✹

Weekend

REAL MEN NURTURE THEIR FAMILIES

JUST A WEEK AFTER LEADING THE Washington Redskins to a Super Bowl victory, head coach Joe Gibbs announced he was giving up football to spend more time with his family. "I'm fifty-two [years old]," the coach explained, "and there's a window of opportunity with my family" that's not going to stay open forever.

Gibbs says he wants to see his wife all year round, not just in the off-season. He wants time to spend with his sons, watch them play football.

"I want to sit in the stands and just be a dad," Gibbs told reporters.

Now, I love rooting for the Redskins, but this Father's day I'm rooting for Coach Gibbs. He's doing something tougher than taking on the Dallas Cowboys: He's standing against a distorted value system—a system that says, in the words of one Christian counselor, that "it's OK for men to be married to their jobs and fail at home."

For decades, fathers have handed over the major responsibility for child rearing to their wives, as though their only role was to bring home the bacon. But today the evidence is pouring in that fathers are crucial in their children's emotional and intellectual development.

Unfortunately, a lot of that evidence is negative: Dark reports from the inner cities about the crime and social pathology caused by what psychologists term "father absence."

But the most prevalent form of father absence isn't in the

inner cities, says one book on the subject. It's in families where fathers simply do not engage in their children's lives—fathers who work sixty-hour weeks and come home to slump in front of the television or behind a newspaper. Fathers are all too prone to what psychologist Robert Coles labels "the teddy bear syndrome": They buy their children toys and Nintendos to compensate for spending so little time together.

Joe Gibbs is one father who's not satisfied with trying to buy father-substitutes. He's cutting back on a brilliantly successful career to give his family what they really want: time with him. My friend Joe Gibbs has set a wonderful example—something far more important than any Super Bowl championship. 🔲

THE BASIS
OF TRUST

Monday

EVERY POLITICAL ORDER MUST REST on a moral order, a shared set of beliefs and values. What binds society together is the trust that we will all regulate our conduct according to an agreed-upon moral framework.

But since the 1960s, the very notion of a common moral framework has steadily eroded. Today many people believe that we can set our own standards—that ethics is just a matter of individual feelings and choice. But when ethics is reduced to feelings, the moral bonds that tie society together quickly dissolve. People have no common standard of conduct they can agree on; they no longer know what to expect of one another.

Mistrust and hostility set in.

You see, in any relationship trust is based not merely on people's good will; we all know *that* can fluctuate. Instead, trust comes from knowing that the other person is committed to a shared standard—a standard binding on both parties.

Think of traffic laws. When we enter an intersection, our confidence is not based on knowing the other drivers feel kindly toward us. It's based on knowing they're going to follow the same traffic laws. If traffic laws were a matter of individual choice, our streets would surrender to chaos.

It's the same with our social life. Trust depends on a shared set of laws and standards. Until recently, the shared standards that bound American society together were derived from our Christian heritage. But no longer.

And the danger is that we are knocking out the moral props upon which all political orders depend. ▨

OFFENDED ABSOLUTES

Tuesday

I N THE GUISE OF PLURALISM AND TOLERANCE, western cultural and political elites have set about to exile religion from our common life. They use the power of the media and the law like steel wool to scrub public debates and public places bare of religious ideas and symbols. But what is left is sterile, featureless, and cold.

Our elites seek freedom without self-restraint, liberty without standards. But they find instead the revenge of offended absolutes.

Courts strike down even perfunctory prayers, and we are surprised that schools, bristling with barbed wire, look more like prisons than prisons do.

Universities reject the very idea of truth, and we are shocked when the best and the brightest of their graduates loot and betray.

Celebrities mock the traditional family, even revile it as a form of slavery, and we are appalled at the human tragedy of broken homes and millions of unwed mothers.

The media celebrates sex without responsibility, and we are horrified by sexual plagues.

Our lawmakers justify the taking of innocent life in sterile clinics, and we are terrorized by the disregard for life in blood-soaked streets.

C. S. Lewis described this irony a generation ago. "We laugh at honor," he said, " and are shocked to find traitors in our midst . . . We castrate and bid the geldings be fruitful." 🖼

PRIVATE MORALITY AND PUBLIC POLICY

Wednesday

D OES A CANDIDATE'S PRIVATE MORALITY have anything to do with his public life?

For years, liberals have said no. But when a person regularly lives a certain way, habitually makes certain choices, over time that affects the way he or she thinks about issues.

Consider a historical example: the life and thought of Jean Jacques Rousseau. In 1762 Rousseau wrote the classic treatise on freedom, *The Social Contract*. But the freedom Rousseau envisioned wasn't freedom from state tyranny; it was freedom from personal obligations: family, church, workplace. We can escape the claims made by these groups, Rousseau wrote, by transferring complete loyalty to the state. In his words, we become "independent of all [our] fellow citizens" only by becoming completely "dependent on the republic."

This idea smacks so obviously of totalitarianism that one wonders how Rousseau came up with the idea.

Historian Paul Johnson offers an intriguing hypothesis. At the time Rousseau was writing *The Social Contract* he was struggling with a great moral dilemma. He had drifted from job to job, from mistress to mistress, until he took up with a servant girl, Thérèse. When Thérèse had a baby, Rousseau was, in his own words, "thrown into the greatest embarrassment." His burning desire was to be received into Parisian high society, and an illegitimate child—by a servant girl!—would be an awkward encumbrance.

So a few days later, a tiny blanketed bundle was left on the steps of the local orphanage. Over the years, four additional children born to Thérèse and Jean Jacques appeared on the orphanage steps. Historical records show that most of the babies in that orphanage died; the few survivors became beggars.

Rousseau knew that, and several of his books and letters reveal desperate attempts to justify his action. In handing his children over to a state orphanage, he argued, he was merely following the teachings of Plato. Hadn't Plato said that the state was better equipped than parents to raise good citizens?

Later, when Rousseau turned to political theory, he recommended that responsibility for educating children be taken away from parents and given to the state. In fact, his ideal state was one where impersonal institutions liberate citizens from *all* personal obligations.

Now, here was a man who himself had turned to a state institution for relief from personal obligations. Were his own choices being transmuted into his political theory? Is there connection between Rousseau the man and Rousseau the political theorist?

In politics and in every other subject, ideas do not arise from the intellect alone but from the whole personality. They reflect our hopes and fears, longings and regrets. When the Reformers talked about "total depravity," they meant that sin affects every aspect of our being, including our ideas.

Most of the tyrants of the modern world have knelt at the altar of Rousseau, from the leaders of the French Revolution to Hitler, Marx, and Lenin. So can we really say private behavior has nothing to do with public policy?

Just ask the survivors of Hitler's concentration camps. 🔲

ARE YOU AN ABSOLUTIST?

Thursday

A GALLUP POLL FOUND THAT 50 PERCENT of Americans are worried about Fundamentalism. What worries them is that Fundamentalists actually believe in moral absolutes.

Why does that send a chill down people's backs? Because they have confused belief in absolutes with absolut*ism*—a rigid mentality that is inflexible, irrational, and hostile.

But there's a world of difference between absolutes and absolut*ism*.

You see, every time you tack "ism" onto a term, you change its meaning. Think of the word *individual*—a good word, suggesting individual dignity and worth. But individual*ism* denotes something altogether different—an egoistic mentality that puts individual interests above everything else. There's also a huge difference between *material* and *materialism*, between *human* and *humanism*, between *feminine* and *feminism*.

When Christians maintain the reality of absolutes, we simply mean we believe that there is a created order. That there are virtues—like courage, fortitude, and patience—which are morally obligatory. That there are normative patterns for marriage, business, and government.

In short, we believe that there are laws for human behavior just as there are laws for the physical world. Believing these things doesn't make you an absolutist in mentality any more than believing in gravity does. And if I try to persuade you of a moral law, I'm not "imposing my views" any more than if I teach you the effects of gravity.

Moral absolutes are not based on private convictions, which we try to impose on our fellow citizens. They are based on objective truths about the created order, and we search them out the same way we search out scientific laws.

So when someone accuses you of being an absolutist, explain the difference between *absolutes* and *absolutism*. And if you demonstrate a loving and patient attitude while you're talking, you will prove by your own action that believing in absolutes *doesn't* make you an absolutist. ▓

Friday

TRUE
TOLERANCE

NO GROUP IS MORE HARSHLY STEREOTYPED in America today than what the media labels the Religious Right. But a look at the facts should make these negative stereotypes crumble.

One of the most significant studies ever done on Christians was published in 1992 by George Gallup under the title *The Saints Among Us*. It found that people with a strong Christian faith are happier, more generous in helping others, and—here's the real surprise—more tolerant.

The survey asked questions such as, "Would you object to a person of another race moving in next door?" Of the highly religious, 84 percent said they would not object, compared to only 63 percent of the nonreligious. They also score higher on related virtues such as compassion and forgiveness.

So much for the stereotype of intolerant hatemongers.

If the empirical evidence contradicts the stereotype, why is it still so widespread? To begin with, Gallup's findings apply only to people highly committed to the Christian faith—about 10 percent of the population. Average churchgoers show little difference from the general population. So when the non-Christian peers through the doors of the average church, he sees people whose lives demonstrate little of the transforming power of God.

Christians are condemned as intolerant for a second reason: Our culture has a distorted view of what true tolerance is. Americans tend to define tolerance as moral neutrality—refusing to judge any behavior right or wrong. The classic definition of tolerance, however, is profoundly judgmental: It means putting up with people *even when we know they're wrong.*

The classic definition stems from a deep Christian sense of sin and error. Since everyone falls short at some point, we are enjoined to tolerate people's shortcomings, so long as they do not directly threaten the communal life—all the while, of course, lovingly seeking to persuade them of the truth.

Real tolerance is a *Christian* virtue—and the empirical evidence shows that it is Christians who practice it best. 🐚

MISUNDERSTOOD REBEL?

Weekend

THIRTY YEARS AGO CHARLES MANSON masterminded an orgy of bloodshed that became a vivid symbol of mindless murder. Today he's becoming a pop celebrity.

Manson was the wild-eyed leader of a gang that murdered several people, including actress Sharon Tate and her unborn baby. But from his prison cell, Manson is evolving into a cult hero. Several rock bands are playing songs he composed. His face is appearing on T-shirts, jackets, hats, hair clips, and even children's clothing. People picking the clothes off the rack told reporters they don't see Manson as evil. He's just "misunderstood," one customer said.

How did our values get so inverted?

There was a time when Western culture held to a universal moral code. A code rooted in divine command. A code that applied to everyone, all the time. But as the West grew secular, people began to realize that without God, all moral codes are man-made. And if you make up your rules, while I make up mine, then for you to try to make *me* follow *your* rules is by definition oppressive.

This is the philosophy of postmodernism. If there's no transcendent moral standard above us all, then whoever has the most power imposes his or her views on everyone else. But in that case, conforming to society's moral code means giving in to an oppressive system. The healthy response is not to give in but to rebel. Ever since the 60s, flaunting social rules has been portrayed as courageous rebellion.

Crime itself can be turned into heroic defiance. This explains why even Charles Manson can be elevated from a repulsive mass murderer into a misunderstood rebel.

As Christians we need to grasp this progression. Unhitched from God's law, morality was reduced to mere private opinion. Calling something right or wrong was then seen as cramming your opinion down another person's throat.

Christians need to make it clear that morality is *not* based on private opinions, it's based on a transcendent truth. ▩

WHAT'S A
GOOD STORY WORTH?

Monday

ON A BALMY DAY ONE SUMMER, a group of teenagers blew their minds out on the hallucinogenic drug LSD. They were all nice kids, the kind who get good grades and lead student council. No one suspected they were indulging in a dangerous drug that night—not their parents, not their teachers, not the police.

No one, that is, except a reporter.

A *Washington Post* reporter stayed on hand all night to observe the party. She calmly watched as minor children broke the law by popping four, five, and six hits of acid. She listened as kids described their hallucinations. The reporter observed and took notes. She made no effort to stop the teens. She offered no moral comment. And when she wrote up a story for the *Post*, she concealed the kids' identities.

Public reaction to the story was swift—and outraged. Was it right for a reporter to stand by passively as teens took an illegal and dangerous drug? What *was* her ethical obligation as a reporter in a situation like this?

Remarkably, the *Washington Post* omsbudsman, Richard Harwood wrote a piece *defending* the reporter. He advanced the utterly crass argument that journalism has no ethics anyway so what was everyone so upset about? He said journalists are "in a business with no fixed moral or ethical formula." Their ethics just "get invented as [they] go along." To tell the truth, Harwood confided, for journalists "ethics is not even [a] concern." Getting a good story is. *How* you get the story doesn't matter.

This is sheer pragmatism, where the end justifies the means.

The article is an amazing admission, revealing just how much journalists have rejected any transcendent, God-given standards to guide their conduct. They have become mini-gods, making up their own rules as they go along.

The Book of Judges describes a time when the people of Israel lived in ethical anarchy—when "everyone did what was right in his own eyes."

What a fitting description of life in America today. ▧

ABORTION RITES

Tuesday

A TEENAGER NAMED DELENIA CAME to her parents with bad news: She was pregnant.

Her father, a minister, was shocked and ashamed. But fortunately a Christian residential ministry took her in and provided maternity care. Eventually Delenia finished her education and was able to support herself and her child.

The story has a contemporary ring to it, doesn't it? But surprisingly enough, it happened nearly a hundred years ago.

Delenia's story is told in Marvin Olasky's book *Abortion Rites: A Social History of Abortion in America.* Olasky discovered that in the nineteenth century, even though abortion was illegal, it was widely available. In fact, the number of abortions relative to the size of the population was about the same as it is today.

In the mid-nineteenth century, America was racked by massive social upheavals. The Industrial Revolution had taken work out of the home, where it had been a family industry, and transferred it to the factory. Cities were flooded with young adults trying to find work.

But that's not all they found. Living alone, without family guidance or protection, many were enticed into relationships that didn't last. Young women found themselves pregnant and abandoned, with no one to help. They were easy targets for abortionists, who profited from their misery.

Then Christians, whose hearts were torn by the decay of the cities, launched a multi-pronged strategy. Laws were passed outlawing abortion. Christian journalists wrote exposés of abortionists.

Equal emphasis was placed on prevention. Scores of Christians started homes for unwed mothers. They founded adoption agencies. They ran job-training programs. They opened Christian residences for young people coming to the cities. They formed recreation centers so young singles could "just say no" and still enjoy fun and friends.

It was hard work, but it paid off: The abortion rate went down. And it stayed down pretty much until the 1960s, when a new cycle of abortion began.

In our day, pro-lifers have tended to focus more narrowly on efforts to change the law. But like our counterparts a hundred years ago, we need to develop a multi-pronged strategy of prevention, including crisis pregnancy centers, Christian youth groups, and inner-city ministries. We must be willing to get our hands dirty ministering to hurting men and women—one by one. ▨

SQUANDERING A HERITAGE

Wednesday

MANY PEOPLE WOULD BE SURPRISED TO LEARN THAT nineteenth-century feminists uniformly opposed abortion. Susan B. Anthony once wrote, "I deplore the horrible crime of child murder." And Elizabeth Cady Stanton wrote, "When we consider that women are often treated as property, how can women turn around and treat our children as property to be disposed of as we see fit?"

The early feminists didn't treat abortion as a purely women's issue, either. They held men responsible for most abortions— realizing that in many cases abortion is a desperate response to male abandonment.

Back then, abortion was generally sought by young women who had been seduced with promises of marriage—then callously dropped when they became pregnant. Even today, most abortions are sought by single women—often pressured by boyfriends who don't want to face the responsibilities of fatherhood. This is what Susan B. Anthony had in mind when she wrote: "The woman is awfully guilty who commits the deed; but oh, thrice guilty is he who drove her to the desperation which impelled her to the crime."

The solution to abortion, Anthony felt, lies in stressing male responsibility. And here we see the starkest difference between traditional feminism and the contemporary version. The early feminists passionately believed they could *reform* men. Their goal was to encourage family formation: to change social mores so that every man would feel morally obligated to marry the mother of his children.

But modern feminists have given up on men. They're so sure the brunt of the responsibility for children is going to fall on them anyway that they angrily demand the right to make a unilateral decision from the start.

But, of course, that will only exacerbate the problem. Defining childbearing as purely a women's issue is guaranteed to erode men's sense of responsibility still further—leaving even more women in the lurch.

So the next time someone says pro-lifers just want to oppress women, tell them about Susan B. Anthony and about feminism's pro-life history.

What a shame modern feminists have lost that proud tradition. 🀰

PRIVATIZED LIBERTY

Thursday

I N 1994, A FEDERAL JUDGE RULED that the citizens of Washington may not outlaw doctor-assisted suicide. After all, the judge argued, the U. S. Supreme Court has proclaimed a constitutional right to end life through abortion; hence there must also be a constitutional right to end life through suicide.

The most frightening thing is the logic *behind* this slide toward the culture of death. Legal reasoning took a sharp turn in the 1992 *Planned Parenthood v. Casey* decision, in which the Supreme Court relegated life-and-death decisions to the strictly private arena.

The Court argued that abortion is protected under the fourteenth amendment right to liberty. Then it defined liberty in the most expansive terms imaginable: "At the heart of liberty is the right to define one's own concept of existence, of meaning . . . of the mystery of human life." If the state were to set a public standard on abortion, the Court argued, it would infringe on citizens' rights to make up their own minds on this "intimate and personal" choice.

The federal judge who struck down Washington's law against assisted suicide quoted directly from the *Casey* ruling—arguing that suicide, like abortion, "involves the most intimate and personal choices a person may make."

As Christians, our response ought to be that all this talk about intimate, personal choices is completely beside the point. Our courts and legal system are not concerned with private metaphysical beliefs; they are concerned with public justice. Christians, atheists, and New Agers may disagree over personal philosophy; yet we can all agree on standards of public justice and order—just as we can all agree to stop when the traffic signal is red.

We may each have different *moral* reasons for stopping at the signal; yet we can still agree that such behavior promotes the public good. This is a crucial distinction if we are to maintain freedom of conscience while also maintaining public order.

But it is precisely this distinction that the *Casey* ruling denied: It gave up any concept of the public good and transferred the most fundamental decisions about life and death to the purely private realm. 🔳

DONUTS AND
DEMONSTRATORS

Friday

ANN SERVES ON THE BOARD OF A pregnancy-counseling center offering alternatives to abortion. One Saturday their center was picketed by University of Michigan students representing an abortion-rights group. Among them were a number of lesbians asserting a woman's right to control her own body. The Christians and the militant homosexuals had little common ground. Television camera crews stood by to record whatever transpired.

But the confrontation did not degenerate into a shouting match. Nor did Ann and her friends huddle inside their fortress, afraid to engage the world. Instead, one of Ann's colleagues suggested that they meet the demonstrators outside with trays of food. Says Ann, "This was either the worst idea I had ever heard or an inspiration straight from the Holy Spirit."

As they emerged from the doors of their center, trays of donuts and cups of steaming coffee in hand, the newspeople and students stared in disbelief. "We wanted to show the demonstrators that we cared about them, that we weren't afraid to talk to them, and that we were willing to answer any questions they might have," says Ann. "We wanted to respond in love rather that in fear or anger."

As we fight the battle for unborn lives, a broken world will see either our faces twisted in hate and anger or the face of Christ, listening, serving, speaking the truth in love. 🪶

Weekend

A MOTHER'S ORDEAL

YOU COULD CALL IT THE ULTIMATE IN workplace harassment. "If you want to keep your job," the woman was told, "you have to get an abortion."

The country was China, and the woman's name was Chi An. Her story is told in Stephen Mosher's book *A Mother's Ordeal*, a firsthand account of China's use of state coercion to enforce a rigid policy of one child per family.

Chi An gives the view from both sides: Not only was she forced to get an abortion herself, but as a nurse in a large state factory Chi An's job was to make sure there were no unauthorized pregnancies.

Every woman in the factory was required to post a record of her menstrual cycles on a public bulletin board. When women became pregnant illegally, Chi An ordered them rounded up and locked in dark storerooms. There they were subjected night and day to harsh "reeducation" tactics designed to break them down until they signed a form agreeing to having an abortion.

Some women tried to escape the population police, hiding out with relatives. But Chi An would send armed soldiers to hunt them down. Even if the women managed to elude their pursuers during their pregnancy, doctors attending the birth would often strangle or drown the infant. The stories are sickening, and Christians ought to stand against government funding of any international family planning agencies that participate in coercive population-control programs.

Chi An's personal story ends on a happy note. She was able to move to the United States with her husband and her "illegal" second child. She has become a Christian, and has learned a profound truth: that children are a gift of God, not a commodity to be regulated by the state. ▩

GERMANY JUST SAYS NO

Monday

THE JUDGES OF GERMANY'S CONSTITUTIONAL Court stood resplendent in their red robes as the chief justice read its most important decision in decades: The Court struck down Germany's liberal abortion law.

The law had been passed as a compromise between East and West German laws. Under Communism, East Germany embraced abortion on demand. To compromise, West Germany accepted a law that was significantly more permissive than its own law had been.

But immediately the new law was challenged as unconstitutional. And therein lies a fascinating story.

Germany's constitution dates back to the end of World War II and was explicitly designed to prevent another holocaust. The Nazi gas chambers were justified on the grounds that some lives are not worth living; that it is morally and legally permissible to snuff them out.

To stand against that idea, the German constitution includes a right-to-life clause, which reads, "Everyone shall have the right to life and to physical inviolability." The Constitutional Court was established to review all federal legislation to ensure that the right to life would never be overridden by law.

This explains the court's decision to strike down the compromise abortion law. The judges declared that the Constitution "obliges the state to protect human life" and that "the unborn are part of human life."

What makes the German debate so interesting is that exactly the same arguments are used on this side of the Atlantic. American pro-lifers argue that abortion rests on the same principle that undergirded the Nazi holocaust: the idea that some human lives are not worthy of living, and that it is morally and legally permissible to snuff them out.

In abortion, of course, that applies only to unborn babies.

But once the *principle* is accepted, it can be applied equally well to other groups. And the result could well be an American version of the holocaust.

Naturally, this argument drives pro-choice activists mad. They steadfastly refuse to see any connection between abortion and Nazism. But the parallels are real.

After all, the holocaust did not start with gas chambers. It started when ordinary people accepted the *principle* that it is permissible to take an innocent human life. ▨

A REASONABLE REVOLUTION

Tuesday   FOURTH OF JULY

ON THE FOURTH OF JULY, WE SALUTE the Declaration of Independence, which is unique in the history of revolutionary documents.

It doesn't rally the masses to overthrow society, as most revolutionary manifestos do. Nor is it an invitation to lawlessness, because the colonists believed their demands were lawful. They weren't destroying a legal order, they were demanding what they felt were legitimate rights *within* a legal order.

To understand how remarkable this really is, compare the American Revolution to the French Revolution, only a few years later.

The French Revolution was driven by a fanatical determination to destroy the existing social order. The leaders were disciples of Jean Jacques Rousseau, who believed that individual corruption is caused by a social corruption. The solution, they said, is to raze the corrupt society to the ground.

The goal of the American Revolution was exactly the opposite: The colonists were revolting to *preserve* their society, not to destroy it. They were determined to protect their country from tyranny.

Another crucial difference: The French Revolution was avowedly atheistic. By contrast, many of the leaders of the American Revolution were devout Christians. A major impulse behind the revolution was a passion for religious freedom.

A third difference: The French revolutionaries were utopian. Just tear down corrupt social institutions, they said, and people's natural virtue will shine through. In their optimism, they placed no restraints on the new government they formed. As a result, it soon became even more corrupt than the government it replaced.

The American founders, however, held the biblical teaching that humanity is intrinsically prone to evil. As a result, they wove a network of checks and balances into the new government to protect against abuses of power.

One final difference: In the end, the French Revolution devoured its own children. Many of its leaders fell before the guillotine. Order was finally restored by the iron fist of Napoleon.

But the American Revolution gave birth to a country both prosperous and free. Its leaders were elected to high office and later died peacefully in their beds.

Our own revolution was so unproblematic that its seminal ideas were quietly forgotten. Today few Americans really understand our revolutionary heritage.

And that ignorance could be a greater threat to America's freedom than any outside force has ever been. ▓

MEASURING MORALS

Wednesday

CAN COMPUTER GAMES TEACH us right from wrong?
In *Parade* magazine, astronomer Carl Sagan says computer games can now simulate ethical decisions. Should I be selfish or generous? Should I cooperate with people or take advantage of them? When wronged, should I punish or forgive?

With computer games, we can try out various strategies and see how other people might respond. Every time you get what you want, you score a point. With games like these, Sagan says, we can test moral systems scientifically.

Computers have been programmed to test the Golden Rule: Do unto others as you would have them do unto you. Then they tested what Sagan calls the Brazen Rule: Do unto others *as they* do unto you. Then they tested the Iron Rule: Do unto others—*before* they do it unto you.

In test after test, Sagan says, the rule that won out was the Brazen Rule: Tit for tat. You're most likely to get what you want by paying people back in kind for whatever they do to you.

Well, the Brazen Rule may get what you want—and earn the most points in computer games. But does that make it moral? For Carl Sagan, the answer is yes. With computer games, he says, we find out "what really works."

But, of course, ethics isn't a matter of "what works," it's a matter of what's *right*. Sagan's words reveal that his own philosophy of ethics is purely pragmatic. Right and wrong are defined by whatever gives us what we want.

The name for this is utilitarianism. And while the idea of computer scoring may be new, the philosophy itself is old. Two hundred years ago, utilitarianism was proposed as a purely rational ethic to replace Christian ethics. It defines good behavior as behavior that accrues the most benefits—health, wealth, happiness, whatever.

But utilitarianism has proved to be a cold and heartless ethic. It justified slavery on the grounds that it was good for the economy. Today it justifies abortion on the grounds that it reduces welfare rolls. It supports euthanasia because it cuts medical costs.

No, we've seen utilitarianism in action, and it is utterly inhumane. The truth is, you can't quantify morality and run it through a computer program. True right and wrong are based on God's holy character. ▦

JUST LET HIM DIE?

Thursday

THERE ARE TIMES WHEN YOU DO something wrong and are dogged by guilt for years afterward. Well, I want to tell you about a time a doctor did something *right*—and was dogged by guilt for years afterward.

The year was 1968, and Kenneth Swan was a young army surgeon, just arrived in Vietnam. When a nineteen-year-old soldier was brought in on a stretcher, Dr. Swan immediately got to work. The soldier had been blown up by a grenade, losing his eyesight and both his legs. Swan labored seven hours at the operating table to repair the injuries.

Afterward he was sharply criticized by his fellow surgeons. For not doing a good job? No, for doing the job at all. "That kid was so badly mangled," the other doctors said, "you shouldn't have even bothered to treat him. He would have been better off dead."

Those words burrowed their way into Swan's mind, and for the next twenty years he wondered whether he had condemned the soldier to a life of helplessness. Finally, he decided to settle the question. It took more than two years, but in the end he found the soldier.

And *what* he found is nothing short of astonishing.

Yes, the man was blind and in a wheelchair. But he is not languishing in a hospital. He is married and has two daughters. He attended college, learned to scuba dive, and is now training to help others cope with debilitating injuries. At age forty-three, the former soldier has a zest for life and a faith in God. When a reporter asked him about his achievements, he responded simply, "I give the credit to God."

The debate between Swan and his colleagues twenty years ago is still being waged in the medical community. Swan is of the old school. He says, "I was taught to *treat* the wounded—not leave them to die." His colleagues represent a new philosophy. They practice selective medicine—weeding out the wounded who, they decide, do not have a life worth living. When the young soldier was flown back to the United States for rehabilitation, he overheard one doctor ask, "Why did they let this guy live?"

Swan knows now that he did the right thing in "letting this guy live." We can only hope the story of the young soldier blown up in Vietnam will stand as a powerful lesson to medical workers that all life should be treated as a gift from God.

And let's hope the Dr. Swans of this world will never feel guilty again—for doing the right thing. ⚜

Friday

HOLLAND'S NETHERWORLD

EUTHANASIA IS OFTEN PROMOTED UNDER the banner of "patient autonomy." But in Holland *voluntary* euthanasia has led straight to *involuntary* euthanasia—where the doctor unilaterally decides to end a patient's life if the patient is deemed incapable of making a choice. The next step on this slippery slope is euthanasia even when the patient *is* capable of choosing—but the doctor disagrees with the choice.

The lesson is clear: Euthanasia does its PR work under the slogan of patient choice. But in the end it leads to coercion—where medical personnel decide unilaterally who shall live and die, based on utilitarian and financial grounds.

On this side of the Atlantic we're setting up the conditions for the same progression. How? By heralding choice as the ultimate virtue.

But choice itself has no moral value. It's merely a process, an act of the will. There has to be a standard, a criterion, before we can judge whether something is a good choice or a bad choice. Empty choice, with no standards, will always end up in coercion—as the Dutch experiment with euthanasia so poignantly demonstrates.

But there *is* a standard—the one given us by God in Scripture: "Behold, I have set before you life and death," God says. "So choose life." Humans don't make things right or wrong by our own choices. There are objective criteria. And the *right* choice is the choice for life. ▨

Weekend

WE'RE ON THEIR SIDE

ALAN MEDINGER WAS A PRACTICING homosexual for seventeen years. Today he is a Christian and the founder of Regeneration, a ministry to homosexuals. "Homosexuality isn't just about sexual relations," Medinger says. "It's a complete personality orientation, a set of attitudes toward masculinity and femininity."

At some point in childhood, Medinger explains, the normal process of maturing is interrupted—often due to emotional trauma or abuse. The normal growth into manhood or womanhood is diverted. Freedom from homosexuality often involves a long, difficult process, going back and retracing the process of development to create a heterosexual identity.

Only then is the homosexual completely healed.

But today our society is blocking the potential for healing— ironically, by becoming too tolerant and accepting. As one former lesbian puts it, pro-gay groups are actually making it *harder* for those who want to break out of their destructive lifestyle.

It's not enough just to fight gay rights. Christians need to help people who are fighting the sin of homosexuality in their own lives.

And who desperately need the church on their side. ▩

TRUTH
AND LOVE

Monday

SUE SEEL FIRST LEARNED THAT HER brother Richard was homosexual when he announced he had AIDS. Deciding how to respond proved to be the biggest spiritual challenge she had ever faced.

The first time Sue flew to San Francisco to see Richard, he met her in a public place. He wouldn't even invite her into his home. Still, she continued to see him every few months, little by little learning what life is like in a gay subculture.

Sue knew the day would come when Richard would be too sick to care for himself. What should she do when that happened? Should she care for him in San Francisco? That would mean being separated from her husband and children. Or should she bring him to her own home?

If she did bring an AIDS patient into her home, how would her friends react? What would the neighbors say? Would her children be ostracized? Sue sought the advice of Christian groups that work with AIDS patients. Finally, she and her family decided they would care for Richard in their home.

The day came when Sue flew her brother home from San Francisco. For Richard, it was a whole new world. Sue's two boys played on the floor around his bed and read stories to him at night. Church friends dropped by to welcome him and pray with him.

In the last few weeks of his life, Richard was surrounded by a living testimony of God's love. Before he died, he committed his life to the Lord. His favorite verse was, "in His presence there is fullness of joy"—words now etched on his gravestone.

As Christians, we often find it difficult to respond to the AIDS epidemic in the spirit of Paul's injunction in Ephesians: to "speak the truth in love." We find it hard to achieve a real balance between the two.

Our culture preaches love—but equates love with tolerance, with passing out moral blank checks. As Christians we know that love sometimes means telling people that they are violating God's law. But how can we couch that kind of hard truth in concrete demonstrations of love?

Through his sister, Richard had the opportunity to learn of a God who hates sin but loves the sinner. ✖

THE POLITICS
OF CHILDBEARING

Tuesday

LITTLE MICHAEL HAS FOUR PARENTS: two lesbian lovers, one of whom gave birth to Michael, and two gay lovers, one of whom donated the sperm for artificial insemination.

In homosexual circles today, having babies is the hottest trend—made possible by technologies of artificial reproduction. Across the country, homosexuals are getting together in what they call "Sperm-Egg Mixers." Lesbian women and gay men meet and mingle, examining each other with an eye not toward marriage but toward selecting good genes.

Reproductive technology is raising some of the most serious challenges to traditional norms of what a family is. Artificial insemination and in vitro fertilization are being used to break the tie between biology and parenthood.

As researchers push the frontiers of reproductive technology, we need to impose some moral limits. Today the United States has no federal rules or guidelines governing fertility clinics. And with the subjectivist view of ethics so common today, it's likely to stay that way. As law professor Susan Estrich told *Newsweek* magazine, "This is an individual matter, an ethical and moral choice, not the business of government."

Notice the assumption that a moral issue is by definition a matter of purely individual choice. The implication is that there can be no public ethic guiding us.

Morality is reduced to whatever the parents want.

Ironically, it's gays and lesbians who recognize that this privatized view of morality is inadequate: Private actions *do* have public consequences. As gay rights leader Stefan Lynch puts it, "For two women to have a kid is a political act"—a direct challenge to the norm of heterosexual marriage and parenthood.

There's just no way to dodge the social and political implications of reproductive technologies. Used *within* traditional norms, they can simply help husbands and wives struggling with infertility. But often they are used to *challenge* traditional norms and dissolve morality into private choices.

Any technology is only as good or bad as the moral vision that guides it. You and I have an obligation to stay abreast of the surge in reproductive technology and to provide a biblical moral vision. ▩

JUDGED BY OUR GENES

Wednesday

THE U. S. GOVERNMENT IS FUNDING the Human Genome Project, aimed at identifying every gene in the human body. The head of the project is an evangelical Christian named Francis Collins. For Collins, the science of genetics "is a form of worship in understanding God's creation." He sees genetic screening as a powerful tool for alleviating suffering and saving lives.

But genetic screening can easily be taken beyond therapy and used in the service of eugenics—the philosophy that people with genetic defects should be weeded out.

This is not some scary prediction for the future. Scientists have identified many genetically based diseases that have no known treatment yet. As a result, the most frequent use of genetic screening is to test babies in the womb—and to abort those that are defective. A mentality is spreading that only perfect babies deserve to be born. As Collins puts it, couples seeking genetic counseling often have a "new car mentality:" If the baby isn't perfect, "you take it back to the lot and get a new one."

We're not talking here about racial or political eugenics—the kind practiced in Nazi Germany, where Jews were labeled genetically inferior. Instead, we might call it commercial eugenics—where parents act like consumers who treat their babies as merchandise that must fit certain specifications.

Ironically, the *bad* use of genetic screening is actually making it harder to practice the *good* use. By aborting defective babies, we're in essence saying that genetically imperfect people have no right to live. And if they have no right to live, why are we working so hard to find genetic cures for them?

As Christians let us never forget that God is not interested in physical and genetic perfection, He's interested in moral perfection. Throughout history, societies have suffered much more because of the *morally* defective and their evil schemes than because of the physically defective.

As Francis Collins says, genetics should be about ending suffering. It should *not* be about ending lives. ※

GENES AND GEEPS

Thursday

OLD MACDONALD WOULD NEVER recognize some of the creatures on today's farms—thanks to modern genetic engineering. Scientists have used cell fusion to create an animal with the face and horns of a goat and the body of the sheep. The animal was dubbed a "geep."

Other scientists extracted florescent genes from fireflies and inserted them into tobacco plants. The result is a plant that glows twenty-four hours a day.

Genetic technology represents an epic step for science. From the dawn of history, farmers have cross-bred plants and animals to create new variations; but they were limited to the existing gene pool. You can interbreed a cow with a buffalo but not with a horse. You can cross cabbage with brussels sprouts but not with watermelon.

Nature has built-in limits to biological change.

But today genetic technology can cross those limits. Geneticists are in a position similar to that of the early chemists, who first discovered how to make synthetic materials. Nowhere in nature do we find plastic, nylon, or polyester; these are manufactured by combining atoms and molecules in patterns that never occur naturally. Now geneticists can combine DNA in patterns that never occur naturally.

What will happen if we release all these engineered organisms into the environment? No one really knows. But our record on these things is not very good. Our polluted air and water prove that we often put human desires and utility above respect for the integrity of God's creation. Who knows what ecological unbalances we may create by introducing completely novel life forms?

That's why it's so important that the new technology is guided by a Christian worldview. On one hand, Christians support the development of technology as a way of cultivating the creation. The cultural mandate in Genesis calls us to nurture God's creation—to develop its hidden power and potential.

But precisely because it is *God's* creation, our work must be morally constrained by His will and His word. We are not to use technology for self-indulgent or destructive ends. We are not to reduce creation to merely a means for amassing personal or financial power. Since the earth is the Lord's, technology must be used for the Lord's purposes: to cultivate, to restore, to heal.

PHARM ANIMALS

Friday

PHARMACEUTICAL RESEARCH HAS MOVED from the sterile walls of the laboratory to the mud and straw of the barnyard. Scientists can now genetically engineer cows and pigs to grow life-saving drugs right in their own bodies. The genetically altered livestock are nicknamed "pharm" animals.

Here's how it works. Many proteins, such as insulin and human growth hormone, have medicinal functions. Scientists can now identify which sections of the DNA molecule contain the code for some of these proteins. If they cut out that section of human DNA and graft it into the DNA of another animal, it will function there exactly as it does in humans: directing the production of the same protein. The medicinal products are then extracted from the animal's blood or milk.

Pigs have been genetically engineered to produce human hemoglobin, used for blood transfusions. Goats are engineered to produce an anti-clotting protein used for heart-attack patients.

Genetically altered sheep produce a human protein for treating emphysema. The engineered animals are called "transgenic" because they carry transferred genes from humans. They are literally live, four-legged drug factories.

Using farm animals for pharmaceuticals may well produce the next generation of wonder drugs. But in our secular age, it could also foster a genetic reductionism that reduces human beings to a read-out of their genetic code. A spokesman for an animal-rights group, People for the Ethical Treatment of Animals, says splicing human genes into animals proves that humans are nothing special—that they are merely part of the animal world and nothing more.

But this is nonsense. The fact that a tiny strand of human DNA can function in an animal tells us nothing about the metaphysical status of human beings. After all, humans are much more than DNA.

The essential mark of humanity is the image of God. DNA is an important molecule—governing heredity and development. But we are not made in the image of a strand of chemicals. We are made to reflect the character of the God who created us. ※

GOVERNED
BY OUR GENES?

Weekend

ALCOHOL AND COCAINE ADDICTION may be written in the genes, says a team of geneticists. They discovered that addicts often have a less common form of a particular gene—the dopamino receptor gene. Roughly half the addicts studied had this unusual form of the gene.

Do genes govern our behavior?

Some scientists think so. Francis Crick, co-discoverer of DNA, wrote a book called *The Astonishing Hypothesis*, subtitled *The Scientific Search for the Soul.* Crick claims that the entire human soul or personality—"your joys and sorrows, your memories and ambitions, your sense of personal identity"—can be reduced to the behavior of the molecules in your brain, acting at the behest of the genes.

Language like this ought to raise a red flag for Christians. When Crick talks about "the soul," he has left behind the realm of science and is expressing his commitment to the philosophy of genetic determinism—that people are no more than walking DNA.

But the facts simply don't support these wild conjectures. Recall that in the study of addiction, only half the people addicted have the unusual form of the dopamine receptor gene—which means the rest got hooked *without* any genetic basis. On the other hand, some people who *do* have the gene succeed in resisting temptation.

Dr. David Persing is a molecular genetics researcher and a Christian. He says the biblical teaching that all of nature is fallen includes our genetic heritage. As a result, we *all* have inborn tendencies toward various forms of sinful behavior—whether it's addiction, a sexual disorder, or a tendency to ruthlessness or cowardice.

Yet our genes give no excuse for sin, Persing says. We still have room for making real moral choices. Everyone is dealt a different genetic hand in life, but we're each responsible for how we play it. The life-giving message of the gospel is that we are not pawns of our genes. Despite our fallen nature, we can still be governed by God, not by our genes. 🔲

CLONES
FOR SALE

Monday

SCIENTISTS SAY THEY HAVE CLONED the first human being. At George Washington University, researchers took human embryos consisting of only two to eight cells, split the cells apart, and allowed each to develop its own. If each cell had been implanted in a woman's womb, the result would have been several genetically identical babies.

Why would anyone want several identical twins? The answer reads like science fiction. Some scientists have suggested freezing the extra embryos for future use. For example, if the original child dies at an early age, a frozen twin could be thawed out, and the parents could raise a clone identical to the child they lost.

Or what if the original child needs an organ transplant? Just unfreeze a twin and use it for spare parts. The tissues would match perfectly.

Some geneticists even propose a catalog allowing parents to select their baby before birth. Parents could peruse photographs of the original children, pick one they like, buy a frozen clone, and raise an identical child. Some entrepreneurs could even specialize in embryos that grow up to be Einsteins or Picassos.

Sound far-fetched? It's not. America already has sperm banks for Nobel prize-winners and champion athletes. In short, we already have a market for pre-selected babies.

The only real barrier to mass-producing babies through cloning is a residual sense of the biblical worldview, which regards each person as valuable in his own right. But that worldview is under severe attack. Listen to the words of geneticist Robert Haynes: "For three thousand years," he says, "a majority of people have considered that human beings were special. . . . It's the Judeo-Christian view of man."

"Well, not anymore," Haynes declares. Genetics teaches that "we are biological machines" and nothing more.

This is the philosophy of genetic reductionism, which treats people as merely DNA on legs. It allows the human body to be manipulated, used, and discarded as though it were an industrial product.

Christians support science as the investigation of God's world. But we must make sure that it's applied in a way that furthers God's purposes. Genetic technology can be a great benefit or it can be a Pandora's box of horrors—depending on the worldview that guides it. ▨

THE SCARLET THREAD

Tuesday

FOR THE CHURCH TO HEAL THE RIFT between evangelism and social action, we need to rediscover a central theme of Scripture: *justice*.

Many think of justice in terms of a political definition: everyone getting his or her due. Conservatives suppose that means wrongdoers receive punishment. Liberals assert it means everyone getting an equal share of society's benefits.

These misconceptions blind us to the glorious scarlet thread that connects the Pentateuch to the Prophets to the Epistles: the true scriptural understanding of justice. When Isaiah admonished the Jews to "do justice" and Amos thundered, "Let justice roll down like waters," the word in Hebrew, *tsedaqah*, literally means "righteousness." It was God's declaration that people and social structures must be in conformity with the standards of a just and holy God.

In the New Testament, God sets forth the same standard, bringing justice to pass through Christ's atoning death on the cross. It is Jesus who pays for our sins, bearing God's just judgment in His own body; as the apostle Paul writes so eloquently in Romans, we are *justified*—declared righteous by our faith in Christ alone.

This definition unlocks the true mission of the church. We no longer see justice as solely the preoccupation of social-activist Christians; nor do we perceive God as the angry Judge whose justice would obliterate us all if He had His way. Instead, we hear the clarion call for men and women to be declared just by faith in

Christ, and then to help create a social order that mirrors God's
righteousness.

THE LURE OF SIN

Wednesday

SAINT AUGUSTINE IN HIS *CONFESSIONS* gave what is perhaps the
classic teaching on the nature of crime, reflecting Paul's argument in Romans 7:

> . . . I willed to commit theft, and I did so, not because
> I was driven to it by any need. . . . . For I stole a thing
> of which I had plenty of my own and of much better
> quality. Nor did I wish to enjoy that thing which I desired
> to gain by theft, but rather to enjoy the actual theft and the
> sin of theft.
>
> In a garden nearby to our vineyard there was a pear
> tree. . . . Late one night a group of very bad youngsters
> set out to shake down and rob this tree. We took great
> loads of fruit from it, not for our own eating, but rather to
> throw to the pigs; even if we did eat a little of it, we did this
> to do what pleased us for the reason that it was forbidden.
> Foul was the evil, and I loved it.

Some scholars mock Augustine. Here, they say, was a phi-
landerer and a heavy drinker. Surely he could think of more
heinous sins than stealing a few pears from a neighbor's tree.

But they miss the point. The fruit, says Augustine, "was de-
sirable in neither appearance nor in taste." We sin not primarily
because of outside influences or factors beyond our control, but
simply because we *choose* to sin.

This is the key to criminal behavior. We are sinners; we *choose*
to do evil. A multitude of other factors influence us. But in the
end we are responsible for what we do.

QUAINT EXPLANATION?

Thursday

IN THE 1960S PSYCHOLOGIST DR. Stanton Samenow and psychiatrist Samuel Yochelson, sharing the conventional wisdom that crime is caused by environment, set out to prove their point. They began a seventeen-year study, published in 1977, entitled *The Criminal Personality*. To their own astonishment, they discovered that the cause of crime cannot be traced to environment: to poverty or oppression. Instead, crime is the result of individuals making, as they put it, wrong moral choices. Samenow and Yochelson concluded that the answer to crime is a "conversion of the wrong-doer to a more responsible lifestyle."

In 1987, professors James Q. Wilson and Richard J. Herrnstein at Harvard came to similar conclusions in *Crime and Human Nature*. They determined that the cause of crime is a lack of proper moral training among young people during the morally formative years, particularly ages one to six.

In other words, the crime problem boils down to concepts that are foreign to our lips today, words that may even sound quaint—like morality and character. The root of our crime problem is the loss of individual character, and the resulting erosion of our character as a people. ▨

CRIME IN HISTORY

Friday

IN THE EARLY 1980S, JAMES Q. WILSON decided to survey our national history to find some trend or cycle that would correlate with crime data. He noticed a startling pattern.

Contrary to common expectations, crime did not correlate with poverty. During the Great Depression, for example, there was widespread poverty—thirty-four million people unemployed—and yet crime dropped.

Nor did it correlate with factors like urbanization—masses of people crowding into the cities. The middle of the nineteenth century, for example, was a period of rapid urbanization. Yet the level of crime actually fell. Why? During that same period a great spiritual revival took place—the Second Great Awakening. Just as industrialization was beginning, a more fervent morality was also taking hold. So from the mid-1800s to 1920, despite all the environmental, economic, and social pressures that should have led to increased crime, the crime rate actually decreased.

Conversely, during the good economic years of the 1920s, crime actually rose. Why? Because, as Wilson concluded, "the educated classes began to repudiate moral uplift and Freud's psychological theories came into vogue." People no longer believed in restraining a child's sinful impulses; they wanted to develop his "naturally good" personality. The weaker emphasis on moral training led predictably to an increase in criminal behavior.

The same philosophy came back into fashion in the 1960s, bringing with it a sharp increase in crime, which still continues today.

The facts show clearly that crime stems from moral factors—the solution to crime must be moral as well. Anything else is merely a Band-Aid to treat a sickness of the soul. 🕮

CHILDREN WHO KILL

Weekend

IN 1993, BRITAIN WAS SHOCKED by a murder that sickened even the most hardened police officers: the senseless butchering of a two-year-old boy by two ten-year-old boys.

The steepest increase in violent crime is taking place among teens and adolescents. In the U. S. from 1985 to 1991, the number of sixteen-year-olds arrested for murder rose 158 percent; the number of fifteen-year-olds rose 217 percent; the number of thirteen- and fourteen-year-olds rose 140 percent; twelve-year-olds, 100 percent.

What's happening to our children?

Two criminologists—James Q. Wilson and Richard Herrnstein—asked that question a few years ago in their book

Crime and Human Nature. Whether a person becomes a criminal depends crucially, Wilson and Herrnstein found, on the development of conscience in the early years. Adult behavior is a reflection of childhood moral training, the development of internal restraints on impulsive behavior.

Scripture teaches that evil is a part of human nature from birth. The Puritans captured the idea in the *New England Primer*: "In Adam's fall, we sinned all." In colonial days, parents knew that their primary task was to instill moral conscience in their children.

But later, the biblical view was rejected as harsh and negative. In the eighteenth century, Jean Jacques Rousseau introduced a new philosophy of childhood. Children are not sinners, he said. They are naturally good. The goal of education ought to be to free children's natural impulses.

In the 1960s, Rousseau's ideas became common currency among educators and child experts. As Wilson and Herrnstein tell it, morality was denounced as repressive and stifling. Child rearing theories rejected self-control in favor of self-expression.

But without moral self-control, there is no check on the innate tendency to evil. No sooner did Rousseau's concept of childhood become widespread than the crime rate began to climb.

And it's still climbing today—engulfing ever-younger children.

The only solution to juvenile crime is to reverse our ideas about childhood. We need to recapture the Puritan insight that children are sinners who need moral training. Without internal moral restraints, any civilization will fall into barbarism. 🏵

CRIME AND CHARACTER

Monday

"T HE MORAL RELATIVISM . . . OF the recent past isn't right."
These are not words we normally expect to hear from a movie
star. But the speaker was actor Tom Selleck, and he was traveling
across the country promoting a new organization called Character Counts.

The very fact that morality has moved to the center of the
public debate over crime shows that the discussion has taken a
new turn—for both conservatives and liberals.

As Myron Magnet explains in *The Dream and the Nightmare*,
traditional liberal thought fixed responsibility for crime on poverty and other social ills—which in turn are shaped by impersonal
economic forces. The liberal solution to crime was to modify those
economic forces through enlightened social policy and government programs.

But this assumes a very low view of human nature—a sub-
Christian view. It treats people as passive products of the
environment—like corn or alfalfa that automatically grows or wilts
depending on the rain and sunshine.

On the other side, traditional conservative thought (especially
its libertarian form) has treated crime as a matter of incentives.
Crime rises when the benefits of criminal behavior outweigh the
costs of punishment. The conservative solution was to increase
the costs through harsher punishments and longer sentences.

But this, too, assumes a sub-Christian view of human nature. It treats people as little more than calculating machines,
totting up external incentives.

Both liberal and conservative approaches have proved im-
potent to stem the tide of rising crime. And the reason is that
both are based on wrong presuppositions. Both begin with a view
of human beings as passive, devoid of dignity and moral significance.

The good news is that today people on all sides of the political spectrum are returning to a richer view of human nature, one
rooted ultimately in our Christian heritage. In this view, people

are active and responsible moral agents. The long-term solution to crime is a reformation of values.

In the end, it's character that really counts. ▨

CRIME WITHOUT CONSCIENCE

Tuesday

THE ROOTS OF CRIME REACH back to early childhood.

In his book, *The Moral Sense,* criminologist James Q. Wilson argues that morality is innate—like the capacity for speech. As Paul writes in Romans 2, all human beings have a conscience, a "law written on their hearts."

But conscience must be trained, just as we must be trained to speak a language. Feral children, raised in the wild, are unable to speak despite an innate capacity; likewise, children raised in a moral "wilderness" never learn to judge right from wrong.

The most crucial training takes place in the family. Parents teach their children by example and by the behavior they require. As Aristotle wrote, virtue consists not merely in *knowing* what is right but also in having the will to *do* right. And the will is trained through repetition. In Aristotle's words, "We become just by the practice of just actions."

But with divorce and dual careers, parents today spend 40 percent less time with their children than a generation ago. And their job is made harder by a weakening of public standards. Modern thinkers have rejected the very idea of objective morality: Charles Darwin, who reduced morals to an extension of animal instincts; Sigmund Freud, who considered repression of impulses the source of neurosis; Karl Marx, who disdained morality as an expression of self-interest.

Under this onslaught, confidence in any common morality has crumbled. When children are raised in this climate, their moral sense remains unshaped, untutored. Like feral children incapable of speech, many children today are incapable of drawing moral distinctions—or controlling their passions and impulses.

The front line in the war against crime, then, is not in Congress or the courts. It runs through every living room in America, where parents teach their children right from wrong. It runs through every classroom, where teachers pass on a culture's common moral heritage. It runs through every film and movie, where virtue is either mocked or praised.

A society cannot survive if the demands of human dignity are not written on our hearts from early childhood. ▨

BEGINNING AT HOME

Wednesday

A FEW YEARS AGO, NINE-YEAR-OLD Jeffrey Bailey, Jr., calmly pushed a three-year-old child into the deep end of a swimming pool. Like a scientist making a detached observation, Jeffrey pulled up a lawn chair and sat down to watch the younger child drown. When police tracked down the young killer, he was nonchalant—and even seemed to enjoy all the attention.

This chilling story is told in *High Risk*, by psychologist Ken Magid. Magid describes children who have little sense of right and wrong—no conscience.

At core, crime is a moral problem—and it requires a moral solution. Ultimately, it depends on the cultivation of conscience. The most chilling stories in the news today are about kids who kill with no glimmer of conscience like young Jeff Bailey.

This utter alienation from normal human emotions has been traced to a breakdown in parent-child relationships. Psychiatrist Selma Fraiburg writes, "Where there are no human attachments, there can be no conscience." Psychologist Richard Herrnstein writes that "shallow emotional attachments" are the cause of much of the random violence by adolescents.

In short, the solution to crime begins right at home—in the commitment to build stable, secure families. ▨

Thursday

THE DEMAND SIDE OF DRUGS

I'M ALWAYS AMUSED WHEN POLITICIANS talk about winning the war on drugs as if we could build enough prisons, hire enough police and judges, and effectively seal off the borders to stop the drug flow into America.

In prison I never went to sleep one night without smelling marijuana burning.

And if you can get marijuana into prison with all the guards and watch towers and security measures, you can surely get drugs into a country. I don't care what kind of treaties we enter into with South American nations. I don't care how many guards we put on the border. I don't care if we send the Marines in to burn all the coca and poppy fields in Colombia. So long as people want drugs they will find them just a few handshakes away.

The problem is not on the supply side. If it were, we could have stopped the drug problem long ago. The problem is on the demand side.

Kids are not given training in the basics of right and wrong in the home. They surely don't get any education in traditional values at school. And the drumbeat message of commercials, television, and music is to live for the moment and go for the gusto. At ten, eleven, and twelve they go out on the street and smoke dope or crack. We bust them, they think we're crazy. So do I.

The problem isn't a lack of law enforcement, and it isn't material poverty. It is a poverty of values. In our violent, inner-city neighborhoods, people are crying for the order that grows only out of moral character and moral courage.

Crime is a mirror of a community's moral state.

F REDEFINING
DEVIANCE

Friday

BRITISH POLICE HAVE REPORTED A STRANGE trend: Crime is going *up* but arrests are going *down*. Authorities say police officers have apparently "reached the ceiling" in their ability to respond to rising crime. They're tolerating behavior they once arrested people for.

The same thing is happening here in the United States, says Senator Patrick Moynihan. He calls the trend, "defining deviancy down." We have adjusted our level of expectations until we tolerate rates of crime once deemed intolerable.

And ironically, our culture is feeding this phenomenon.

An article in the *Journal of the American Medical Association* discussed the first longitudinal studies on the effects of television violence on young people. And the results are chilling.

Babies are born with an innate capacity to imitate adult behavior, the article noted. They will imitate anything they see. And until they are five years old, children do not understand that the programs they watch on television are not real.

As a result, the earliest and deepest mental impressions are made during a time when the child sees television as a source of factual information. The child learns that the outside world is a place where violence is frequent, colorful, and exciting.

What happens when this child becomes a young adult? At moments of severe anguish or stress—moments when we all revert to our earliest, most visceral feelings—this child's memory will activate deep-rooted images of violence. The instinct to imitate what we see may trip him into committing a violent crime.

Clearly, we need to monitor own children better. We also need to put pressure on the television industry to clean up their programs. What if every CEO in America pledged to review the television programs his company sponsors? What if every CEO asked not only about ratings but also about the *content* of the programs supported by his corporate dollars? This is a prime opportunity for business to practice social and ethical responsibility.

If we keep redefining deviance down, we will be like the proverbial frog in the kettle—who keeps redefining the level of heat he will tolerate . . . until he boils to death. 🕮

SICK
—OR SINFUL?

Weekend

IN 1981 I VISITED DEATH ROW AT the maximum security prison in Menard, Illinois, and one of the prisoners asked to speak with me alone. He was a middle-aged man with neatly brushed, silver-streaked hair, a warm smile, and intelligent eyes. Except for his shackles and chains, he could have been a genial high school principal or a friendly pharmacist.

In reality, he was John Wayne Gacy, Jr., the man who had sexually abused and murdered thirty-three young men. As we sat in a small interview room and talked, Gacy spoke quite rationally. And as I thought of his crimes, I kept telling myself that he had to be sick.

He *was* sick. Sick with sin that had erupted into horrific evil. Only as I reminded myself that he was sick with the same sin that dwells in us all was I able to spend one hour facing him across a table—and then to pray with him.

More recently, the trial of serial killer Jeffrey Dahmer revolved around the issue of his sanity. No one disputed that Dahmer had committed the unspeakably grisly crimes. But how could a sane person have done that? Yet a Milwaukee jury, confronted with ghastly murder, cannibalism, and necrophilia, concluded that Dahmer was not insane. Just evil.

The terrifying truth is that we are not morally neutral. A friend of mine who is a renowned psychologist and Orthodox Jew often makes the point that left to their own devices, with the assurance they would never be caught or held accountable, individuals will more often choose what is wrong than what is right. We are drawn toward evil; without powerful intervention, we will choose it. And that sin can be cleansed only by Christ's shed blood. 🕮

FIGHTING
CRIME ON SCREEN

Monday

IDENTIFYING THE CAUSE OF CRIME means entering the mysterious realm of human motivations. But in the case of Marvin, in prison for robbery, there was nothing mysterious at all.

In a survey of prisoners conducted by Prison Fellowship, Marvin wrote, "Watching TV and seeing people do robberies—and the way it has been glamorized on TV—made me think of doing it myself."

TV was his tutor in crime.

Psychologists debate endlessly over whether television causes crime. But maybe they should ask those who know best: criminals themselves. People like Marvin tell us without hesitation that they were inspired by television.

Criminals' favorite programs are true-to-life cop shows. Many are so detailed and specific that they are virtually how-to manuals for an aspiring criminal. They've become the equivalent of the Frugal Gourmet: Tune in, take notes, and try it yourself.

I'm not saying television executives set out on purpose to encourage crime. But with their single-minded concern for the bottom line, the shapers of the mass media often do play a significant role in the downward spiral of our society's moral health.

If we want to get tough on crime, we have to get tough on the cultural forces that contribute to crime. Today the media moguls can count on depictions of crime and violence to boost the ratings. Why? Because millions of average citizens like you and me watch those programs.

As a result, the first line of defense against crime runs right through our own living rooms, where we make decisions about what our families watch and listen to. The apostle Paul lived before the days of television, but he knew how important it is to monitor what we put into our minds. He wrote, "Whatever is true, whatever is noble, whatever is right, whatever is pure . . . if anything is excellent or praiseworthy, think about such things" (Phil. 4:8).

A modern-day Paul would have to do a lot of channel surfing before he would find anything on television meeting that high standard today. ▨

CHEERLEADERS AND CRIME

Tuesday

WHEN FOUR CHEERLEADERS SHOWED up at a Texas high school visibly pregnant, the school board kicked them off the team. Immediately the protectors of liberalism took up arms. And what they said reveals a lot about why the social fabric in America is unraveling.

The National Organization for Women threatened a lawsuit. *The New York Times* scolded the school board for even *thinking* of banning the cheerleaders. "The realities of American adolescents' sex lives are understandably hard to confront," the *Times* intoned. "But confront them we must."

Yet it seems to me that the school board *did* confront adolescent sexuality—and in a very direct way. Cheerleaders are looked up to as student leaders, and leadership positions ought to be reserved for students who model exemplary behavior. Getting pregnant outside marriage is not exemplary behavior.

But that's not what *The New York Times* had in mind when it talked about "confronting" teenage sexuality. What it really meant is that we must *accept* it. "These girls should neither be stigmatized nor stopped from joining in any school activity," *The Times* editorialized.

But in today's cultural climate, a little "stigmatizing" of pregnancy outside marriage might not be such a bad thing. Studies reveal that children without fathers are more likely to grow up in poverty, to have problems in school, to commit crimes. Charles Murray of the American Enterprise Institute wrote that "illegitimacy is the single most important social problem of our time—more important than crime, drugs, poverty, illiteracy, welfare, or homelessness." Why? Because illegitimacy "drives everything else."

David Blankenhorn of the Institute of American Values says, "Fatherlessness is . . . the most important predictor of juvenile crime—a greater predictor than either race or income." The major reason the ghettos are the focus of violent crime is that they have the highest rates of illegitimacy.

Crime begins when the middle and upper classes allow the moral consensus to break down. And the brutal truth is that if society does *not* take a moral stand, then the pathology of the underclass will continue to spread to the middle class.

So if we're worried about crime, there's something we can do about it: We can bring biblical ideals of marriage and family to our own neighborhoods, our own high schools.

Starting with the cheerleaders and football players. ※

"ROBBERY! ROBBERY!"

Wednesday

IT WAS A TYPICAL TUESDAY NIGHT in a quiet neighborhood in Washington, D. C., and a pedestrian was strolling down the sidewalk. Suddenly, he was attacked by a young man, who beat him and tried to take his wallet.

That too, unfortunately, is typical.

But then something happened that is definitely *un*typical. A boy riding by on a bike began peddling up and down the street, yelling "Robbery! Robbery!" Neighbors stopped what they were doing and rushed to help. A man taking groceries out of his car dropped them and ran over. Others poured out of their homes, clad in pajamas and bathrobes. In minutes the mugger was pinned against a parked car under a pileup of angry citizens, who held him until police arrived.

"This is a real community," the local police captain said. "They get involved and they take initiative."

To Americans who are desperately searching for an answer to crime, I suggest we could learn something from a quiet neighborhood in Washington, D. C. When we rely too heavily on centralized government, we become disconnected from our neighborhoods. We look to Capitol Hill to safeguard our rights, to protect us.

But when someone is beating you up on a dark street, there's no time to write your congressman a letter about better law enforcement. You need real people right there. You need an active, caring community.

The untypical response by the Washington neighborhood was the result of people deciding to build a caring community. Months earlier they had met together and agreed to put their lives on the line to help one another in trouble.

This is a profoundly biblical principle. When Jesus taught His followers to be Good Samaritans, He illustrated by telling a story about a man who was attacked by robbers. A man who was mugged.

The best anti-crime programs are ones that empower ordinary citizens to be Good Samaritans.

CHAOS IN THE CITY

Thursday

I N CITIES ACROSS THE NATION THERE are areas so dangerous that police officers no longer walk the beat but cruise the neighborhood behind the locked doors of their patrol cars. This ought to set off all our mental alarm bells. If local governments surrender our streets, in time entire cities will be ruled by the law of the jungle.

The Bible teaches that the primary task of government is to maintain civic order. As Paul says in Romans 13, the purpose of government is to commend those who do right and punish those who do wrong. But in America these days we ask the government to take on all sorts of additional tasks: to conduct surveys, subsidize the arts, mandate ethnic policy, and even police gender relations in the workplace. As a result, the government is spread too thin. The state is overextended into so many social engineering projects that it no longer has the resources to attend to its primary task of keeping our streets safe.

The only way to turn things around is for you and me to stop expecting government to supply a vast array of services—and to start pressing it to protect our streets. A government asked to do too much ends up failing in its primary task. If we give up the streets, we give up a free society.

YOUR LIFE OR YOUR LIBERTY

Friday

A S CRIME SOARS, SO DOES PUBLIC FEAR—a cycle that ends in a clamor for greater government control to quell the chaos.

Crime has so unsettled political leaders that some cities are imposing curfews on young people, despite objections that the curfews are unconstitutional. "Curfews are basically martial law," argues an ACLU lawyer. And so they are. Still, they have almost uniform approval from frightened citizens.

In another ominous sign, police in St. Petersburg, Florida, are stopping cars randomly and searching for drugs. This despite the fact that it violates the Fourth Amendment's protection against unreasonable search and seizure. Yet a *Miami Herald* poll found that 71 percent of residents favor police roadblocks to stop drugs. As one inner-city resident told reporters, people "shell-shocked" by crime welcome higher levels of police intrusion.

In his novel *When the Almond Tree Blossoms*, journalist David Aikman portrays a fictional future when civic disorder infects society so deeply that Americans are willing to give up their freedom for tyranny—as long as it restores order. But the scenario is not merely fictional. Aikman believes it's a plausible prediction of what could actually happen—and soon.

Aikman is right. Faced with social chaos, people will always exchange liberty for order—even if enforced through the barrel of a gun.

The need has never been more urgent for a biblical approach to crime. Unless we work for moral reformation across the whole society, we will surely see the strong arm of the state come crashing down on our liberties.

Weekend

BIBLES
OR BAYONETS

IN PUERTO RICO, TROOPS IN camouflage uniforms are patrolling the beaches, M-16s in hand, as they weave through crowds of children playing in the sand. The National Guard was called in as an emergency response to skyrocketing crime.

As civil disorder spreads, governments inevitably resort to military might. A hundred years ago, Lord Acton foresaw the process leading to a police state. Acton is best known for the dictum memorized by civics students that absolute power corrupts absolutely. But few students know how he proposed to *avoid* absolute power: through religion. The Christian religion, Acton argued, "creates and strengthens the notion of duty." It creates an invisible bond of duty that yokes every citizen.

I witnessed this profound sense of duty in a Czechoslovakian priest, Vaclav Maly. In the early 80s, Maly was defrocked by the Communists and dispatched to clean subway toilets. Yet he continued to preach the gospel.

When Czechoslovakia's "Velvet Revolution" broke out, it was Maly who led hundreds of thousands of exuberant demonstrators through the streets of Prague. "Maly! Maly! Maly!" the crowds shouted. Later, when a democratic government was formed, he was offered a position of power. But he declined public service in favor of spiritual service.

When I met Maly in his tiny Prague apartment, I told him what a hero he was to many of us in the West. He smiled but shook his head. "Oh, no. A hero is someone who does something he doesn't have to do. But me—I was merely doing my duty."

This is the vital sense of duty we need to rekindle among our own compatriots. When religion decays—as it has in the West today—duty loses its hold on our hearts; we are left with no reason to restrain our impulses or obey the law. Crime and lawlessness are unleashed, as our rising crime statistics demonstrate. And the government, no longer able to motivate its citizens by duty, falls back on force and fear.

If people are not governed by *internal* values, they must be governed by *external* force. Take away the Bibles that direct a nation's soul, and the government will bring out the bayonets. 🔲

DEGENERATING FAMILIES

Monday

COLUMNIST WILLIAM RASPBERRY WARNS that the family is not merely "changing," as experts once reassured us; instead, it is "degenerating."

Raspberry cites a study comparing two groups: One group waited to have children until after they had finished high school, reached the age of twenty, and got married; only 8 percent of their children lived in poverty. The other group consisted of people who waited for none of those things; they had a staggering 79 percent poverty rate.

All our vaunted poverty programs, welfare programs, and drug programs have less effect, it turns out, than decisions made by individual men and women to wait for marriage and maturity before having children. Our most pressing social problems stem from moral decisions made in the heart of family life.

For decades public policy was pursued as though it could ignore moral questions. But now policy makers recognize that when a society's moral sense decays—particularly in regard to the family—the center cannot hold.

THE EPIDEMIC OF ABSENT FATHERS

Tuesday

SINCE THE 1960S, AMERICA HAS seen a staggering increase in broken families. Liberal social scientists don't like to use phrases like "broken families"; they glibly describe them in neutral terms like "new family forms" and "single-parent homes."

But in the eyes of a child, what's nearly always happening is the loss of a father.

Statistics show that the results of that loss are devastating. While the national poverty rate is 6 percent, the poverty rate for female-headed households is 30 percent. Among black female-headed households, it jumps to 50 percent.

And with no-fault divorce, poverty is rapidly making inroads into the middle class as well. Half of all new welfare recipients are recently divorced women and their children. Today the most reliable indicator of whether a child is poor is whether or not he lives in an intact family.

But a missing father means much more than a missing paycheck. A father's love and discipline are crucial to character formation. And for children growing up without that love, the statistics are grim.

Fatherless children display more antisocial behavior, do worse in school, and are twice as likely to drop out than children from intact families. They are more likely to use drugs and become sexually active at an early age. Approximately 70 percent of juveniles who end up in long-term correctional facilities grew up without a father at home.

Even health rates are affected. A study by the Department of Health and Human Services found that after controlling for age, sex, race, and socioeconomic status, children from broken families are twenty to forty times more likely to suffer health problems than children living with both parents.

Our nation can no longer afford to be morally neutral about family forms. For the sake of our children, we must begin to design social policies that support and encourage intact families. We need to encourage men to take their family responsibilities more seriously.

There's a reason God created the family the way He did. Children need fathers as well as mothers in order to thrive. And even more important, in order to learn to trust God as their *heavenly* Father. 🔳

CRITICAL CONDITION

Wednesday

D EBATES OVER ISSUES LIKE FAMILY structures and sexual conduct have become so politicized that we have nearly lost all shared definitions of such terms as *family* and *values*—a loss that renders us incapable of reasoned moral discourse.

A poignant illustration was a report entitled "Code Blue," issued a few years ago by several professional organizations. "Code Blue" is a phrase used by hospitals to signal a life-threatening emergency; the emergency in this case was a steep rise in adolescent suicide, school failure, pregnancy, sexually transmitted diseases, and drug and alcohol abuse.

"Code Blue" pinned the blame directly on changes in family structure. A central factor in the youth crisis, the report said, is changing families and neighborhoods, which has left many children "on their own . . . isolated from adults." The mobility of American families and the need for second incomes, the report added, "have robbed too many young people of stable families and communities where they are surrounded by caring adults to guide their growth and behavior."

This is great, I thought. Finally we're hearing mainstream institutions admit that many of our social problems stem directly from family decline. I turned the pages to see what solutions the report would offer.

Alas, in "Code Blue," the disorders plaguing youth today, from depression to drug use, were labeled *health* problems. And the solution recommended was guaranteed access to health services, both medical and "psychosocial" services.

But think about it: If the problem is that children are being left "on their own," to use the report's own words, is the solution really another health clinic? If the problem is that children have been "robbed . . . of stable families and communities," is the solution really a visit to the doctor?

No, what children need most are strong families, and family cohesion is a direct result of moral choices. What "Code Blue" illustrates is a massive failure among health and education professionals even to conceptualize the moral dimension. We have lost the language of moral discourse.

Americans are finally groping their way toward a correct diagnosis of the problem: namely, that modern society has given adults permission to adopt lifestyles out of tune with the needs of their children. But too many cultural leaders refuse to recognize that this is fundamentally not a health disorder, nor a result of inadequate "services"; it is a moral disorder.

FAMILY TIME
FAMINE

Thursday

A MERICAN FAMILIES ARE SPENDING less time together than ever, says sociologist Sylvia Hewlett. She calls it the "family-time famine." Statistics show that today's parents spend 40 percent less time with their children than their parents did.

That's a staggering decrease in adult investment in children.

The good news is that some parents are trying to reverse the trend. A recent story in the *Washington Post* announces that fast-track professionals are slowing down, exploring things like part-time work and flexible schedules to create more family time.

Lynn Myers is a pediatrician who began working part-time when her first son was born. Today she still restricts her work to school hours so she can help with homework or drive to soccer practice.

Caroline Hull is a computer specialist, who started her own business at home when her children were born.

Bob Hamrin was economic advisor to a national political figure when he decided he wanted more time with his growing family and started a home-based consulting firm. Now he can adjust his work schedule to attend a child's school function or sports event.

Stepping off the fast track isn't easy. As I think back on my own life, my biggest regret is not spending more time with my kids. Making family your top priority means standing against a culture where materialism and workaholism are rampant. It means realizing that you may not advance as fast in your career as some of your colleagues—at least for a few years. It means being willing to accept a lower standard of living.

Call it the "Parent Penalty."

In today's high-powered career world, parents who really invest in family life pay the Parent Penalty. But the trade-off is knowing you're doing the right thing for your children, giving them the emotional security they'll draw on for the rest of their lives.

There's a professional trade-off too. People who enjoy a healthy family life make better workers. The Association for Part-Time Professionals says part-time workers invest more productive effort into the hours they do spend on the job.

Good parents make good workers. Encouraging a healthy family life is not only a biblical principle. It also happens to be good business. 🔲

BEATING UP ON DAD

Friday

IT LOOKS LIKE A CHARMING CHILDREN'S story—three little bears on a scouting escapade. But who's this? Papa Bear is coming along. And at every step of the way, Papa makes a complete fool of himself. If Papa suggests the direction to take, the path is sure to end up in a swamp. If he makes the campfire stew, it's sure to taste awful.

Just what is this book teaching kids about fathers?

The story I just described is from the highly popular Berenstein Bear picture-book series. In several of the books, Papa Bear is portrayed as a bumbling oaf. The sensible one in the family is Mama Bear.

In the story on junk food, Papa is the worst offender. It's Mama who enforces the switch to a healthy diet. In the story of manners, again, Papa is the worst offender. It's Mama who enforces politeness.

Isn't there anything Papa does best? Well, yes, he's given one distinction. In a book on fitness, the children outdo Papa on every skill except one: Sister Bear can run the fastest, Brother Bear can jump the farthest, but when the exercise session is over, Papa Bear can sleep the longest.

Ha, ha. Let's all have a good laugh at Papa's expense.

This treatment of fathers is not the exception but the rule in children's books. In a *Newsweek* article, a young father complained that he has a terrible time finding books for his children that show fathers in a positive light.

What will happen to a society where children's imaginations are filled with images of fathers who are oafs and fools? It's no good saying this is all "just" fiction. When children read story upon story with incompetent or abusive fathers, that can't help but shape their expectations.

Psychologists recognize the emotional impact of books—so much so that there's even a branch of counseling today called "bibliotherapy," which uses story books to change children's attitudes. And if stories have power to do good, then clearly they have power to do harm.

That's why the women's movement has worked so hard to change the image of women in children's books. And the civil rights movement has worked to root out negative images of black people.

Maybe it's time to start a movement for fathers. ■

VIRGINS
SPEAK OUT

Weekend

GLAMOUR MAGAZINE HAS MADE a shocking discovery: Many of its readers are virgins.

It all started when the magazine asked its readers a question: "Are there any virgins left out there?" Two thousand women wrote in to say *they* were virgins—and proud of it. The magazine summarized the responses in a March 1992 article entitled, "2,000 Virgins: They're *Not* Who You Think." In other words, they're not ugly wallflowers. They're intelligent, "with-it" young women who are articulate, who know what they want, and who read sophisticated magazines. Like *Glamour.*

They've simply chosen not to have sex outside of marriage.

Judging by their letters, it is not an easy choice to make these days. The women told of being teased and humiliated and made to feel like freaks. Some women even sent in photos to prove that they're really just normal human beings.

In the face of such intense opposition, why are there still young people who stand against the current? The women who wrote in listed several good reasons.

Almost all of them listed AIDS and other sexually transmitted diseases as good reasons to remain chaste. Others said they didn't want to be pressured into sex by peers and the media. Many said sex is too meaningful for a casual relationship. As one woman put it, "a lot of feelings, trust, and intimacy are put into a relationship once sex is involved." That's why she wants to save it for a relationship that's going to last. Others warned that sex outside marriage loses its deep meaning. One woman told *Glamour* that sex is for expressing love—and you can't possibly love a new person every few months.

The virgins who wrote in didn't express a low view of sex. On the contrary, they saw it as something intensely meaningful— so special that it should be saved for a special context: for the committed relationship of marriage. One letter-writer said, "God doesn't forbid sex before marriage because He wants to put us in a box with a list of rules and no fun. No, it's because He wants the best for us."

That hits at the core of the issue.

God's laws are not capricious or arbitrary. They tell us who we are and what is truly best for us. 🔳

WOULD COSMO LIE TO YOU?

Monday

I T'S TAKEN THREE DECADES, BUT *Cosmopolitan* magazine may finally be catching up with biblical morality.

Thirty years ago, *Cosmo* editor-in-chief Helen Gurley Brown wrote a best-selling book called *Sex and the Single Girl.* But more recently, the magazine sounded an entirely new note: It warned that living together could sink your chances of a good marriage. One national survey found that couples who live together before marriage are one-third more likely to separate or divorce within ten years. A Swedish study was even more disturbing. There, women who have cohabited experience an 80 percent greater risk of divorce.

The *Cosmo* article was taken from a book by family therapist Laura Schlessinger. Why, Schlessinger asks, does living together so often lead to disaster? Her answer is that people who move in before making a marriage commitment are people who haven't learned to practice delayed gratification.

They want the *benefits* of a solid relationship before investing the time and effort to *build* a solid relationship. Later, when the road gets rocky, these folks won't invest the time and effort to *sustain* the relationship either.

The word must be getting around. At the same time the *Cosmo* article appeared, the *Washington Post* published a similar piece. Written by William Mattox of the Family Research Council, the article describes a study designed to find out if moral values have any impact on sexual happiness. The study found that of people who are married and hold traditional sexual morality, 72 percent report high sexual satisfaction.

By contrast, non-traditionalists—defined as people with no moral objection to sex outside marriage—report far less happiness. Non-traditionalists who are married fall 13 percentage points lower than traditionalists; non-traditionalists who are single fall a whopping 31 percentage points lower.

The data is finally in on the sexual revolution—and what it shows is that a happy sex life is firmly linked to marriage and traditional sexual values.

We can be confident that what God commands in Scripture is always best for us. After all, it was God who invented sex and marriage in the first place. ▨

WEDDING FACTORIES

Tuesday

T HERE'S A MYSTERIOUS EPIDEMIC that renders adult males twice as likely to die from heart disease, stroke, hypertension, and cancer. No, I'm not talking about smoking or eating too much salt. I'm talking about divorce.

Studies show that the stress of divorce puts both men and women at a significantly higher risk for a whole host of physical illnesses—not to mention emotional problems.

And what are Americans doing about it? Virtually nothing.

When have you ever heard a sermon on divorce? Yet most marriages that end in divorce *began* at the altar. Obviously, too many churches have become little more than "wedding factories." They help couples prepare for elaborate wedding ceremonies but not for lasting marriages.

How can your church become a real force for building strong marriages? Mike McManus, in his book *Marriage Savers*, says a marriage ministry needs to begin with teens and dating couples. After all, when are people's ideas about relationships formed? In those crucial years *before* a couple actually walks the aisle.

The church's first message to the dating couple ought to be strong and clear: If you want a good marriage, don't have premarital sex. The National Survey of Family Growth found that women who were not virgins when they got married had a divorce rate *71 percent higher* than virgins. These are statistics every church ought to be teaching high school and college groups. Saying no to premarital sex means saying yes to a stronger marriage.

The reason behind the numbers is simple: Dating couples who abstain from sex are more likely to build emotional and intellectual companionship. What's more, they're building the self-restraint so crucial to being a successful husband or wife later on. After all, fidelity in marriage takes self-control too!

It's time for churches to break the silence on divorce. It's up to God's people to begin teaching people *how* to have a marriage that lasts. ※

TRIAL MARRIAGES ON TRIAL

Wednesday

IN A PROGRAM CALLED TRUE LOVE WAITS, thousands of teenagers have signed public pledges that they will practice sexual abstinence until marriage.

Television host Rush Limbaugh sent a cameraman out on the streets to gauge public response to the program. Bystanders were asked, "Do you think teens should practice sexual abstinence?"

"Absolutely not," replied one well-dressed woman. "I think couples should live together to see if the relationship will work out." Those words express one of our society's most harmful myths. A national survey discovered that 90 percent of people who live together *want* to get married; about half believe that cohabiting will help ensure that they're compatible.

But the truth is that living together is almost certain to destroy your chances of a good marriage.

Just listen to the numbers. A 1985 study found that only a quarter of women—and a fifth of men—end up marrying the person they live with. That means if you decide to cohabit, you're taking a 75-80 percent chance of breaking up before signing a marriage license.

Even if you do marry, your chances of divorce skyrocket. The *National Survey of Families and Households* found that couples who live together before marriage are almost twice as likely to divorce. Thinking of cohabitation as a trial marriage is profoundly mistaken.

The Bible says, "a man shall leave his father and mother and be united to his wife, and the two will become one flesh." Then, speaking of Adam and Eve, it says, "the man and woman were both naked and felt no shame."

The sequence here is crucial: First comes leaving one's father and mother; then being united to a spouse; and finally becoming one flesh—physical intimacy without shame.

Couples who live together are reversing that sequence: They're trying to be "one flesh" *before* marriage. And the result is that they *do* feel shame . . . and fear and rage and all the other feelings that erupt when a relationship lacks commitment.

So don't be tongue-tied when you talk to friends who are living together. Give them the statistics: Tell them that cohabitation literally sets them up for a failed marriage. 🔳

PROMISE
ME FOREVER

Thursday

I CAN'T PROMISE YOU FOREVER," a Hallmark card says. "But I can promise you today." It's the quintessential love card for the 90s: No commitment, just warm feelings . . . as long as they last. No wonder 60 percent of marriages are failing. Young people are literally training themselves for relationships without commitment.

America has the highest divorce rate in the world. Ironically, it also has the highest rate of church attendance among the modern nations of the world. Clearly, churches are not doing much to stem the tide of family breakdown.

This is scandalous. The church needs to boldly proclaim the biblical teaching on marriage. It also needs to offer practical help to couples considering marriage. As family psychologist James Dobson comments, "A dating relationship is designed to conceal information, not reveal it." Couples need help in honestly assessing their relationship *before* they walk down the aisle.

In *Marriage Savers*, Mike McManus lists several excellent programs churches can use. One is called Relationship Instruction, designed by Jim Talley, author of *Too Close, Too Soon*. It's a four-month course for seriously dating couples, teaching them how to identify problem areas in their relationship and to resolve conflicts. After using Relationship Instruction with more than one hundred couples, Jim Talley knows of only one that later divorced. That's a 99 percent success rate!

For engaged couples, there's a program called PREPARE (Premarital Personal and Relationship Evaluation). Couples fill out a questionnaire whose results give an objective snapshot of the state of their relationship—its strengths and weaknesses. Then they're taught concrete strategies for tackling the weak areas. PREPARE's questionnaire has proven so reliable that it can predict with 80 percent accuracy which couples will divorce. It's a diagnostic tool that every church ought to use.

If your own children are planning to marry, don't wait. Find a church that has premarital programs your children can attend.

Think of it as divorce insurance. It's the best wedding present you'll ever give your children. ▓

WHEN THE
HONEYMOON IS OVER

Friday

THE ECONOMY HAS BEEN SLUGGISH since the recession, but one industry has proven recession-proof: bridal magazines. Pages are filled with shimmering wedding gowns and countless tips for planning the perfect wedding—but almost nothing about what really matters: how to make a marriage work.

After the honeymoon, many couples are shocked by the conflict that erupts in their relationship. This is a critical period for marriages. On one hand, it can be the time when the seeds of divorce are planted. On the other hand, this period can be one of the teachable moments in a person's life when the church can effectively intervene.

For example, a program called ENRICH provides a survey that gives a penetrating x-ray of any relationship.

Even Christians often score low on relational skills: on ability to communicate, resolve conflicts, and manage finances. Through its questionnaire, ENRICH highlights weak areas and helps couples work on them—*before* the weaknesses become entrenched habits.

The idea that newlyweds need special nurturing goes back to the Old Testament. Deuteronomy 24 says, "If a man has recently married, he must not be sent to war or have any other duty laid on him. For one year he is to be free to stay at home and bring happiness to the wife he has married."

A whole year! That's how long newlyweds in ancient Israel were to be free of stressful outside responsibilities. Clearly the lesson for us today is that the church is meant to tenderly nurture its young couples.

LOVE AND THE LAW

Weekend

A TWELVE-YEAR-OLD GIRL, I'LL CALL her Rachel, was seeing a counselor who asked her to write down the best and the worst things that had ever happened to her. Rachel had no trouble identifying the worst thing: It was, she wrote, "when my parents got divorced."

Ironically, Rachel was just a toddler when her parents divorced, and she doesn't even remember the actual event. Yet she has a deep, visceral sense that was the moment her world was shattered.

Unfortunately, America's legal system actually helps create tragedies like Rachel's by treating marriage and divorce casually. Nearly all fifty states have no-fault divorce laws that allow anyone to get a divorce—regardless of whether the other spouse wants it or not. *No other* legal contract can be broken so easily.

What no-fault divorce laws have done is remove the moral dimension from family law. Under previous laws, the person who broke the marital contract suffered negative consequences. If a man ran off with his secretary, he had to leave his home to his wife and pay child support and alimony. But today the same man can demand the sale of the family home and pocket half its value; he rarely has to pay alimony or child support. It's his innocent wife and children who suffer the adverse consequences.

In effect, the law punishes the innocent party who *fulfills* the marriage contract . . . and rewards the guilty party who *flaunts* it.

These laws are unjust and ought to be changed. For example, in California judges may now defer sale of a family home until children are older, so that kids who lose a parent don't lose their school and friends at the same time. The state also makes it easier for a mother to get alimony if she has foregone a career to raise children.

Church leaders, activist groups, and attorneys ought to line up behind reforms like these. Christians are called to be salt in the broader society: a force for preserving the institutions God has ordained as the basis of the social order.

We need to find ways to build moral accountability back into family law. ☒

Monday

BERKELEY'S "NAKED GUY"

AFTER HAGGLING FOR SIX MONTHS, officials at the University of California in Berkeley expelled the "Naked Guy"—a student named Andrew Martinez who had been coming to class stark naked, wearing nothing but a house key on a chain around his neck. Martinez said his goal was to make a philosophical statement: He wanted to teach people that clothes have absolutely no use—that they're just "a form of cultural repression."

Like Berkeley's "Naked Guy," many Americans have forgotten the reason *behind* our social mores. Even such common-sense conventions as wearing clothes are being questioned. Beyond simple utilitarian reasons—like keeping warm—people no longer remember why these social rules were established in the first place.

The biblical teaching on modesty goes back to the beginning, when God first created human society. When Adam and Eve were created, Genesis tells us, they were naked without any sense of shame. But when they fell into sin, that changed. Suddenly being naked made them feel vulnerable.

Notice that God didn't tell Adam and Eve to free themselves from their hang-ups and repressions. Instead He fashioned coverings for them; He *reinforced* their newfound sense of modesty.

Genesis is teaching us that in a fallen world modesty is an expression of respect and restraint. It gives us the freedom to *choose* the people with whom we want to associate intimately. It permits us to keep full self-disclosure within the protection of the loving, committed relationship of marriage.

Even students at Berkeley sense this instinctively. When the "Naked Guy" took to walking around campus naked after dark, he frightened some of the female students. When imposed on people unwillingly and uninvited, nudity is a form of aggression. It breaks down social boundaries that normally act as a protection.

This ought to be common sense. But in today's "anything goes" society, even the most fundamental social conventions have to be justified.

To paraphrase Dostoyevsky, without God, everything is up for grabs. ※

NATIONAL INSECURITY

Tuesday

WHAT WOULD YOU THINK IF YOU called a baby-sitter for your kids, and when you opened the front door, he turned out to be a teenage boy . . . sucking a pacifier? Well, that's exactly what happened to a startled New York father not long ago.

You might be a lot less startled if you knew that pacifiers have become the latest fad. In nightclubs across the country, twenty-year-olds suck on pacifiers and lollipops. They wear Dr. Seuss hats, while dancing with bears and stuffed Big Bird dolls.

Has the world gone mad? No, says self-help guru John Bradshaw. It's all part of the recovery movement, part of searching for the inner child.

Recovery leaders tell us that beneath the layers of our adult experience is the child we once were. Recovery is about getting in touch with that inner child and nurturing it. People "in recovery" come to group meetings clutching teddy bears and baby dolls.

From the religious fervor that permeates some recovery books, you might think they were bringing a message of salvation for today's dysfunctional world. Gloria Steinem, in her book *Revolution from Within,* promises that "there is always *one true* inner voice," the voice of the "untamed and spontaneous child."

Where have we heard that before? Back in the nineteenth century, Jean Jacques Rousseau first preached the gospel of the untamed child. What is the source of evil in the world? Rousseau asked. And he answered: Civilization. The traditions, customs, and rules that cut us off from our natural goodness. And where do we see humanity in its natural goodness? Rousseau asked. Mostly in the child, who is not yet trained into adult hang-ups and inhibitions.

But anyone who has actually raised a child knows that the romantic portrayal of childhood is a sham. Without adult guidance, what comes naturally isn't all love and sweetness; it's also selfishness and greed.

The Bible is utterly realistic about human nature. It teaches that there is no time in our lives when we are pure and without sin. There is no time when we can save ourselves. It is God alone who saves us. ▨

SPOILED ROTTEN?

Wednesday

WHEN BOTH PARENTS WORK—AND admittedly for many it is a necessity—they are forced to leave their young children during the morally formative years from one to six. When the choice is between the financial flexibility of a two-income family or a tighter budget with one parent at home, the answer should be clear: a well-raised child is worth a lot more than a new VCR or microwave.

In fact a tighter budget might even be good for some families. A book entitled *Spoiled Rotten—American Children and How to Change Them* argues that when affluent middle-class children are showered with toys and amusements, they are not taught the value of what they have. The author's answer is to teach children there are limits. If they want name-brand shoes, make them pay for the difference over plain label brands. And let them work for that money. It's part of a value system they'll carry with them for life.

In the home, children first learn the importance of individual responsibility. Until we reclaim our families and our children, we will never deal with the moral crisis in our society. ▨

DOWN THE TUBE

Thursday

I HAVE A CONFESSION TO MAKE. I recently bribed two people—my grandchildren—a boy of eleven and a girl of eight. I had noticed that the children were watching TV more and more frequently.

Television was eating up the time they might have spent reading, playing sports, or chatting with their parents.

So I offered them a challenge. I said, "Keep the set turned off for a complete thirty days, and I'll give you each a hundred dollars."

Both kids took me up on my challenge, and to my surprise they were absolutely faithful. There are now two children in this world who are one hundred dollars richer. But they're richer in many other ways as well. That month of refraining from TV gave them a chance to rediscover a whole range of other activities.

The harmful effect of TV isn't just its content—the violence and the junk shows. Even more serious is its effect on the thinking process itself. As television critic Neil Postman says, "Each form of media encourages a different kind of mental process." Reading, for example, requires long periods of sustained attention and fosters rational thinking. The printed page unfolds its narrative line by line, teaching a coherent, linear thought process.

Television, on the other hand, erodes the ability to concentrate with its fast-moving images. It discourages analytical thinking by reducing complex ideas to images and condensing complex events to a forty-five-second sound bite.

And so, ironically, as our machines grow more complex, our thinking is growing simpler. One study found that children who are heavy TV watchers tend to be less informed and less able to concentrate.

Television has become a bane of family life as well. Statistics show that most fathers today spend only a few minutes a day with their children; mothers, too, are spending less time than they used to. The average preschooler spends about six thousand hours watching television before entering kindergarten. Face-to-face interaction is being replaced by electronic images.

So maybe you'd like to try a little bribery, as I did with my grandchildren. They now recognize they were hooked; they've agreed from now on to put a strict limit on how much TV they watch.

GARBAGE IN, GARBAGE OUT

Friday

WHEN A CALIFORNIA SCHOOL DISTRICT participated in a creative writing project, the students' response was shocking. The assignment was to write a story imagining coming to school on a "misty, foggy morning" to find a strange car on the field, with the teacher's voice coming from the car.

But the stories the children came up with were spiked with savagery, violence, and sexual innuendo.

One child's story told about his teacher holding the class hostage with a machine gun—until police blew her up; another was about a teacher kidnapping a student and stuffing him into the trunk of the car; another told about taping the teacher's mouth shut and pointing a gun at her head.

Other children laced their stories with sex. One child wrote about his teacher being brutally raped; another wrote about finding his *father* in the car with his teacher.

How old would you suppose these kids were?

Incredibly, they were only third-, fourth-, and fifth-graders. What a stark testimony to the early age at which children are absorbing the sordid, ugly side of life.

Just thirty years ago parents could pretty much control their children's access to unwholesome material. Society cooperated by protecting kids from explicit sex and violence. But today it is just the opposite: Everywhere, from movies to television to paperbacks, kids are fed a steady diet of murder, suicide, abortion, incest—you name it.

And with the rapid increase in divorce and two-career families, there's been a sharp drop in the amount of time parents spend supervising their children's activities.

The result is that children are no longer protected from the corrupt and dangerous side of life. In fact, some scholars say we are losing the very concept of childhood as a special and protected place in the life cycle. Several books on the subject have appeared, with titles like *The Disappearance of Childhood* and *Children Without Childhood*.

Christian parents need to stand against the tide. It may mean rethinking our priorities so we spend more time with our children. But it's time we gave them back their childhoods. 🕮

RENTING LOVE

Weekend

HELLO," SAYS A CHIRPY LITTLE BOY'S VOICE. "My name is Yoshi. I'm five years old, and I'm your grandson." An elderly woman hugs him, and smiles at the young man and woman who are with him. She coos at the baby in the woman's arms. The meeting looks for all the world like a family reunion.

But it isn't.

The four visitors are actors, paid to play the part of a family for an elderly couple whose own children have moved away or are too busy to visit. It's called Rent-a-Family, a service offered by a handful of enterprising companies in Japan. News reports say the companies are doing a brisk business. The market consists of elderly couples who are so lonely they're willing to rent a family for an evening of fake reminiscing and pretend conviviality.

Japanese sociologists say the demand for rented families is a result of a culture addicted to work. Since World War II, Japan has been determined to increase the nation's productivity. Many Japanese put in sixty- to eighty-hour work weeks. But in the process, they've created an emotional void—a void some people are so desperate to fill, they'll pay by the hour for mock family time.

The idea may sound outrageous, but before you scoff at the Japanese, ask yourself whether America is all that far behind. Here, too, an obsession with making money is threatening to destroy family life. Companies think nothing of uprooting young families and sending them across the country, separating them from their elderly parents. And so, like the Japanese, we've become more willing to pay other people to spend time with our parents than do it ourselves.

Oh, it's not as blatant as Rent-a-Family. But we build Leisure Worlds where paid assistants help the elderly shop and cook, or take them to a concert. Retirement communities can be pleasant places to live, but they're also a symptom of the way Americans have glorified material prosperity over family relationships.

Honoring our parents is clearly one of those responsibilities; it's one of the Ten Commandments. Among God's people, there should never be a market for services like Rent-a-Family. ▨

Monday

TRENDIER THAN THOU

SCAN A MAGAZINE RACK THESE DAYS, and you'll see titles like "Children's Crusade for Somalia"; "Green Watch: . . . the fight to save our environment"; "Inside Germany: Confronting the Neo-Nazi Nightmare."

From the titles alone these could be news magazines. But they aren't. They're women's fashion magazines.

Perhaps you were still under the impression that fashion magazines were about, well, fashion. Forgive me for saying so, but that only shows that you're terribly outdated. As columnist Richard Grenier comments, "Today's Fashionable Woman must not only wear fashionable clothes, she must also wear fashionable ideas."

Fashion magazines have always reflected the styles and tastes of the upper classes. The articles express the political views of the upper classes, the trendsetters. They're a way for ordinary women to find out what the chic ideas are.

A generation ago the chic ideas were pretty staid. But not any more. *Harper's Bazaar* carried an article called "Gender Defender," a profile of a feisty prochoice lawyer. *Vogue* had an article called "A Few Nice Men," about sexual harassment in the military. *Glamour* featured a sympathetic article on gay men. *Mademoiselle* ran one on "Young Lesbians" that started out, "They're fresh, they're proud, and they're comfortable with their sexuality."

From the glossy pages a picture emerges of the modern Fashionable Woman: She's into abortion rights, gay rights, and she's sexually emancipated. These are the up-to-date attitudes women are learning along with the new shades of make-up and the correct accessories.

If sociologists are right when they say there's a culture war going on, then surely one of the battle sites is women's magazines. But Christian women—and men, too, for that matter—need to stand against the pressure. Our concern should be to cultivate the inner beauty of a good and generous spirit, which not only is biblical but also protects us from being swayed by every new wind of fashion.

Whether in clothes *or* in ideas.

FAMILY MATTERS

Tuesday

IN A NATION TROUBLED ABOUT RISING health-care costs, we ought to ask what's pushing costs up in the first place. The factor most frequently overlooked, says Bryce Christensen of the Rockford Institute, is the moral factor. Study after study shows that health costs go up when families break down.

Christensen cites studies spanning hundreds of years and several cultures. One study examines mortality rates in Europe over the past four hundred years; another examines records in twenty-six developed countries. The pattern is consistent across the board: People in stable families are healthier and have lower mortality rates than divorced people or single parents. These findings hold for men and women, for whites and nonwhites, for adults and children.

What's the explanation behind the statistics? Some studies show that living in a family is a deterrent to unhealthy behavior. People bound by love and responsibility to other family members are less likely to smoke, drink, use drugs, and so on.

Emotional factors count just as much. Families are healthier because people are happier in committed relationships. One medical researcher even published a book on the health problems that follow family breakdown. It's called *The Broken Heart: The Medical Consequences of Loneliness.*

Family stability is the great overlooked factor in keeping health care costs down. And even when there *is* an illness, families pay less because they care for their own. Statistics show that people in intact families spend less time in expensive hospitals and nursing homes.

What about single folks? Christensen cites studies showing that singles enjoy similar health benefits if they, too, avoid unhealthy behavior and are tied into a strong social support system—such as a church. The church ought to be providing love and care for those whose families have broken down.

We always knew religion was good for the soul. Now research shows it's good for the body as well. ⚜

THE INMATE, MY BROTHER

Wednesday

I WAS IN PRISON BECAUSE I HAD to be there, a price I had to pay to complete the shedding of my old life and to be free to live the new. God was chastening me for the future perhaps, but for what purpose *now*?

The first time I opened the Bible in prison, I read Hebrews, 2:9-11: "What we actually see is Jesus, after being made temporarily inferior to the angels (and so subject to pain and death), in order that he should, by God's grace, taste death for every man . . . . It was right and proper that in bringing many sons to glory, God . . . should make the leader of their salvation a perfect leader through the fact that he suffered. For the one who makes men holy and the men who are made holy share a common humanity. So that he is not ashamed to call them his brothers" (Phillips).

Something wonderful appeared to me from these words: God became one of us. He as Jesus could for a time be flesh, understand our sins and temptations, feel our fears as we feel them. He could speak to us in our own language, forgive us, and offer us the way of salvation. What an awesome thought—knowing God as our *Brother* through Christ!

Just as God became man to help His children, could it be that I had to become a prisoner the better to understand suffering and deprivations? If God chose to come to earth to know us better as brothers, maybe God's plan for me was to be in prison as a sinner, and to know men there as one of them. Could I ever understand the horrors of prison life by visiting a prison? *Of course not.* No one could understand this without being part of it, knowing the helplessness, living in the desolation. On a tiny scale, it was the lesson of Jesus coming to us. *Of course,* I thought to myself. *There is a purpose for my being here, perhaps a mission the Lord has called me to.*

For the rest of my life I would know and feel what it is like to be imprisoned—the steady, gradual corrosion of a man's soul. Just as God in the Person of Christ was not ashamed to call us His brothers, so I should not be ashamed to call each of these fellow inmates my brothers. 🔲

BLESS YOU, PRISON

Thursday

WHAT MIGHT SOUND LIKE TRIVIAL THINGS can become desperate matters to prisoners. In a prison journal, I wrote of having all my possessions, including my wallet, taken from me and sent home: "I protested that I might be called back to Washington to testify and I would need identification. The officer explained that if I were taken back I would be in custody, with a set of government orders, a government-provided ticket, and I would need no identification.

"'What if someone released me,' I asked, or if there were some emergency, or if somehow I would be pardoned? 'No,' the officer insisted. 'Regulations are regulations—no personal identification.'

"One is overcome by the sudden desperate feeling that he is no one," I wrote in my journal. "I was to become no more than an anonymous number."

The depersonalization continued with the experience of standing naked while the officer decided whether I needed to be scrubbed with a disinfectant soap, standard practice for any inmate coming from a jail. He then handed me a well-worn pair of underpants with five numbers stenciled on them; I was the sixth person putting them on.

It was the low point of my life. I had only a whisper of hope that something might come of it. I wrote to my Christian friends in Washington, "I want you brothers to read this back to me when I am out of here and have forgotten what the initial shock was like—and in the event I ever forget I have an obligation to try to improve the fate and circumstances of many in this plight."

As I relive those days, I come to a renewed appreciation of God's total sovereignty. And with Alexander Solzhenitsyn I can say, "Bless you, prison, for having been in my life." For now I see clearly what I dared not dream then. Just when I thought that everything I had worked for was destroyed, God began His greatest work. He used those days in my life to deepen my spiritual commitment. Then out of my helplessness in prison has come His help to thousands of prisoners around the world.

Amazing how God chooses to work! 🕮

RADICAL POWER

Friday

A MAGAZINE ARTICLE ABOUT MY PRISON ministry concluded that "prison radicalized the life of Chuck Colson." But it is simply not so. I could have left prison and forgotten it; I wanted to, in fact. But while every human instinct said, "Put it out of your mind forever," the Bible kept revealing to me God's compassion for the hurting and suffering and oppressed; His insistent Word demanded that I care as He does.

What "radicalized" me was not prison but taking to heart the truths revealed in Scripture. For it was the Bible that confronted me with a new awareness of my sin and need for repentance; it was the Bible that caused me to hunger for righteousness and seek holiness; it was the Bible that called me into fellowship with the suffering.

It is the Bible that continues to challenge my life today. It is irresistibly convicting. It is the power of God's Word, and it is, by itself, life changing. 🕮

FORGOTTEN HEROES

Weekend

I ONCE TOOK A GROUP OF SUPPORTERS to a Maryland prison, where a Prison Fellowship seminar was in progress. We were welcomed by the bright lights of TV cameras. Reporters scribbled notes while officials greeted us warmly; the governor had even issued a proclamation for the occasion.

By the time we got to the prison chapel, it was exploding with excitement. Wintley Phipps, a well-known gospel singer, was with us. When Wintley let loose in that cinder-block chapel, the walls shook. Then Herman Heade, converted in a solitary-confinement cell during a seven-year prison term, gave his dramatic and convicting testimony. The excitement continued as I then challenged the men to accept Christ. When the time came to leave, inmates pressed around, hugging us and weeping.

The next day at the closing meeting, a tall inmate stood to speak. "I really appreciated Chuck Colson's message," he told the group, "and Wintley Phipps's singing stirred me beyond words.

"Frankly, though, those things really didn't impress me so much as what happened after all the celebrities and TV cameras left: The ladies among the volunteers went into the dining hall and sat at the table to have a meal with us. That's what really got to me," he concluded, his voice choked.

What was the witness of Christ at the Maryland prison? Certainly Wintley's singing and Herman's testimony and my sermon were appreciated. But the most powerful message came from the volunteers—ordinary people whose names never appear in the headlines—who went into the dingy dining hall to share a prison meal with the inmates.

It does not take celebrities or institutions to make a difference. The way God builds His kingdom is through those who follow His example of sacrifice—as those unknown volunteers prove so beautifully.

WORKING CHIC

Monday   LABOR DAY

FASHION MAGAZINES ARE AGHAST OVER the latest fashion craze: work clothes. Carharrt hunting jackets are the rage on the streets of London and New York. Blundstone boots, until recently worn only by sheep farmers and miners, are now counted as hip footwear.

The workwear craze actually has a long tradition in America. And it's not a bad image to take with us from Labor Day—a tribute to the fundamental dignity of the worker.

Christians have a special reason to celebrate Labor Day. We worship a God who labored to make the world—who created human beings in His image to be workers. When God made Adam and Eve, He gave them work to do: cultivating and caring for the earth. In the ancient world, the Greeks and Romans looked upon manual work as a curse, something for lower classes and slaves. But Christians viewed work as a high calling—a calling to be co-workers with God in unfolding the rich potential of His creation.

This high view of work can be traced throughout the history of the church. In the Middle Ages, the guild movement grew out of the church. They set standards for good workmanship and encouraged members to take satisfaction in their labor.

During the Reformation, Martin Luther preached that all work can be done to the glory of God. Whether ministering the gospel or scrubbing floors, any honest work is pleasing to the Lord.

Christians were also active on behalf of workers in the early days of the industrial revolution, when the factories were "dark satanic mills," to borrow a phrase from William Blake. John Wesley preached the gospel not to the upper classes but to the laboring classes—to men whose faces were black with coal dust, women whose dresses were patched and faded.

Two of Wesley's disciples, William Wilberforce and Lord Shaftesbury, were inspired to work for legislation that would clean up abuses in the work place. The British parliament passed child labor laws, safety laws, and minimum wage laws.

So go ahead, let your kids wear hunting jackets and Blundstone boots, as long as workwear is the fashion. But this Labor Day, remember that labor derives its true dignity as a reflection of the Creator. 🕌

CRIME AND SHALOM

Tuesday

H OW DOES THE BIBLE DEFINE AND deal with crime? The place to begin is with the concept of *shalom*, commonly translated as "peace." While we generally think of peace as public order and security, the Hebrews meant something more. *Shalom* meant the existence of right relationships, harmony, wholeness, completeness. It characterized the ideal relationship between individuals, the community, and God. As a result of these right relationships, the community knew security, prosperity, and blessings from God.

Crime destroys *shalom*. Offenders break the harmony between themselves and their victims, their community, and God. The biblical response to crime aimed to restore right relationships—*shalom*—between the affected parties.

Restitution—paying back the victim—was essential to this process. The Hebrew language reflected the linkage between restitution and peace: the word for restitution was *shillum*, from the same root as *shalom*.

Did this mean there was to be no punishment? Not at all. Restitution was understood to be retributive. And *shillem*, another word related to *shalom*, meant "recompense" or "retribution." The goal of biblical justice, then, was restored relationships through restitution and vindication.

How does American criminal justice measure up to this standard? Our nation's system focuses completely on maintaining public order and punishing offenders. It views crime only as an offense against government, not an injury to the victim or community. It does not require that victims be repaid, or that offenders make things right, or that the community take responsibility to see justice done. No wonder crime has become a crisis in America today. ※

PRISONERS OR PENITENTS?

Wednesday

A MERICAN PENAL PHILOSOPHY IS NOT based on biblical principles. It is founded on a humanistic view that crime is an illness to be cured.

The pattern was established two centuries ago, when well-meaning Quakers converted Philadelphia's Walnut Street Jail into a facility where offenders were confined to repent and be rehabilitated. Though a number of those early "penitents" simply went mad, the idea flourished. Soothed by the comforting illusion that these miscreants were being "treated," the public called such places *penitent*iaries, *reformat*ories, and *correct*ional institutions.

This illusion was reinforced in the twentieth century when liberal sociologists argued that crime was not the individual's fault but society's. Societal failures like poverty, racism, and unemployment were to blame.

If the criminal was but a victim of the system, prisons were places for him to be vocationally trained, "socialized," and educated. Society, which had caused the disease of crime, would now cure it—and ever-increasing thousands were packed into institutions as wards of the state.

Prisons proved themselves not places of rehabilitation, however, but breeding grounds for further crime.

It's a travesty that in this so-called Christian nation we consistently ignore the most basic of Christ's teaching: sin comes from within the individual (Mark 7:20). Crime is the result of morally responsible people making wrong moral decisions, for which they must be held accountable.

As C. S. Lewis said, "To be punished, however severely, because we have deserved it, because we 'ought to have known better,' is to be treated as a human person made in God's image." In the biblical sense, punishment is very often redemptive—to the offender, the victim, and society at large. ※

GETTING TOUGH ON CRIME

Thursday

W HAT DOES IT TAKE TO BE TOUGH on crime? The answer on
   Capitol Hill is simple: Put more cops on the beat to catch
more criminals and build more prisons to house them all. But
that assumes putting people behind bars is itself a tough anti-
crime measure.

A serious misconception.

Putting people in prison *does* get them off the streets—but
only temporarily. In a little while, they are back again, meaner
than ever.

No one can pretend any longer that our criminal justice system strikes a tough blow at crime. Given today's revolving-door
prisons, it can actually be much tougher to impose alternative
forms of punishment: house arrest, electronic surveillance, and
community-based work programs.

Rick Templeton of Justice Fellowship has firsthand experience with both forms of punishment. After being convicted he
was first locked up in solitary confinement in a maximum-
security federal prison. Later he was transferred to a
minimum-security prison where he was much less restricted and
even went out to work during the day.

Ask Rick which regimen was "tougher," and he'll answer
without a moment's hesitation: the work program. "Being required
to get up every day, report in regularly, go to work, support my
family—that was much more demanding than watching TV all
day," Rick says.

The biblical teaching on justice does not call for simply ware-
housing criminals. It calls for restoring the peace—the *shalom*—of
the community. In ancient Israel, when a thief was caught stealing,
he didn't sit passively in jail. Instead he had to work to pay back
what he had stolen—with interest. When someone committed ag-
gravated assault, he didn't vegetate in a prison cell. Instead, he
had to work to pay restitution to the victim—and repay his lost wages.

Work and community programs are socially redemptive,
mending the tear in the social fabric caused by crime. Prison

Fellowship operates programs that put prisoners to work rehabilitating inner-city homes and community centers. I've talked with countless participants who say they are grateful for the chance to pay society back—to make up for evil deeds with good deeds.

Alternative punishment is the real way to get tough on crime—because it requires criminals to change from the inside out. ▩

ELECTRONIC JEWELRY

Friday

SIXTEEN-YEAR-OLD RONNIE WAS IN juvenile court for breaking and entering. But the judge decided to take a chance on the boy. Instead of sending him to an institution, he sentenced Ronnie to house arrest, enforced by an electric monitoring system.

As Ronnie left the courtroom with his mother, he was fitted with an ankle bracelet—a tamper-resistant device that transmitted a radio signal every few seconds to a receiver in his home. The home receiver was linked to a central computer at a corrections department, which kept tabs on whether Ronnie was sticking to his curfew rules.

When he first laid eyes on the ankle bracelet, Ronnie told the *Christian Science Monitor*, "my whole leg was shaking." But today he's grateful the judge took a chance on alternative sentencing. The electronic monitor turned out to give Ronnie just the supervision he needed to change his ways. For example, when it was time for him to go home early, he could tell his friends without losing face—just by pointing to his ankle. They understood immediately. Ronnie calls the ankle bracelet his "guardian angel."

Overcrowded prisons and high rates of repeat offenders are forcing a search for alternative sentencing for nonviolent offenders: community service, house arrest, work-release programs, boot camps.

Electronic monitoring, one study found, is especially effective with offenders who have lifestyle problems—from alcohol and drug abuse to gang activity. "I stopped drinking," said one offender. "Haven't missed a day of work in six months," said another. What's more, an offender under house arrest can work during the day, earning the money to cover the cost of his own supervision. In fact, electronic monitoring demands so much responsibility that some convicted criminals beg judges to send them to prison instead!

If we want to "get tough on crime," the answer may not always be locking more people up. For nonviolent offenders, alternative sentencing often imposes tougher punishment and greater accountability than prison.

And that should be our real goal: not just to get criminals off the streets but to hold them responsible for their actions. ▨

A SECOND CHANCE

Weekend

O N INTERSTATE 25, AS HER VEHICLE crested a hill, Sherry Kuehl saw another car barreling at her from the wrong side of the four-lane highway. As a result of the collision, Sherry spent the next six months first in traction, then on crutches.

The man driving the other car was named Steven. The combination of prescription drugs and the .275 alcohol level in his blood was nearly lethal. Steven was taken into custody at the hospital, charged with four counts of vehicular assault—a possible sixteen years in prison. Unable to pay bail after pleading guilty, Steven sat in jail three months awaiting sentencing.

As soon as she was released from the hospital, Sherry visited Steven. Seeing him frightened and embarrassed in his jail coveralls, she was filled with compassion. Sherry did not want to see this young man imprisoned. But what could she do?

In Colorado, crime victims receive a victim impact statement, asking them to recommend punishment for the offender. Sherry suggested four years of probation, medical treatment, revocation of Steven's driving license, and most important, 1,296 hours of community service in a hospital—as many hours as Sherry had spent as a patient.

At the sentencing hearing the judge gave Steven the sentence Sherry recommended. Sherry's compassion for Steven was a witness to the judge of God's power. "I am overwhelmed by the forgiveness these people have shown," he said.

Sherry had never heard of restorative justice. But she saw only two options: prison—where Steven would be untreated and allowed to grow bitter—or forgiveness and a chance to change. Sherry's compassion, and a sympathetic judge, gave Steven another chance.

Meanwhile, Steven has experienced God's healing. He went to work in a geriatric center, where the gratitude of the people he served gave him new confidence. Throughout his sentence, he wrote to Sherry often: "Thank you for giving me a second chance." ▨

THE GREAT CIVILIZER

Monday

TEN COUPLES SIT IN A CIRCLE ENGAGED in a lively biblical discussion about marriage. Why can't he communicate? Why does she coddle the kids? At the end, all ten couples rededicate themselves to putting Christ at the center of their homes.

This sounds like a Marriage Encounter weekend in a middle-class suburban church. But it's not. It's a Prison Fellowship Marriage Seminar, and it's being held behind bars.

The men are convicted criminals. Their wives are struggling to survive alone on the outside. And this Marriage Seminar could be the most important factor in restoring these families from the scourge of crime.

Sociologist George Gilder says marriage is the great civilizer of men. Statistics show that married men work harder than single men, are healthier, more stable, and less prone to crime, drug use, and other social pathologies.

Church programs emphasizing marriage and family have proven highly effective in reducing crime. Studies by the National Bureau of Economic Research show that church attendance is the single most accurate indicator of whether urban black men will become criminals.

Churches can recreate a place of dignity and responsibility for men within the family. And men who are respected as husbands and fathers develop the confidence they need to become leaders in their communities. As an article in *Policy Review* magazine comments, "More than law, police, jail, or fear of death, having a family induces men to become good citizens."

Prison Fellowship Marriage Seminars are one way the church is helping to rebuild families and rebuild inner-city communities. But as divorce cuts into the suburbs, middle-class churches need the same message.

The Bible's answer to social decay is men and women coming together in obedience to God to build strong families. There is no more potent prescription for moral and social renewal.

HAWKS IN
THE DRUG WAR

I JUST CAN'T DO IT ANY MORE, THE federal judge said. *I cannot rule in cases where I'm compelled to impose sentences I feel are unjust.*

Judge Jack Weinstein was referring to laws that set mandatory minimum sentences. Laws passed by Congress decree that crime x shall receive punishment y—no matter what the individual circumstances may be. And when that means sentencing low-level, nonviolent, first-time offenders to several years in prison, some judges are rebelling.

A lot of the people taken prisoner in the war are mere foot soldiers: a man who drove a friend to a drug deal; a wife who knew her husband was growing marijuana and failed to call police; a teenage girl who directed someone to her boyfriend's house to close a drug deal. To free up prison cells for these people, officials are granting early release to murderers and rapists . . . who are then free to prowl the streets again.

This is costly and dangerous. Yes, minor players in drug deals have broken the law and deserve to be punished. But years behind bars is a punishment sharply disproportionate to their crime. They lose marketable skills, their families fall apart, and they often become hardened to a life of crime.

The best response to low-level, nonviolent drug offenses is community-based sentencing: house arrest; electronic monitoring; and, for addicts, mandatory drug treatment. Community sentencing keeps minor offenders closely tied to the very things that motivate people to straighten out: their families, their friends, their jobs.

A Christian view of justice takes into account a person's entire motivation and circumstances. Before the days of mandatory sentencing, that Christian principle was the working ideal in our courtrooms. Judges took into account an offender's personal history, his likelihood of repeating the crime, his willingness to undergo treatment. But today judges are forced to impose a one-size-fits-all sentence—which sometimes doesn't fit well at all.

As a result, the war on drugs is producing too many needless casualties. ▓

THE TOUGHEST DAY IN PRISON

Wednesday

CRAIG HAS SPENT FOURTEEN YEARS of a life sentence behind bars for murder. But if you ask him what was the hardest thing he's faced so far, it wasn't a prison riot or an attack by a fellow inmate. What really hurt, Craig says, was sitting down face to face with the family of the man he murdered—and hearing firsthand how his act of rage shattered their lives.

Craig met the family through a program designed to reconcile criminals and their victims. Programs like these are catching on across the United States, and often they do more than years in prison to change a criminal's outlook.

In the American criminal justice system, a crime is prosecuted as an offense against the state, not against the victim. In this impersonal system, the offender rarely confronts the personal pain and trauma he has inflicted.

Most criminals never even talk with the person they have wronged. At best, they might catch a glimpse of each other across a crowded court room. That's where Victim-Offender Reconciliation programs can make all the difference. As Craig puts it, meeting with the victim's family "brought me to grips with my own culpability and personal feelings of guilt." And an awakened sense of personal responsibility is much tougher to deal with than any punishment meted out in a prison yard.

Reconciliation programs can benefit everyone involved in a crime. For victims, it gives a chance to express their deep pain and anger over the trauma they have suffered. For offenders, it gives a chance to face the consequences of their actions—and to set things right again as much as possible. Often the meetings end with the criminal apologizing and offering to pay restitution.

Finally, reconciliation is good criminal justice policy. A scandal of our current system is the high number of criminals who return to prison—again and again. Clearly, we need to look for programs that go beyond simply locking criminals up—programs that change them from the inside. Reconciliation programs can be catalysts for such a life-changing experience.

Biblical teachings on justice aim not only at punishment for crime but also at restoration of the community. Crime tears a jagged hole in the fabric of our social life, but reconciliation and forgiveness mend that hole.

They can help restore the community peace that the Bible calls *shalom*. 🏶

BUSINESS
BEHIND BARS

Thursday

PICTURE IN YOUR MIND HUGE ROLLS of fabric, blocked out with patterns. Imagine workers at sewing stations, stitching the fabric into stylish coats and slacks. Now imagine all this happening not in a factory but in a prison—because that's where it *is* happening. In addition to the garment section, the prison boasts a print shop and a wood-working shop where inmates make furniture.

Employment is voluntary—no slave labor here. And inmates receive wages competitive with the outside economy, which they can use to support their families and to pay restitution to the victims of their crimes. When their sentences are up, the marketable skills inmates have gained become a passport to normal life.

Prison industries have a long and respectable history in the United States. When our prison system was inaugurated two centuries ago, inmates worked to pay the cost of their upkeep. But at the turn of the century that tradition began to decline. Business and labor leaders complained that prison workers posed "unfair competition." By 1990 only 10 percent of inmates were gainfully employed.

But this change has been a regressive one for our prisons. Enforced idleness eats away at the human spirit. In prison after prison, I have witnessed the apathy and despair that builds up in people who lie on their bunks and stare at the ceiling all day. No wonder our prisons are simmering cauldrons of bitterness and rage.

It doesn't have to be that way. Some prisons are putting inmates to work and restoring their sense of dignity. Some private industries hire prisoners too, like Best Western Motels, which employs a couple hundred inmates as telephone reservationists. Control Data, a major electronics firm, has trained one-hundred fifty Minnesota prisoners to assemble computers.

Currently, two-thirds of offenders are rearrested within a few years of their release. But a recent study by the Federal Bureau of Prisons found that inmates who had participated in prison work programs were better able to hold jobs and less likely to commit more crimes.

Why not talk with your state representative about the need for prison industries? With a little lobbying by Christians, we might just get other industries to join Best Western in putting their business behind bars.

MADE
FOR WORK

Friday

SOMETIMES WHEN I DESCRIBE MY VISITS to Third-World prisons, people shrink back in horror, visions from movies like *Midnight Express* stalking their minds. But during my trip to the Far East I discovered that "Made in the U. S. A." doesn't always assure the best quality—particularly when it applies to prisons.

In the Philippines I visited Muntinlupa Prison. Two years ago it housed twelve thousand inmates and was run by prison gangs. Then General Goyena, a member of the Prison Fellowship Philippines board of directors, was appointed head of the prison system. He cracked down on the gangs, reduced the prison population by putting nonviolent offenders in nonprison punishments, and introduced new work programs.

As I walked through housing units, the prisoners were busily making crafts such as picture frames, wooden boxes, and handsome sculptures. These are sold through a prison industry arrangement; the inmates are able to send money to their families, who would otherwise fall by the wayside.

And in this maximum-security unit, the men were carving with razor-sharp knives. I asked the warden if this created a security risk. "Oh, no," he said. "They realize that if there were any trouble, their knives would be taken away. And their knives are their livelihood."

Their work gave the inmates a sense of pride and dignity. They enthusiastically showed me the fine details of their carving. The act of productivity was giving them something that U. S. prisons often rob from inmates.

In the U. S., relatively few prisoners are gainfully employed. The rest are often idle and apathetic. In Muntinlupa the inmates were alert, smiling, productive. Their attitudes showed that purposeful work, by its very nature, ennobles. As Carl Henry has said, "Locking up a person to idleness would be a contradiction of his essential dignity because man, by creation, was a creature made for work rather than for idleness." ※

CRIME'S SILENT VICTIMS

Weekend

ONE MORNING GREG BROWNING WAS washing his car when a young man suddenly appeared beside him, wrestled him to the ground, broke his arm, and drove off with his car. Fortunately, the police quickly chased the thief down. Now justice would be done.

Or would it?

Greg and his wife, Joan, soon discovered that many courts have no place for victims of crime. They were not informed of hearing dates; they were not told when Greg's attacker was released. To this day, they don't even know if the man was ever convicted.

When Greg and Joan complained to the district attorney, they were told, "This is not your case. . . . This was an offense against the state." No matter that it was Greg who was assaulted, who paid the doctor bills, whose sense of security was shattered. Criminal cases are not considered crimes against the victims but against the state.

As a citizen, you may believe that the criminal justice system exists for your sake: to give you justice, help reclaim your losses. But if you're ever a victim of crime, you will be sadly disappointed. Prosecutors don't represent victims, they represent the state.

In fact, in a court of law the victim's only status is to be a witness for the prosecution. Most likely you will be given a chance to tell your story only if the prosecutor feels it will help the case. Otherwise, there is no official channel for you to express your pain and loss.

The good news is that victims' rights organizations in several states are working to change that. Thirteen states have passed constitutional amendments that guarantee victims the right to be present at the trial and sentencing of their attackers. Some also give victims the right to receive restitution for their losses.

These are measures we should press for at every level of the criminal justice system. We cannot claim to be "fighting crime" unless we are fighting the *effects* of crime in the lives of real people. ▩

THE CELEBRITY ILLUSION

Monday

GOD HAS ALWAYS USED THE HUMBLE both to confound the wisdom of this world and to accomplish His purposes. A friend of mine from Madagascar provides an example. Pascal, a university professor, was thrown into prison after a Marxist coup. There he became a Christian.

After his release he started a small import/export company. But he was drawn back to his prison to preach the gospel. During one visit in early 1986, he stopped in shock as he passed the infirmary: there were more than fifty corpses piled on the veranda, naked except for ID tags between their toes.

Pascal went to the nurse, asking if there had been an epidemic. Of sorts, he was told. Prisoners were dying by the dozens—of malnutrition.

Pascal left the prison in tears. His church was too poor to help feed the starving inmates, and there were no big relief agencies around. So he began to do what he could, cooking meals in his own small kitchen. Today Pascal and his wife continue to cook—and without the benefit of a government agency or Christian organization they are making the difference between life and death for seven hundred prisoners. ▨

WHERE I BELONG

Tuesday

AT A LUNCHEON FOR PRISON FELLOWSHIP supporters, one of the instructors for our in-prison seminars, Larry Yarrington, rose to speak. Larry is the picture of confidence—a Ph.D. and business executive. But Larry didn't talk about the glories of our seminars. Instead, he spoke deliberately: "I'd like to share what goes on inside a prisoner. I'd like to give you a sense of that—because I was once a prisoner."

He went on to talk about his feelings of rejection, rooted in childhood by a domineering father. He had compensated by excelling in school, in business. But then he had ended up going to prison. He described his recurring feelings of inadequacy: "It's as if I'm a stranger at a party, dressed in shabby clothes," he said. "Meanwhile all the other guests know one another and are dressed in tuxedos."

Wait a minute, I thought. Larry was not following the accepted public relations script. *Tell us about the seminars. Our supporters don't need to hear all this.*

My unease grew to near-panic as Larry explained that he still felt a deep insecurity, even after his conversion. *What is he doing? Christians are supposed to conquer their weakness—and this man's a leader. . . .*

Then came the unexpected. As Larry explained how he felt like one of the inmates every time he taught a seminar, I forgot about the others in the room. Overwhelmed by long-dormant memories, I was back in prison: Dormitory G at the Maxwell Federal Prison. I could smell it; I felt the horrible loss of freedom and identity. I could look around and see the men lying on their bunks, alone and helpless. I had *known* the deep sense of loneliness and worthlessness that incarceration breeds.

I also remembered that after my release, when I had returned to speak in prisons, I had felt that instant identification with the inmates.

I still felt a passion for prisoners to come to Christ, but caught up in leadership responsibilities, I had lost that vivid sense of being *one of them*. But that day Larry Yarrington brought me back to prison.

And that's where I belong. ▩

A HOLY
SUBVERSION

Wednesday

ON OCCASION, GOD PROVIDES AN UNUSUAL glimpse of His kingdom. I witnessed one in an unlikely place—a prison in Brazil like none I've ever seen. Twenty years ago, in the city of

San Jose dos Campos, a prison was turned over to two Christian laymen. They called it Humaita, and their plan was to run it on Christian principles.

The prison has only two full-time staff; the rest of the work is done by inmates. Every prisoner is assigned another inmate to whom he is accountable. He is assigned a volunteer family from the outside that works with him during his term and after his release. And every prisoner joins a chapel program or else takes a course in character development.

When I visited Humaita, I saw clean living areas. I saw people working industriously. The walls were decorated with biblical sayings from Psalms and Proverbs.

Humaita has an astonishing record. Its recidivism rate is 4 percent compared to 75 percent in the rest of Brazil and the United States. How is that possible?

I saw the answer when my inmate guide escorted me to the notorious punishment cell once used for torture. Today, he told me, that block houses only a single inmate. As we reached the end of the long concrete corridor and he put the key into the lock, he paused and asked, "Are you sure you want to go in?"

"Of course," I replied impatiently. "I've been in isolation cells all over the world." Slowly he swung open the massive door, and I saw the prisoner in that punishment cell: a crucifix, beautifully carved by the Humaita inmates—the Prisoner Jesus, hanging on the cross.

"He's doing time for all the rest of us," my guide said softly.

In that cross carved by loving hands is a holy subversion. It heralds change more radical than mankind's most fevered dreams. Its followers expand the boundaries of a Kingdom that can never fail. A shining Kingdom that reaches into the darkest corners of every community, into the darkest corners of every mind. A Kingdom of deathless hope, of restless virtue, of endless peace. ✺

KEEPING THE GARDEN

Thursday

A CCORDING TO THE GENESIS ACCOUNT, GOD ordered Adam to "cultivate and keep" the garden. "To cultivate" means increasing creation's bounty, while "keep," means literally "to guard." Adam was to guard the garden against anything that might jeopardize its reflection of God's goodness.

The Fall did not negate this mandate. It just made it harder to obey. The curse extended into every arena of life. But so did Christ's redemption.

Eventually, because of Christ's completed work on the cross, all creation will be restored to its former glory. Until His return, however, Christians must persevere in their role of "cultivating and keeping" the garden of a fallen world.

Even before Christ came, the men and women of the Old Testament understood this. The Psalms are filled with King David's exultation over God's rule and His mandate to us. David's son Solomon understood his father's words: His Proverbs touch on everything from child raising to neighborly relations to work to economic justice to international relations.

Throughout His public ministry, Jesus evoked the Kingdom mind-set that consciously takes "every thought captive to the obedience of Christ" (2 Cor. 10:5, NASB). Likening the kingdom of heaven to leaven, Jesus described God's rule as having a transforming effect on everything it touches. And in the parable of the talents He taught that God expects a "return on investment" from His faithful stewards, who are to bring glory to Him as they cultivate and keep that which He has entrusted to them.

The apostles took pains to teach the church not to be conformed to this world but to be transformed by the renewing of the mind, to guard against being taken captive by the empty deceptions and philosophies of the world or cleverly devised tales, and to seek truth according to Christ.

From creation onward, God's rule extends to everything. From our bank accounts to our business dealings to our educational curriculum to social justice issues to environmental concerns to our political choices—everything must reflect the fact that God's righteous rule extends to all of life.

Abraham Kuyper, Dutch pastor and scholar, was one of the great modern exponents of a Christian world-view. "If everything that is, exists for the sake of God, then the whole creation must give glory to God," he wrote. The Scriptures disclose "not only justification by faith but the very foundation of life and the ordinances that regulate human existence."

THE CHRISTIAN MIND

Friday

I F THERE ARE SO MANY CHRISTIANS IN the U. S., why aren't we affecting our world? I believe it's because many of us treat our faith like an item on our "Things to Do Today" list. We file religion in our schedules as just one of the many concerns competing for our attention.

Not that we aren't serous about it. We go to church and attend Bible studies. But we're just as serious about our jobs and physical fitness.

In *The Christian Mind*, Harry Blamires says the typical believer prays sincerely about his work but never talks candidly with his non-Christian colleagues about his faith. He is only comfortable evaluating his spiritual life in a "spiritual" context. This results in spiritual schizophrenia as the Christian bounces back and forth between the stock market and sanctification.

Such categorizing would be plausible if Christianity were nothing more than a moral code, an AA pledge, or a self-help course. But Christianity claims to be the central fact of human history: the God who created man invaded the world in the person of Jesus Christ, died, was resurrected, ascended, and lives today, sovereign over all.

If this claim is valid—if Christianity is true—then it cannot be simply a file drawer in our crowded lives. It must be the central truth from which all our behavior, relationships, and philosophy flow. We must set all earthly issues within the context of the eternal. 🕮

OUT OF THE SECULAR SAND

Weekend

W E SHOULD BE CONTENDING FOR TRUTH in every area of life. Not for power or because we are taken with some trendy cause, but humbly to bring glory to God.

For this reason, Christians should be the most ardent ecologists. Not because whales are our brothers, but because animals are part of God's kingdom over which we are to exercise dominion. Francis of Assisi should be our role model, not Ted Turner.

We should care for human life. Not because of a desire to interfere in people's private lives, but because every human being is created in the image of God.

We should be passionate defenders of human liberty and civil rights. The very term our founding fathers used, "*unalienable rights*," reflects a Christian view of human liberty that is nonnegotiable. Governments can neither confer nor take away human rights because they are given by God. This conviction put Christians in the forefront of the campaign for the abolition of slavery, the civil rights movement, and the crusade for human rights in oppressed nations.

We should zealously seek reforms in the prisons and in criminal justice laws. Not because it's part of some party platform or vague humanistic idealism, but because our view of institutions must always be measured by God's clear standard of justice.

Christians should celebrate the arts and all creative expressions that bring glory to God, the Great Artist.

Christians must champion ethics. Not because it is good business—the dominant pragmatic view—but because moral norms come from God.

Since no area of life is beyond the glorious rule of God, the Christian world view embraces every arena of experience and opportunity. We need to get our heads out of the secular sand and stop being intimidated by the post-Christian culture that surrounds us. Only then will truth be heard above the chaos and discordant din of modern life. 🔲

SALTY
SUBVERSIVES

Monday

"Y OU ARE THE SALT OF THE EARTH," Jesus said to His disciples. In the ancient world salt was a vital staple, both as a preservative and as a seasoning.

The first function was particularly critical, since it was the only preservative available.

Farmers would slaughter animals, carve the meat, and then rub raw mineral salt into it until the flesh was penetrated and the salt was dissolved. This prevented the meat from decaying.

When it came to seasoning with salt, the principle of penetration also applied. If it was to flavor the food, salt had to penetrate and be absorbed.

The church as salt is not only a biblical mandate, it is also particularly applicable in our modern world. For we are dealing with a culture that has lost its fundamental Christian presuppositions, and the guardians of that culture—the gatekeepers of television, radio, newspaper, and other public forums—are for the most part unsympathetic to a Christian perspective.

Frontal assaults only mobilize the opposition. Start an organized campaign against pornography, for example, and before long the ACLU and the pornographers will marshal a better-funded defense.

We are more effective when we penetrate behind the lines, influencing the culture from within.

How does an army fight behind enemy lines? It doesn't move its forces *en masse;* it can't. Rather, it infiltrates small units to disrupt the enemy's communication and attack strategic targets.

That's exactly what Christians must do in a post-Christian culture. 🔲

A TRANSFORMED MIND

Tuesday

IT IS IN THE HEART THAT MOST conversions begin. The baby believer's blissful world is filled with exciting new experiences: love of a kind not known before, forgiveness, inner peace. Emotions of the heart.

So it is understandable that sins of the heart, such as temper, hatred, jealousy, and pride, are the first to be affected in one's conversion. But that is only the beginning, only one part of the transforming process God intends for our lives. If we are to be new creations, much more is demanded: heart, body, spirit, *and* mind.

The *mind* is the key. Experiences and emotions can carry a person only so far and often, in fact, can be undependable supports.

Romans 12:2 says, "Do not be conformed to this world, but be transformed by the renewal of your mind, that you may prove what is the will of God, that which is good and acceptable and perfect" (RSV). The Greek word for "transform" means more than a natural change. The only other time the word is used in the New Testament is to describe the Transfiguration of Jesus. "His face shone like the sun, and His garments became as white as light" (Matt. 17:2, NASB). Man was given a magnificent glimpse of the age to come: the unspeakable joy literally of looking into heaven.

This leap from the sin of this world to the holiness of the next is breathtaking even to contemplate.

Yet that is the precise parallel for this passage of Romans: The Christian *must* make a break with the past so radical that his mind is filled with the thoughts of Christ Himself.

KING OVER ALL

Wednesday

CHRISTIANITY IS MORE THAN SIMPLY A relationship between man and God. The kingdom of God embraces every aspect of life: ethical, spiritual, and temporal.

In announcing an all-encompassing Kingdom, Jesus was not using a clever metaphor; He was expressing the literal theme of Jewish history—that God was King and the people were His subjects. This tradition dated back to the days of Abraham and the patriarchs, when God made His original covenant with the Jews to be His "holy nation."

David, the first great king of the Jews, consolidated a visible kingdom for the people of God. But it was to be only a reflection of the ultimate rule of God, their true King. Later, when the Jews were conquered and sent into exile, the prophets promised the coming of Messiah and the eventual establishment of the kingdom of God. Christ was the fulfillment of that prophecy; He was the final king in David's royal line.

But Jesus was not just a king for Israel; He was King for all people.

This totality of God's authority is a major reason many non-Christians resent Christianity, seeing it as an excuse for religious zealots to try to cram absolute orders from their God down others' throats. But when Christ commanded His followers to "seek first the kingdom of God," He was exhorting them to be ruled by God, to gratefully acknowledge His power and authority over them. That means that the Christian's goal is not to strive to rule, but *to be ruled*—by God. ▧

EVERYTHING UNDER THE SON

Thursday

AN ASSOCIATE OF MINE WAS HAVING LUNCH with a staffer from another Christian ministry when their conversation touched on the subject of recycling programs. My associate commented that Christian ministries should be the first to recycle, but her companion burst out, "What is it with you? Not *everything* is about God, you know!"

Sometimes I get letters telling me that in my writing I should stick to devotional issues: After all, not everything is about God, is it?

Let me show where that line of reasoning leads.

I know a Christian business executive who attended a three-week course in business ethics at Harvard. The course gave him some practical pointers for ethical conduct, he said. "I can sum it up: When you're making a serious business decision, never do anything you think might end up in the newspapers."

I can only conclude that this man left his faith at the door when he walked into the classroom. Despite his apparent Christian maturity, he didn't realize that he had consumed a blitz course in secular utilitarian ethics: Ethics is about not getting caught.

This lack of discernment is not unusual. A Search Institute survey found that only one out of three Christians believe that Christianity should have any effect on how they live.

Christians need to realize that every decision they make reflects their core values. Choices about voting, budgeting, marriage, and movies are all philosophical issues. Christians who don't have a distinctively Christian philosophy will easily be suckered into living by the world's philosophies. Like my friend at Harvard.

This is why church pews may be full on Sundays, but secular values dominate our culture. America's halfhearted religion leaves plenty of room for an anti-Christian value system.

Friday

THE MIND
OF A SPY

ALDRICH AMES WAS RESPONSIBLE FOR the most serious security breach in the history of the CIA. For nine years he fed top military secrets to the KGB, the Soviet secret police. In an interview from his jail cell, Ames was asked how he survived the stresses of his double life. How could he sell sensitive state secrets after taking loyalty oaths? How could he turn over the names of U. S. agents to the Soviets, knowing he was sending them to certain death?

Ames's answer is highly revealing: "I tend to put some of these things in separate boxes" in my mind—to "compartment[alize] feelings and thoughts." That way, he added, "I avoided . . . thinking about" those things. In short, Ames survived by putting his life as a CIA operative in one box and his life as a Soviet agent in another box—fragmenting his life and mind into watertight compartments.

The troubling fact is that Ames is not unique. As Francis Schaeffer writes, fragmentation has become the mark of the modern mind. Even Christians often compartmentalize their minds: They put their religious beliefs in a little box shut off from the rest of their lives. We may be biblical in our spiritual beliefs, yet follow unbiblical views in our everyday attitudes and behavior.

For example, pollster George Gallup compiled candid admissions from people who call in sick when they are not, who puff their resumes, who cheat on income taxes. Astonishingly, Gallup reports "little difference in the ethical views and behavior of the churched and the unchurched." Similarly, religion reporter Terry Mattingly cited surveys showing that students at Christian colleges cheat on exams at the same rates as students at secular colleges.

What does all this tell us? That many Christians are guilty of compartmentalizing our lives into separate boxes so that our faith never informs our everyday attitudes and opinions. Many of us are as fragmented in our minds as any double agent.

This is not the pattern God wants for our lives. The Bible gives a comprehensive view of the world that is meant to integrate all of life. And like Aldrich Ames, spiritual double agents will ultimately be brought to justice. ※

OUR CULTURAL HERITAGE

Weekend

ONE OF THE MOST HIGHLY ACCLAIMED French films is about the life of the Dutch artist Vincent van Gogh. But you'll never learn what van Gogh was really like from this movie. It omits the central fact of van Gogh's life: his deep Christian faith.

As a young man, van Gogh wanted to become a pastor. But his hopes were dashed when he flunked out of seminary. Undaunted, he preached the gospel to destitute coal miners, living among them and sharing their poverty. His goal was thwarted once again when he began to show signs of mental instability and lost the financial support of his mission society.

It was only then that he turned to art. Van Gogh went on to produce hundreds of great paintings. He continued to battle with mental illness until at age thirty-seven, he committed suicide.

It's a tragic story. But almost equally tragic is the fact that the full story is usually suppressed. Books on art history carefully scrub out any reference to van Gogh's strong Christian faith.

And van Gogh isn't the only one. Many people know the name of the great painter Rembrandt; but they don't know that he, too, was a devout Christian. The poet Samuel Coleridge was elevated to an icon by the drug culture of the 1960s because he composed many of his poems under the influence of opium. But no one mentions that Coleridge found freedom from his opium addiction by turning to Jesus Christ.

In music, most people know that Bach and Handel were Christians. But what about Vivaldi? Vivaldi was a man of the cloth, nick-named "the Red Priest" for his bright red hair. Antonin Dvorak, with his lively Slavic melodies, was a sturdy Christian believer. Felix Mendelssohn had Jewish parents but was himself a devout Lutheran.

In science, the notebooks of Copernicus, Kepler, Newton, and Pascal overflow with praise to the Creator.

In virtually every field, Christians have made major artistic and scholarly contributions. Yet modern history books rarely mention the role faith has played in building our culture.

For non-Christians, that makes it easy to belittle Christians as bumbling know-nothings. For Christians, it means we've been cut off from a rich cultural and intellectual heritage that is rightfully ours.

THE MUSES
AND THE MIND

Monday

WHEN CHRISTIANS HEAR THE WORD *art,* we're liable to think first of the controversies surrounding the National Endowment for the Arts. What a shame. The first thing that *ought* to come to mind is our own rich artistic heritage.

Some of those riches were on display at the Museum of Fine Arts in Boston, in a show featuring the seventeenth-century Flemish painter Peter Paul Rubens. Figures painted by Rubens are rich in color and emotion: they look much heavier and fleshier than modern ideals of beauty.

That much you could learn from any art history book. But most books don't tell you *why* Rubens painted that way.

Rubens was a devout Catholic. He lived during the Counter-Reformation, a movement that sought to clean up the corruption of the medieval church. The Counter-Reformation sanctioned the use of images, icons, and other physical representations of spiritual reality. This gave rise to the idea that the physical world itself can be, in a sense, an "icon"—a means of reminding the faithful of spiritual truths.

Catholic artists like Rubens picked up this theme by reveling in the color and motion of the physical world, painting things as heavy and fleshy. It was a way of saying that Christians don't have to be otherworldly, that *this* world is where God Himself dwells—that it carries a weight of spiritual glory.

Many of you may have studied Rubens in art appreciation courses, but history books rarely mention an artist's religious or philosophical convictions. Yet every artistic style is ultimately shaped by a set of presuppositions, a world-view.

Impressionism, with its shimmering, shifting colors, was motivated by a philosophy of skepticism: a philosophy that humans cannot know anything about the ultimate nature of reality, that we know only our own sense data—the play of light hitting the human eye.

Or think of Cubism, where every object is painted from several perspectives—front, side, and back—all at the same time. This wasn't just an artistic technique, it expressed the philosophy that there is no universal truth, only a diversity of private perspectives.

Christians are right to oppose the use of taxpayer money for decadent art. But that should be just the first step. To bring new life to the art world we have to bring a new world-view to *artists*—grounded in the gospel of Jesus Christ. 🔳

BUT IS
IT ART?

Tuesday

MORLEY SAFER, A REPORTER FOR "60 MINUTES," offered a blistering critique of contemporary art, titled "Yes, But Is It Art?" He showed the work of Robert Gober, who creates sculptures shaped as urinals. He zoomed in on Robert Ryman, who paints entire canvases plain white. He showed works by Jeff Koons—like two basketballs floating in a fish tank.

Then Safer asked, Is *this* art?

How do we define art in the first place? The ancient philosophers defined art as that which appeals to our aesthetic sense—our sense of beauty. They believed that beauty is an objective standard. In fact, the ancients listed three absolutes by which we judge things: the true, the good, and the beautiful.

But today the art world rejects any standards. The philosophy of existentialism has taken over, teaching that without God there *are* no absolute standards. Many works of art—like Andy Warhol's famous paintings of soup cans—were intended to debunk the very idea of objective standards for art.

But without standards, how do we decide what qualifies as art? If the definition is not objective, then it is subjective—rooted in the artist himself. As the director of the Whitney Museum in New York stated, "A work of art is whatever an artist *says* is a work of art."

With this philosophy, no wonder artists have grown arrogant. When Morley Safer ran his "60 Minutes" segment, he was savaged for weeks. Artists who feel they have an unchallenged right to define art take offense when they are challenged.

Christian activists often try to curb the worst excesses of contemporary art by limiting government funding, and that's a good start. But we also need to address the underlying cause—the rejection of standards that makes it impossible to distinguish art from junk.

In Romans, Paul says we can avoid being conformed to this world only by being transformed in our minds—our thinking, our world-view. If we want to renew art and culture in America, we have to reach out to artists and challenge their world-view. ※

DRIVING OUT
BAD ART

Wednesday

THE ANCIENT PHILOSOPHERS LISTED three absolutes that should guide our lives: the true, the good, and the beautiful. Most Christians study diligently to know the first two: what Scripture teaches as true and what it teaches about how to be good. But we rarely think about *beauty*.

As author Ken Myers says, Christians largely ignore the realm of art and culture until it hits close to home: until *Penthouse* shows up at the corner drugstore or we discover our taxes are funding blasphemous paintings. Even then our response tends to be political and economic—protests, boycotts—making it easy for our enemies to paint us as anti-intellectual, anticultural reactionaries. Myers comments, "There is more talk about de-funding the National Endowment for the Arts than there is about funding creative work that could be a healthy cultural force."

The biblical justification for art is clear: We are called to live out the full image of God in every area of life. When God created the world, He cared enough to make it beautiful. His people ought to value creativity and beauty as well.

In *State of the Arts*, Gene Edward Veith describes a little-known biblical hero named Bezalel. In Exodus 31 we read that Bezalel directed the construction of the tabernacle, that God equipped him "to devise artistic designs to work in gold and silver and bronze." The Lord "filled him with the Spirit of God, with ability, with intelligence, with knowledge, and with all craftsmanship."

This is a remarkable passage. It teaches us that the Spirit of God does not equip people for spiritual ministry alone but for artistic work as well. Creating "artistic designs" can be a call from God.

The best way to drive out bad art is to encourage good art. As C. S. Lewis wrote, "If you do not read good books, you will read bad ones. If you reject aesthetic satisfactions, you will fall into sensual satisfactions." Since human beings are created in the image of God with imagination and aesthetic sense, they *will* create culture of one kind or another. The only question is whether it will be a decadent culture or a godly one.

In 1703 Andrew Fletcher wrote, "Give me the making of the songs of a nation, and I care not who makes its laws." He was right. Cultural change precedes political change. The first line of attack for Christians should not be attacking the government but reforming the culture.

IN-YOUR-FACE ART

Thursday

WHEN STUDENTS AT THE UNIVERSITY of Maryland came to campus one day, they found hundreds of fliers saying, "Notice: These men are potential rapists." Below were listed the names of fifty male students.

In the outcry that followed, it turned out that the men were not, in fact, suspected rapists. The names had been taken at random from a phone directory as part of a project intended to highlight the problem of date rape.

Well, the project was a disaster. But what few people noticed is that it started out as an *art* project.

The idea was hatched in a class on Contemporary Issues in Feminist Art. The fliers were accompanied by a piece of performance art, where female students in black gowns and hoods read lists of randomly chosen girl's names—who, they said, are all "potential victims" of rape. It was a vivid example of art degraded to pure politics.

Art was once regarded as the expression of a civilization's highest ideals. The great painters and sculptors gave visual form to a shared communal vision of the good and the beautiful. But modern artists would laugh at that definition. The West no longer *has* a shared communal vision of what is good and beautiful.

You see, when intellectuals and artists began to give up belief in God, it was soon followed by a loss of belief in *any* transcendent ideals or standards—whether standards of truth or goodness or beauty. This explains why you can walk into a museum of modern art and see things like a stack of bricks, a box of kitty litter, or an empty picture frame—all labeled as "art."

But people cannot live without standards, without ideals to give significance to their actions. So today many artists try to find a wider purpose for their art in politics. The students with their lists of potential rapists and victims were subverting art to feminist politics.

Ironically, when Christians object to politicized art, we're denounced as anti-cultural bigots, as enemies of art. But the truth is just the opposite: The real enemies are the radicals who *reduce* art to a tool of a political agenda. ❖

MUSIC
FROM HELL

Friday

SOME PEOPLE CALL IT DEATH METAL. It's a style of music that glorifies death, blood, and Satanism. The bands sport names like Megadeth, Slayer, Carcass. Their songs feature titles like "Under the Rotted Flesh," "Covered with Sores," "Raining Blood."

One radio station described it as "Heavy Metal from Hell."

Fortunately, some radio stations refuse to carry death metal music. And retailers objected when an album came out entitled "Butchered at Birth," with graphic pictures of mutilated babies. Still, death metal albums are selling by the hundreds of thousands. Concert halls are packed.

Why do some teenagers *like* this music?

Defenders of death metal say that it helps kids let off steam. Megadeth says their music gives kids "an outlet to vent their frustrations, their anxieties, and their hostilities." A record producer says, "Kids are angry. They want to go out and kill people. This way, they can get it out in a civilized manner."

This is known as catharsis theory—the idea that art gives people a harmless way to get hostility out of their system. Unfortunately, it doesn't work that way. When a television talk show ran a program about children who had committed murder, every one said they listened to death metal.

No, art is not catharsis. Just the opposite: Art is rehearsal. Watching or listening to other people do something is a way of mentally rehearsing it—which makes it easier for us to do the same thing. After all, that's why businesses spend untold millions of dollars on advertising every year.

When it comes to psychology, the Bible is right. It tells us that sin gets a foothold in our minds through the things we see, hear, and talk about. As Job says, we need to make a covenant with our eyes—and with our ears—not to indulge in things that could cause us to sin.

Surely that includes music glorifying blood and violence and Satanism—music that even non-Christians call "music from hell." 🔳

 GRUNGE AND GORE

Weekend

STROLL THROUGH ANY RECORD SHOP TODAY, and your eyes are assaulted with images of destruction and decay.

A CD by Alice in Chains shows plastic flies imbedded in someone's spine. An album by Prong features a gouged-out eye impaled on a dinner fork.

Why does so much popular music celebrate gore and violence? Martha Bayles, in her book, *Hole in our Soul*, says the degradation of popular music has roots in art theory. In the classic tradition, from the ancient Greeks to the Enlightenment, art found its home among the three absolutes: Truth, Goodness, and Beauty. Art was thought to embody objective norms of Beauty, while expressing what is True and Good.

But the rise of modern science led to a philosophy called *scientism*—which anointed science as the only valid approach to truth. Art was cut off from the "objective" world, now defined by science alone. Artists tried to create a purely subjective world where each artist creates his own truth, his own rules.

But it's impossible to create a private world in a vacuum. So artists began defining creative freedom in purely negative terms— as freedom *from* bourgeois society and traditional morality. In the late nineteenth century, the European avant-garde adopted the image of the artist as a rebel, who kicks up his heels at conventional society.

The avant-garde movement immigrated to America, where it merged with our own musical traditions—jazz, blues, folk, and gospel—producing rock and roll and other forms of popular music.

But in the 1960s, the avant-garde gained the upper hand. Members of the Beatles, the Rolling Stones, and other groups attended art colleges and incorporated radical art theories into their music. Making music became less important than mocking the middle class. Today, in punk and MTV, the relentless attack on mainstream values has built to a fever pitch of profanity and perversity.

A reformation of popular music must begin by rejecting scientism, which severed art from truth and cast it adrift on a sea of subjectivism. We must reassert the intimate connection between Truth, Goodness, and Beauty.

It's not enough to denounce perverse popular music and forbid it in our homes. Jesus also calls us to be salt in society—to renew our culture.

We need to create a culture where music that exalts perversity can no longer "go platinum." ※

THE MORAL IMAGINATION

Monday

SOCIETIES ARE NOT HELD TOGETHER BY rules and laws; order cannot be enforced by swords or guns alone. People must find their motivation and meaning in powerful ideas—beliefs that justify their institutions and ideals.

To put it another way, societies are legitimized by "myth," in the sense of grand images, ideas, and words with the power to inspire people to acts of commitment and sacrifice.

People don't pick a vision or myth about the world piece meal, as they might pick a bouquet of flowers in a garden. They come to such convictions within the framework of a broader set of historical assumptions and ideals—more like accepting a story, with all of its internal rules and consistencies.

Here and there in the history of the West there have been people that struck the chord of the moral imagination, and thereby transformed not only policies and practices but a whole manner of thought.

One could point to such writers as C. S. Lewis, J. R. R. Tolkien, and Charles Williams, who were equally fluent in debate and allegory. Or G. K. Chesterton, who as poet, journalist, novelist, and debater championed a vigorous and joyful orthodoxy. Or T. S. Eliot, who, as the most prominent poet of his age, shocked the world by his conversion and vocal defense of Christian culture. Or Dorothy Sayers, whose wit and writing articulated the intellectual fruit of a lively commitment to Christ. Or Alexander Solzhenitsyn, who writes of spiritual freedom with the passion born of suffering.

These men and women did not merely engage in controversy, though they seldom turned down a good argument. Instead, they presented a new perspective, they told a new story.

They provided an alternative to the rotting myths of modernity and presented a compelling vision of the good. 🔳

POETIC LICENSE

Tuesday

MANY OF THE GREATEST MASTERS OF the English language throughout history have been Christian poets. Think of John Donne, who wrote such memorable lines as "Death be not proud," "No man is an island," and "Never ask for whom the bell tolls, it tolls for thee."

Or think of John Milton, who composed the magnificent epic poem *Paradise Lost* in order to "justify the ways of God to man."

And the rich language of Gerard Manley Hopkins is always a call to worship. Listen to the opening lines of "God's Grandeur": "The world is charged with the grandeur of God. It will flame out, like shining from shook foil." Hear the way Hopkins evokes the dreariness of the human condition: "Generations have trod, have trod, have trod; And all is smeared with trade; bleared, smeared with toil." Rich, evocative words like these are far more powerful than a simple factual description.

The writer Percy Shelley once said, "Poets are the unacknowledged legislators of the world." What he meant is that through their vivid imagery and memorable rhythms, poets have the power to shape how people think.

It's a power Christians need to understand—and use to the glory of God.

TELLING STORIES

Wednesday

WHAT MAKES A BOOK GOOD LITERATURE is not the themes it deals with but how it *treats* those themes—the moral stance it takes. As Gene Edward Veith argues in *Reading Between the Lines*, even immoral themes can be treated with moral sensitivity.

Take the story of King Arthur. It deals with the theme of adultery, but in a way that clearly portrays it as wrong. The illicit relationship between Lancelot and Queen Guinevere eventually destroys the court of the Round Table.

And think of ancient Greek dramas. *Oedipus Rex* deals with patricide, self-mutilation, and suicide; yet it manages to maintain dignity and a serious moral tone throughout.

The Bible itself deals with murder and adultery in the story of David and Bathsheba, yet in such a way that the reader comes to understand why these things are wrong.

This is what makes good literature: It deals with deep human problems in a way that teaches us right and wrong. Not by preachy moralizing but by a gripping story. That's why Jesus used parables: Hearing a story, we identify with the characters and enter into their hearts and minds.

This is especially important in teaching children. Bruno Bettelheim, the great child psychologist, said a child's moral choices are not based on abstract standards of right versus wrong; they are based on the people he admires and wants to emulate. In Bettelheim's words, "The question for the child is not 'Do I want to be good?' but 'Who do I want to be like?'"

What makes bad literature so harmful is that it reverses this process. Bad literature encourages readers to identify with evil characters and draws them into a vicarious experience of sexual fantasies, or dreams of wealth and power, or dark obsessions with violence.

But the Bible clearly teaches that even imaginary indulgence is sinful. In the Sermon on the Mount, Jesus warns that lusting is just as bad as committing adultery; hatred is as bad as murder.

This gives a standard that Christian parents can use to evaluate books intelligently. Does the book depict sin to encourage its practice? Or to show how destructive it is?

Good literature is literature that makes us *want* to be good. ▨

A GOOD
READ

Thursday

HOW CAN CHRISTIANS FIND GOOD BOOKS to read? Not just by closing our eyes to the junk and smut, says literature professor Gene Edward Veith, but by learning to recognize good writing.

In *Reading Between the Lines*, Veith argues that there are aesthetic laws for literature—objective principles of art beauty—and that we can learn to recognize.

In literature, aesthetic laws start with the artistic use of language: crisp phrases, colorful imagery, and vivid descriptions. When you pick up a book, skim a few pages to see whether the language is artistic—or whether it is marred by clichés, slang, and obscenities.

Good writing flows from good character. To write an effective story, an author must have empathy to portray characters realistically. He must understand personal motivations to weave a convincing plot. He must be morally sensitive to portray the battle between good and evil—the struggle of conscience. Even if not a Christian, the author must understand the world as God created it.

This means that once we learn to recognize artistic language and an effective story, that alone is enough to steer us through most of the mindless material spewed out by today's presses. Immoral literature is generally bad literature—*artistically* bad.

Consider what happens when an author goes for shock value by spiking a story with graphic scenes. The reader is engrossed in a dramatic plot, he is identifying with the characters, and suddenly the story erupts into sex or violence. The reader is jerked away from the story line by sexual reactions or disgust or morbid fascination. The artistic mood is completely shattered.

Of course, it's far easier to shock readers than to create real art, so the bad writer is quick to resort to it. "Original sin has great marketing potential," Veith quips.

When Christians object to bad literature, we are quickly caricatured as anti-cultural, anti-intellectual, and anti-art. But it's really the smutty writers themselves who are anti-art—because they are *subverting* art to sex and sensationalism. The best literature is not only artistically good but also morally good. ▓

Friday

LOPSIDED LITERATURE

DEATH, DIVORCE, POVERTY, CRIME—it's all in contemporary teen literature. Anyone who objects to such bitter fare for teens is attacked as a censor: "Don't you want kids to learn how to face the real world?" The answer is, of course we do; but these books raise problems without offering solutions.

In *What Are Your Kids Reading?* Jill Carlson reviews the most frequently recommended books for teens. A full quarter of the books, Carlson says, revolve around death as a major theme. Yet none offers a biblical perspective on death or suffering.

Another common theme is teen sex. But it's never portrayed as morally wrong, Carlson notes. It's never even followed by negative consequences, like teen pregnancy or sexually transmitted diseases.

And the portrayal of adults is sharply skewed. Fathers take a real beating, Carlson reports: They're overwhelmingly portrayed as cruel and abusive. When you can find them, that is. Most have died, divorced, or deserted their families.

Mothers have been dressed up by Women's Liberation and usually appear as career women.

And clergy are almost always bad guys—lecherous and lewd.

This new teen literature is described as "contemporary realism." But realistic is just what it's not. To portray *most* American fathers as abusive, *most* mothers as careerists, *most* preachers as hypocrites, and teen sex as fun without consequences is statistically and morally inaccurate.

What are your teens reading these days? If you're a parent, I suggest you find out. When teens read, they enter into a dialogue with the author. As Carlson puts it, "From cover to cover, your child is alone with a skilled author whose beliefs may not be yours." Make a habit of reading with your teens. Acquaint your family with Christian fiction—from *Pilgrim's Progress* to J. R. R. Tolkein, C. S. Lewis, and George MacDonald. Contemporary Christian novels are exploding onto the market these days as well.

What the critics say is true: Kids do need to be prepared for the real world. But that means being armed with the truth. 🔲

Weekend

HOT
DOG CITY

ONE OF THE MOST FAMOUS SCENES in film history is in Fellini's *La Dolce Vita*. To symbolize Rome's historical religious significance, Fellini starts with a statue of Jesus sweeping across the skyline, arms outstretched, hanging from a helicopter.

Steve Martin liked the scene so much that in *L. A. Story*, he did a take-off: As the movie opens, we see something sweeping across the skyline, hanging from a helicopter. The camera zooms in and we see it is . . . a giant hot dog. The perfect symbol for L. A., center of America's mass-produced, lowest-common-denominator popular culture.

Ken Myers, author of *All God's Children and Blue Suede Shoes*, says "the challenge of living with popular culture" may well be the most serious challenge facing Christians today. Popular culture is a very subtle threat: It can cause a gradual erosion of character that many Christians don't even recognize.

What do you mean, we don't recognize it? you may ask. Any Christian can tell you that the level of sex and violence has risen sharply in movies, rap music, and dime-store novels.

True enough, Myers says. But those are concerns about *content*; what we often overlook is *form*. The form of popular culture can shape the way we respond—regardless of the message. For comparison, consider a classical poem or symphony. It has a complex structure that challenges the mind; you have to *work* to appreciate it. But Harlequin romances, soap operas, and rock music don't require any intellectual discipline. They're easy to understand; they grab our attention with catchy lines, loud music, and sensational visual effects.

By focusing on immediate experience, pop culture discourages sustained attention. By angling for an emotional response, it discourages the use of our minds to analyze what we see and hear. Pop culture is a bit like junk food: too much of it can spoil our appetite for healthy food.

Paul writes in 1 Corinthians 10, "Everything is permissible, but not everything is beneficial." There's no harm in popular culture per se, but there *is* harm in making it a steady diet.

How can Christians survive in a junk-food culture? By working to cultivate a taste for higher culture. As families, we ought to delve into good literature, listen to classical music. Learn to love the things that feed the mind—and the soul. 🔖

CHRISTIAN
SOAP OPERA

Monday

CHRISTIANS OFTEN SIMPLY IMITATE the culture around us. We wash out any objectional *content* but keep the same *format*. So today we have Christian theme parks, Christian exercise videos, Christian rock bands, and Christian rappers.

We're rapidly creating a parallel culture, different in content, identical in style.

But in *All God's Children and Blue Suede Shoes*, Ken Myers says some styles may have an effect all their own, which comes through regardless of any Christian message attached. For example, not long ago a Christian broadcasting company experimented with a Christian soap opera. It had the standard soap opera style of acting, the same melodramatic music. The only difference was that at some point the main characters got saved. But until then, they were just as decadent as any secular soap opera character.

The problem here is that soap opera *as a genre* is inherently contrary to Christian values. As Myers puts it, soaps are "the dramatic equivalent of gossip." They arouse the same prying curiosity that gossip arouses—regardless of any Christian message we might tack on.

Like soap opera, some styles of music or film or fashion may be inherently contrary to Christian values. That's because many forms of popular culture were developed expressly as a *rebellion* against traditional culture. And if defiance of traditional values is built into the warp and woof of popular culture, then redeeming it will be no easy task.

RELIGION IN THE NEWS

Tuesday

AMERICA'S MEDIA EMPIRE HAS acknowledged that there's one area of life it does a poor job of covering: religion. And one network is doing something about it: ABC News hired Peggy Wehmeyer, an evangelical Christian, as network television's first full-time religion correspondent.

Wehmeyer's own story is revealing. She started out at a local ABC affiliate as a writer, where she approached the news director with a list of thirty great story ideas. All the stories dealt with religion, and all had the right elements for an engaging TV piece.

The news director was baffled. He took the list to his regular staff and asked how they had missed such good stories. The reporters could only shrug, saying they "didn't know anything about this stuff."

That's exactly what's wrong with network news today. Important and interesting events are missed by a secular media that simply doesn't have eyes to see. A study by the Media Research Center found that stories with a religious focus make up only 1 percent of news programming.

"Do you have to fight to cover politics? Do you have to fight to cover education . . . or entertainment?" Wehmeyer asks. Then "why do we have to fight to get good coverage of a subject that is as controversial, colorful, and exciting as religion?"

One answer is that the secular world regards religious believers as inherently biased. Fellow journalists often ask Wehmeyer how she can cover religion if she is a committed Christian. She fires the question right back at them: "How can you cover politics and then go vote?"

The truth is that all reporters have a point of view, whether religious or secular. And all reporters have to learn how to write objective news in spite of their prior commitments. Being religious is not any more biased than being antireligious.

In fact, Christians who believe God made the world should be the most highly motivated of all to see that world as objectively as possible. While the modern world wallows in subjectivism, we believe in objective truth—and that gives us a rigorous standard lacking in the secular media.

The church's job is to raise up *more* people like Peggy Wehmeyer—talented Christian writers who are committed to the truth. 🗷

"WASTING TIME" ON DEATH ROW

Wednesday

BEFORE PREACHING AT MISSISSIPPI'S Parchman Prison, I visited death row. Most of the inmates were in their bunks wrapped in blankets, staring blankly at little black-and-white TV screens, killing time.

But in one cell a man was sitting on his bunk, reading. As I approached, he looked up and showed me his book—an instruction manual on Episcopal liturgy.

His name was John Irving. He'd been on death row for more than fifteen years, and he was studying for the priesthood. John told me he was allowed out of his cell one hour each day. The rest of the time, he studied—preparing to meet Christ or to serve Him here.

Seeing that John had nothing in his cell but a few books, I thought, *God has blessed me so much, the least I can do is provide something for this brother.* "Would you like a TV if I could arrange it?" I asked.

John smiled gratefully. "Thanks," he said, "but no thanks. You can waste an awful lot of time with those things."

"Waste time" on death row?

The psalmist prayed that God would "teach us to number our days, that we may apply our hearts unto wisdom" (Ps. 90:12, KJV). For the fifteen years since a judge placed a number on his days, John Irving had done just that, determined not to waste the one commodity he had to give to the Lord—his time.

The real evils of the entertainment industry are not the violence and profanity—offensive though they are. No, it's the banality: the sheer waste of time. When we turn the TV on, we turn our minds off.

The Scriptures are clear: "Be careful how you walk, not as unwise men, but as wise, making the most of your time, because the days are evil" (Eph. 5:15-16, NASB). We are to be stewards of time, just as we are of funds or any other resources. ▨

MORALITY IN MOVIES

Thursday

ONLY A FEW DECADES AGO, FILMS conveyed a moral message. Like "Mr. Smith Goes to Washington," a classic by Frank Capra. It's about a young senator who stands up for moral principles in the face of practical politicking.

We don't hear that kind of message from Hollywood anymore. Today's filmmakers insist that art should be free of moral overtones. But look what they give us instead: tired formulas—endless rehashing of chase scenes, slashers, nudity, and gore. Sure, today's special effects are spectacular. But when the film itself has no substance, that's like frosting with no cake. Glitz and glitter that leave the viewer feeling empty afterward.

Many modern filmmakers feel that morality gets in the way of serious art. But Frank Capra proves them wrong. He successfully portrayed characters who stood for traditional moral values—honesty, courage, sacrifice, loyalty—characters who turn to prayer as easily as breathing. In *It's a Wonderful Life*, when George runs into financial trouble, his wife asks the children and her neighbors to pray. And they do, right there on screen.

Frank Capra described his goal in these words: "I deal with the little man's doubts, . . . his loss of faith in himself, in his neighbor, in his God." And then, "I show the *overcoming* of doubts, the courageous renewal of faith."

This is the stuff of real life. Homey, yet heroic.

Capra's creative period, the 1930s and 40s, is considered the golden age of film. Even feminists say the old studios cast women as strong, interesting characters. By contrast, today's films portray women one-dimensionally, either as sex objects or female Rambos.

The truth is that a moral framework doesn't *limit* art, it makes *better* art. Characters who demonstrate moral integrity are complex and interesting. But characters who live for pleasure and self-gratification are shallow and childish.

The American public is so used to shallow characters and formula films, we've almost forgotten what a good movie can be. Why don't you try renting some of the older classics and see the contrast?

If Christians start demanding real quality in films, we just might spark a cultural revolution—where movies once again portray the moral drama in the souls of ordinary men and women. 🕮

WHEN SCHOOLS ARE BATTLEGROUNDS

Friday

STEPHEN BATES IS A SECULAR JOURNALIST but his book, *Battleground*, shows a real sensitivity to Christian concerns. Public education has undergone a philosophical shift in the past few decades, Bates says. The Christian perspective has been virtually blanked out of textbooks, and Christians are much less successful than other groups in influencing public education.

For example, Bates describes a set of files subpoenaed during a trial from a major textbook publisher: Holt, Rineholt, and Winston. Internal memos showed that when complaints about textbooks came from feminists, minorities, and multiculturalists, the editors at Holt were polite, accommodating, even apologetic.

But when complaints came from conservative and Christian groups, accommodation went only so far. Then the memos became hostile, calling the groups "reactionary" and even "totalitarian."

The inescapable fact is that all educational materials are shaped by the beliefs of the people who write them. As Bates puts it, "the mission of public education *forces* the government to do what the First Amendment as a rule frowns on: select particular ideas, package them, and present them with the imprimatur of the state." No matter which ideas the state selects, some parents will disagree.

That's why the battle over education is one front in the broader culture wars. And Christians had better be sure we understand where the battle lines are drawn. 🕮

A GENERATION OF BARBARIANS

Weekend

S TANDING BEFORE A HUGE AMERICAN FLAG, Barbara Walters looked sternly into the television camera. "The alarm has sounded," she said. "The clock is ticking. But most of us are still asleep."

Nuclear threat? Acid rain? An epidemic?

No, Walters was referring to the deterioration of American education. Most high school students she surveyed thought the Holocaust was "a Jewish holiday." Many couldn't locate the United States on a world map.

But the real crisis, Walters argued, is one of character. "Today's high school seniors live in a world of misplaced values," she said. They have no sense of discipline. No goals. They care only for themselves. In short, they are "becoming a generation of undisciplined cultural barbarians."

We shouldn't be surprised. Teachers and school administrators encourage students to choose from a smorgasbord of what they term morally equivalent lifestyles: homosexuality, adultery, premarital promiscuity. Gorge yourself on one or sample them all. And this smorgasbord morality, which is itself a value system, tramples on the sensibilities of any who hold to moral absolutes—particularly Christians.

Every area of education has been infected by this value-neutral philosophy. This is not only tragic but ironic: At one time the pursuit of virtue was the specific goal of education. "If you ask what is the good of education," said Plato, "the answer is easy—that education makes good men, and that good men act nobly." We have lost the ideal of educating for virtue. ▩

EDUCATING FOR ETHICS

Monday

CAN ADULTS TELL YOUNGSTERS WHAT TO do? The dominant method in education today says no. Adults can only help youngsters explore their feelings and make their own decisions. For example, one sex education textbook advises teachers to tell children, "Although we adults feel it's in your best interest to delay intimate sexual behaviors, you and only you will decide when you will become sexually involved."

Students are not having their minds trained by confrontation with the great principles of truth and justice expounded through centuries of Western culture. Instead they are told that all they have to do is look within, judge their own feelings, and choose what "feels right" to them.

The result is people who approach ethics as though it were a consumer choice—who insist that they are free to choose their own value systems just as they are free to choose between, say, a Sony or a General Electric radio. In fact, one prominent sex educator says a good program is one that "supports the decision to say 'yes' as well as the decision to say 'no'" to sexual involvement.

"Yes" is a Sony, "no" is a GE. It is just a matter of personal preference.

The implicit message to youngsters is that junior knows best. Making up their own minds means rejecting the teachings of home and church. In fact, ethical maturity is actually defined in educational theory as the autonomous individual making his own choice. Any external authority is suspect. If you listen to anything outside your own feelings, you are not truly mature, independent, and autonomous.

But moral education stressing autonomy yields disappointing results. Studies show that youngsters who take courses teaching individual decision-making as the basis for ethics end up with higher rates of drug use and sexual activity.

The reason should be obvious. Without a timeless, universal set of ethical guidelines that they can rely on—an absolute standard beyond themselves—young people have no means to withstand temptation. They have no defense against the pushers and the dealers.

With this form of moral education, there is little hope that kids will just say no. 📖

MORAL ILLITERACY
Tuesday

A SURVEY OF HIGH SCHOOL STUDENTS HAS forced teachers to think twice about the way they teach ethics. Two-thirds of all high school students admitted to cheating on an exam within the past year. One-third said they'd stolen something. More than a third said they would lie on a job application.

These were not inner-city kids brought up in crime-ridden neighborhoods; most of them were from middle-class communities. The Josephson Institute of Ethics, which conducted the survey, says part of the problem is the way values are taught in schools. Most public schools use a decision-making approach, which tells kids that there is no right or wrong, that they're entitled to make up their own minds.

In *Why Johnny Can't Tell Right From Wrong*, William Kilpatrick says classrooms have taken on the style of talk shows, where the only rule is that everyone has a right to his own view, no matter how bizarre.

But the Donahue-style classroom is not a very good way to teach kids morality—as the recent survey shows. The alarming thing, however, is that most teachers are still fiercely attached to it.

Kilpatrick is often invited to speak in schools, where he asks audiences to suppose their own child's school is instituting a course in moral education. The school is considering two programs. Program A exposes students to provocative ethical dilemmas, tells them there are no right or wrong answers, and encourages them to make up their own minds. By contrast, Program B holds up certain virtues as admirable, such as justice, charity, and self-control; it exposes students to illustrations from history and literature, and encourages them to practice the virtues themselves. Which of these programs would *you* choose? The vast majority of parents, Kilpatrick says, choose Program B the one that stresses character training. But teachers invariably choose Program A, the one based on individual decision-making. In fact, many teachers tell Kilpatrick they would *never* use Program B under any circumstances!

Clearly there is a wide gap in outlook between parents and many educators.

Proverbs 22:6 says, "Train up a child in the way he should go." When we fail to teach children standards of right and wrong we are abdicating our adult responsibility, no matter what the education experts say.

Donahue is bad enough for television; we *certainly* don't want Donahue-style classrooms in our schools.

COMPUTER CONFUSION

Wednesday

AN ARTICLE IN THE *CHRONICLE OF HIGHER Education* describes a set of computer videodisks for teaching ethics. The disks present students with ethical dilemmas to solve. For example, there's a disk called "A Right to Die?" showing the true story of a young man named Dax, severely burned in a car explosion. For months, Dax underwent excruciating burn therapy. He pleaded with doctors and nurses to let him die. Eventually he recovered, and today he is married and practicing law.

But the students don't know all that. The videodisk shows Dax before the accident, shows him horribly burned—and then stops. The students are asked to decide whether Dax should be allowed to live or die.

Whatever they choose, the computer challenges them. If they say Dax should live, they are shown film clips of the patient begging to die. If they say he should be allowed to die, they see clips of him today, in his successful law practice.

So what's the right answer? The computer doesn't tell.

What's the point of teaching ethics this way? It doesn't teach students right or wrong; it doesn't teach them about the great ethical systems of the world. So what *does* it teach?

The answer is simple: It teaches relativism—that there *is* no right or wrong in ethics. Dilemmas are chosen that are so difficult, it's hard for students to see how ordinary ethical categories apply—the ones they learned from parents and teachers.

The goal is to free students from everything they've been taught before so they can develop their own ideas about ethics. Lawrence Kohlberg, who pioneered the dilemma approach, says the situations are meant to be so hard that "the adult right answer is not obviously at hand," and the student is free to think up his own answers.

This idea comes straight from the eighteenth-century philosopher Immanuel Kant, who said the inner self should be absolutely free and autonomous. For Kant, that means we should not accept any moral laws from outside ourselves—not from parents, not from teachers, and especially not from God. The Autonomous Self creates its own moral law.

If you've ever wondered what's wrong with secular courses in ethics, this is it. Not just that they teach relativism, but that they idolize the human Self.

The Autonomous Self, and not God, becomes the legislator of morality. ※

VALUES AND VIOLENCE

Thursday

NEARLY THREE MILLION CRIMES ARE committed on school property every year, writes William Kilpatrick in *Why Johnny Can't Tell Right from Wrong*. And the problem is not that students aren't getting any values education. "In fact," says Kilpatrick, "more attention and research has been devoted to moral education in recent years than at any [other] time in our history."

The problem is that most of these programs have been resounding failures. Why? Because they are based on the wrong moral philosophy—a philosophy that reduces morals to a matter of "likes" and "dislikes."

Those are the very words used by Sidney Simon, a guru of values education, in an interview with *Newsweek*. In his approach,

Simon explains, "children's responses are never judged right or wrong." Every decision is treated as a matter of personal taste, no different from deciding between Coke and Pepsi.

But the decision-making approach, as it is often called, makes real moral education impossible. Kilpatrick tells the story of a teacher who used Simon's approach with low-achieving eighth-graders. The program told students to list the things they loved doing. As it turned out, the most popular activities were "sex, drugs, drinking, and skipping school."

The teacher was hamstrung, Kilpatrick says. Her students had clarified their values, and Simon's system gave her no way to persuade them otherwise—no way to challenge them to aim for something higher in life.

This story paints a dark picture of what's wrong with the decision-making approach to values education: It encourages people to look inside for answers to questions of right and wrong. The Bible teaches that human beings are fallen, with a deep-rooted attraction to evil. If we take our impulses as our only guide, we are certain to be led astray.

If we really want a solution to crime—in schools and in society—we need programs that train people in virtue—that restrain our impulses with godly principles. 🔲

THE HUMAN ANIMAL

Friday

ACCORDING TO THE *NEW YORK TIMES*, there's a fad at city pools called "the whirlpool." Twenty to thirty boys link arms in a circle and surround a solitary girl. The boys close in on her, dunk her head under water, and frequently tear off her bathing suit and grab at her.

The problem has grown so severe that in New York City several teenage boys have actually been arrested for sexual assault.

Reporters asked several teens how they accounted for the boys' predatory behavior. "It's nature," one boy replied. "Look at a female dog and a male dog. It's the same thing: You see twenty male dogs on a female dog. It's the male nature, in a way."

How utterly repugnant. But how utterly consistent with what these kids are being taught in public schools.

The great prophet of sex education was Alfred Kinsey, who built his theory of sexuality squarely on the foundation of scientific naturalism. Humans are part of nature, Kinsey taught—nothing more. As a result, he evaluated every form of sexual activity in terms of its role in the lives of the lower species. Any behavior found among the lower animals Kinsey regarded as natural for humans as well.

In his words, it is "part of the normal mammalian picture."

Kinsey was working on the assumption of evolution. Evolution teaches an unbroken continuity between humans and the animal world. And if we are simply advanced animals, then our guide to behavior is whatever the animals do. As Kinsey puts it, in sexual matters humans should follow the example of "our mammalian forebears."

Kinsey's philosophy has been gospel among sex educators ever since the 1950s. And it sounds to me as though some New York boys have grasped it precisely. "Look at a male and a female dog" is merely a vernacular translation of Kinsey's more sophisticated talk about "the normal mammalian picture."

Christian parents need to promote sex education programs that acknowledge that humans are more than animals. The Bible does not teach that we are merely dogs in heat. It teaches that we are bearers of the image of God. ※

Weekend

PUMSY, THE MAGIC DRAGON

FIVE-YEAR-OLD STEPHANIE SAT ABSOLUTELY still, her hands folded, her eyes closed. For a lively little girl, this was unusual behavior, and her mother was puzzled.

"Stephanie, what are you doing? Stephanie!" Finally, the little girl opened her eyes. She explained it was an activity she had learned at school. And she went on to describe what her mother recognized as classic Eastern meditation.

Stephanie was in a program called PUMSY: In Pursuit of Excellence. There's a dragon named Pumsy, along with a guide simply called Friend. Friend teaches Pumsy that her mind is like a pool of water: There's a muddy mind, which tempts her to think negative thoughts, and a Clear Mind, which can solve all her problems through positive thinking. Friend tells Pumsy, "Your Clear Mind is the best friend you'll ever have. . . . It is always close to you, and it will never leave you."

This sounds suspiciously like religious language: "I will never leave you nor forsake you." And a few pages later in the story, we read "You have to trust [your Clear Mind] and let it do good things for you."

This "mind" sounds like divine power.

And that's exactly what it is. The Pumsy story is just a fairy-tale way of teaching Hinduism. Hindu doctrine teaches that the human mind or spirit is part of God—a spark in the divine fire, a drop in the divine ocean. The Clear Mind is a euphemism for the divine spark within. What we're seeing here is New Age pantheism wedging its way into education—often marketed as a way to teach self-esteem.

The rationale is that teaching kids to look within to solve their problems makes them more self-reliant. PUMSY teaches youngsters to chant slogans like "I can handle it," "I can make it happen," and "I am me, I am enough."

But there's that religious language again—like God's name in the Old Testament: I am who I am. What PUMSY teaches is not self-esteem, it's self-worship.

Educational programs like PUMSY are popping up all across the country. The cover may say it's a program in self-esteem or drug education or whatever. Teachers often don't even recognize the underlying philosophy. So it's up to parents to find out what their children are learning; to teach them to discern true from false religion; and to equip them with spiritual weapons to fight the spiritual battle. ▨

PC FOR THE
PLAY-DOH SET

Monday

PICTURE BOOKS ABOUT BABAR, THE elephant king, are being pulled from the shelves. The stories have been judged to be dangerous for the tender minds of preschoolers.

Just what is Babar's crime? In the words of a prominent educator, Babar is a poor role model for children because he "extols the virtues of a European middle-class lifestyle."

In short, Babar is not politically correct.

We've all heard about the PC movement on college campuses. Now it's trickling down to the younger grades.

It's PC for the Play-Doh set.

For example, one guide advises teachers to explain to young children that witches are not evil hags but good women who use herbal remedies to help people. Another guide encourages teachers to use story time to instill politically correct attitudes. It suggests reading "Twas the Night Before Christmas" and pretending there is no Papa in the story. Apparently the original poem's family values are not inclusive enough.

Even playtime must be regulated. In the dress-up corner teachers are urged to stock more briefcases than purses to encourage careerism in little girls. They're told to get rid of dump trucks and earthmovers because these reflect the American desire to "conquer nature."

These stories may sound silly, but they reflect an underlying worldview that is anything but silly. Multiculturalism does not simply mean teaching children about the culture, history, and geography of other lands. Instead these programs are out to change our values. They send a subtle message that Western culture is bad and should not be held up as a standard.

In fact, the message is that *nothing* should be held up as a standard, that there is no standard of right or wrong—no transcendent, absolute truth. A report on multicultural education by the New York state board of education actually talks about "multiple truths"—as though each racial and ethnic group has its own truth.

So the issue is not just over whether kids should read Babar. It's over whether we acknowledge a single, universal truth that transcends all our differences. ▨

A "SACRED" RIGHT?

Tuesday

SEPTEMBER HAD ARRIVED, SCHOOL was opening, and in Washington, D. C., the superintendent was fired up. There will be "a lot of changes" this year, he told a back-to-school rally. We've got to prepare "youngsters to be successful in the twenty-first century."

What was he referring to? Stronger academic programs? Tighter discipline? New computers?

No, what the D. C. superintendent decided students needed was condoms.

The school system authorized school nurses to hand out condoms to any student who asked. The service was offered "confidentially," which means without informing the students' parents.

When parents heard of the plan, they were outraged. Many requested an opt-out program to exempt their child. Initially the superintendent agreed, but he was overruled by the D. C. public health commissioner.

No one will be allowed to "interfere" with the condom program, the commissioner thundered. *No one* will be allowed to disrupt the "sacred" right of confidentiality between school nurse and student. And so D. C. officially decreed that the relationship between school and child is more sacred than the relationship between parent and child.

What we're seeing played out in the office of the school nurse is a philosophical battle over who bears responsibility for children. Biblical teaching gives the primary responsibility to parents, with the support of the church community. Historically, schools were established as an extension of parent and church authority.

But the rise of a public school system challenged all that. As one Princeton scholar puts it, "There is a struggle between the family and the state for the minds of the young." The public school system has become "the chief instrument" for state officials to make "a direct appeal to the children over the heads of their parents."

The condom issue is just one front in a larger battle over the role of the public school system. American schools are in the throes of being redefined: Are they going to be an extension of parental authority—or an arm of the state?

There is no middle ground. ❧

LITTLE VICTORIES

Wednesday

CHRIS THOMPSON, A PETITE, ENERGETIC mother of four, has quietly salted her suburban neighborhood for years—starting with her children's school.

When Chris learned that some of the school's teachings didn't square with her Judeo-Christian values, she asked her daughter's first-grade teacher if she could help him in the classroom once a week. He agreed, and Chris began spending every Thursday doing odd jobs.

As they talked from time to time, Chris took the opportunity to explain how she was trying to equip her children to live in a world where the lack of absolute values is destroying society. She explained why self-esteem isn't dependent on how much we like ourselves, but on the fact that we are created in the image of God. Gradually, bit by bit—a friendship and trust developed. Soon the teacher was checking with Chris regarding any films he planned to show the class.

One day a little boy brought a picture book with the David and Goliath story to the class for Show and Tell. Chris's little girl, Claire, raised her hand and asked the boy if the story was true. The teacher told the class that it was not a true story.

The next Thursday as she helped out in Claire's classroom, Chris mentioned to the teacher that she was teaching her children at home that the Bible *is* true and that it didn't seem appropriate for him to label a biblical account fictitious.

The next day, Claire's teacher pulled her aside. "It's really good that you tell your mom everything that happens," he told her. "And you're right. David and Goliath *is* a true story!"

It was a little victory. But think what a difference it would make if thousands of Christians were salting our culture in similar ways. 🔳

WHOSE MORALITY?

Thursday

IT IS TIME FOR UNIVERSITIES TO PAY "real and sustained attention to students' intellectual and moral well-being," said Cornell President Frank Rhodes at a meeting of educators. But immediately an indignant student challenged him: "Whose morality are we going to follow?" The audience applauded thunderously, believing the young man had posed an unanswerable question. Rhodes sat down, unable or unwilling to respond.

Even a generation ago, the obvious answer to the question "Whose morality?" would have been to point to 2,300 years of accumulated moral wisdom in the Western tradition or to a rationally defensible natural law or to the moral law revealed by God in Scripture.

But none of these carry much weight in the current discussion. As Allan Bloom has written, "There is one thing a professor can be absolutely certain of: almost every student entering the university believes, or says he believes, that truth is relative."

But basic human nature dictates that when an individual is left to make moral decisions without reference to some standard above the self, he or she invariably chooses on the basis of self-interest. As sociologist Robert Bellah writes, Americans have two overriding goals: personal success and vivid personal feelings.

But the survival of society depends on people acting on motives superior to personal self-interest. Keeping the law, respecting human life and property, loving one's family, fighting for the common good, helping the unfortunate, paying taxes—these depend on individual virtues such as courage, loyalty, charity, compassion, civility, and duty. Cultures cannot survive without relying on the selflessness of people of character. 🔳

WHY SAIL
THE SEVEN SEAS?

Friday

IN 1992 WE MARKED THE FIVE hundredth anniversary of the ar-
rival of Christopher Columbus on American shores. And what
a fire storm it ignited.

On one side were Columbus supporters, who painted him
as an enlightened and progressive explorer. Their account is not
much different from the glossy, simplistic stories we learned about
famous people when we were in grade school.

On the other side were the protesters, who set themselves
up as debunkers of cultural myths. They've made a new interpretation popular: that Columbus set sail for America merely to gain
wealth and extend Spanish dominion. They mutter angrily about
exploitation and greed.

But the new story is just as simplistic as the old myth. If we
really want to know who Columbus was, we need to read balanced literature on the subject, like Robert Royal's *1492 and All
That*. These books cast new light on the controversy. What motivated Columbus above all else in his ventures on the high seas
was his Christian faith.

Yes, Columbus was a committed Christian. Like Joan of Arc
and Saint Francis of Assisi, he was convinced that God had personally called him. "With a hand that could be felt," Columbus
once wrote, "the Lord opened my mind to the fact that it would
be possible to sail from here to the Indies, and He opened my will
to desire to accomplish this project."

That's genuine religious conviction.

Columbus' desire to travel was first inspired by the Franciscan
monks, who taught that the end of the world would come as
soon as the gospel had spread to the ends of the earth. Columbus
believed he had been called by God to accomplish this task, to
become an instrument of universal evangelization. Whenever he
encountered native peoples, he sought to bring them the Word of
God.

This is the real Christopher Columbus—a man set on fire by
missionary zeal. Columbus saw himself not as a representative of
Spain but of Christendom.

Both sides of the Columbus controversy are overlooking the real story. It's the story of Christopher Columbus as a sincere Christian, doing his best to follow God's call on his life. Now, that's a story worth passing on to our children. ▨

IS LIFE A GAME?

Weekend

THE NUMBER OF AMERICANS WHO play the lottery these days is staggering. During busy hours, Lotto machines in Florida churn out as many as fifteen thousand tickets per second.

Why are so many people willing to sacrifice their time and money for something as elusive as luck?

The Lotto mania signals a shift in fundamental beliefs about life. More people are giving up the historic Christian belief in a personal God, who exercises divine providence over our lives. Instead, they are worshiping at the altar of Almighty Chance.

The same basic philosophy is showing up in the academic world as well. John Rawls, an influential professor at Harvard, teaches a theory of justice that starts with the premise that life is a lottery, that wealth and privilege are dealt out like cards in a poker game. From biological traits, like race and gender, to social traits like family and education background, they're all distributed by chance in what Rawls calls "the lottery of life."

From the university campus to the convenience store with its lottery machine, Americans are abandoning belief in a personal God who lovingly guides our lives. They're reverting to an ancient belief in chance and fate. America is beginning to resemble the pre-Christian Greek culture, with its myth of the Fates—three goddesses who measured out each person's life as a thread from a cosmic spinning wheel. . . and then cut it off.

The fact that Americans spend billions of dollars today on lotteries means that many of them place their real faith in the god of Luck. And the money they spend on lottery tickets is nothing less than their tithes and offerings laid on the altar of Fortune. ▨

Monday

THE NEW APARTHEID

M ANY COLLEGE CAMPUSES HAVE DROPPED required courses that treat Western culture as a whole. Instead, the curriculum has splintered into East Asian Studies, Judaic Studies, Latin American Studies, Women's Studies, Black Studies.

Black students want to read only books by black authors; women want to read only books by female authors. The assumption seems to be that race and gender determine how people think.

This is nothing less than intellectual balkanization. Some may try to justify it in the name of ethnic pride, but it's much more than that. It's a blow at the very principles upon which America was built. America is a nation of immigrants. What gives us cultural cohesiveness is not a common ethnic background but a common belief—belief in such principles as the rule of law, the value of the individual, the freedoms outlined in the Bill of Rights.

Indeed, America depends for its very existence upon the conviction that we can *transcend* our native cultures and commit ourselves to a unified national vision. This is expressed in our national motto: *e pluribus unum,* "out of many, we are one."

That motto is a secularized version of a biblical vision of unity. In the first century, Jesus' apostles scattered across the globe with the message that the gospel is for Jews and Gentiles, Greeks and barbarians, men and women, rich and poor. But today's university students are being taught that there is no single set of principles that can command allegiance from all people.

As a result, we are in danger of splintering into a thousand squabbling nationalities, each hiding out in its own cultural and intellectual ghetto.

The breakup of the universities is not just a disaster for American culture. It's a disaster for anyone trying to communicate the Christian truth. It will be impossible to preach that Christianity is true . . . when truth itself is splintered into a thousand ethnic fragments.

A NEW
IDOLATRY

Tuesday

MASCOT MANIA IS SWEEPING THE land, transforming mascots into ideological battlegrounds.

Bradley University replaced its tomahawk-wielding Indian with a bobcat. Students at the University of Alabama turned thumbs down on "Blaze," a cartoon-like Nordic warrior; they objected that the mascot was overly Teutonic. At the University of Massachusetts at Amherst, the school's mascot—the "Minuteman"—came under multiple attacks: for being sexist (because he's male), for being racist (because he's white), and for being violent (because of his ever-ready musket).

In the 90s, even mascots are supposed to be multicultural.

We might be tempted to dismiss mascot madness as trivial. But there's a serious theme underlying it: The attack on cultural symbols signals a new way of thinking, a philosophy called postmodernism.

Until recently, Americans were immensely proud of our tradition of individual rights and individual dignity. Many of our great freedoms derive from our high view of the individual. But today individualism is being crowded out by the new philosophy of postmodernism, which replaces the individual with the social group. Postmodernism teaches that there *is* no real self—that individuals are merely constructs of social forces, like culture, race, gender, ethnic background. The important thing is not self-identity but social identity.

This explains why all aspects of education—from mascots to classroom curricula—are being scrutinized for sensitivity to blacks, women, Native Americans, and every other conceivable social group.

In *Postmodern Times*, Gene Edward Veith says the social group has become the new icon of our times. Whereas Christianity teaches that God creates reality, postmodernism teaches that social forces construct reality. Culture has been elevated into a god.

As Christians we are called to stand against the spirit of the age. Today's spirit is a worship of race and culture. We need to help people to see that the petty posturing over mascots and logos is really a symptom of something much deeper: a dangerous new idolatry. ❧

COLLEGE BLUES

Wednesday

A RECENT SURVEY OF IVY LEAGUE COLLEGE students revealed gaping deficiencies in their knowledge of American history and civics. Three out of four students could not identify Thomas Jefferson as the author of the opening words of the Declaration of Independence. The same number could not identify Abraham Lincoln as the author of the Gettysburg Address.

These are things taught in a typical ninth-grade civics course—things every immigrant has to master to gain U. S. citizenship. Yet they are unfamiliar to students in our elite Ivy League colleges—people destined to become our nation's next generation of leaders.

The problem stems from the politicizing of education. Educators no longer agree *which* version of American history to teach. Do we teach it as the development of impartial principles of freedom and civic virtue? Or do we teach it as the story of ideological oppression by a band of white males?

The second version is what's taught on most campuses today. Many professors completely reject the ideal of impartial principles. They adopt an approach called the "sociology of knowledge"—derived ultimately from Marxism—which treats all ideas as an expression of class or economic interest. Frederic Sommers of Brandeis University, writing in *The New York Times*, says the main concern of many educators is not to pass on our American heritage but to "empower" students in the struggle against patriarchy, racism, and classism. No wonder, then, that even Ivy League students don't know basic American history.

Politically correct professors reject the ideal of objective truth, with its roots in the biblical teaching of divine revelation. And when that happens, a decline in learning is absolutely predictable.

Those of us who hold the biblical ideal of truth ought to be standing for real scholarship, real education—firmly rooted in the understanding that all truth is God's truth. ▨

WHEN IDEAS
ARE IDOLS

Thursday

IN THE 1960s, REBELLIOUS YOUNG people grew their hair long and sang songs about love and peace. In the 1990s, rebellious young people are shaving their heads bare and singing about hatred and violence. Skinheads, they're called. In Europe, skinheads beat up foreigners, throw firebombs into their homes, and set their cars ablaze. Their slogan is "Foreigners get out!"

What we're seeing here is the revival of Nazism. Nazism was not just about shouting "Heil Hitler" and erecting concentration camps. It was based on a philosophy called fascism. Fascism denied all spiritual truth and idolized what is tangible and earthy: the nation, the race. Fascist philosophy was not completely defeated after World War II. It simply went underground. Today we're seeing its re-emergence in the skinhead movement.

And not just there. The academic world is reeling from the discovery that two of the most influential scholars of modern times—Martin Heidegger and Paul de Man—were once Nazis.

But perhaps it should not really be so surprising that fascism is re-emerging. Human beings are incurably religious. The Russian novelist Fyodor Dostoyevsky once wrote that a person "cannot live without worshipping something." Anyone who rejects the true God must worship an idol.

An idol is not necessarily a figure of wood or stone. It can also be an idea or a set of ideas put forth to explain the world without God. An ideology.

The decline of Communism has created an ideological vacuum. Fascism is rising to fill that vacuum. And no wonder. Fascism resonates with the exaggerated sense of race and ethnic identity emerging all around the globe today—the tendency to break into competing groups, Hispanics versus Jews versus blacks versus whites.

In polite company, we call it "multiculturalism." But it's really an expression of the same impulse that drives fascism—the impulse to identify people foremost by race and ethnic group. One idol, Communism, is toppling, while another idol, fascism, is being resurrected.

The rise and fall of idols has occurred since biblical times. And it will continue throughout the rest of human history. As long as humans revolt against God and raise ideologies to take His place. ※

GENDER WARS

Friday

F EW PIECES OF CLASSICAL MUSIC ARE better known than Beethoven's Ninth Symphony, a paean to freedom and joy. One section has even been turned into a hymn: "Joyful, Joyful We Adore Thee."

So it's startling to hear what some feminist music critics are saying today about this symphony. Radical feminists insist that all music is shaped by themes of male domination and control. Professor Susan McCleary writes that in Beethoven's Ninth, what she hears is not an ode to freedom but frustrated sexual energy— energy that builds up until it "finally explodes in the . . . murderous rage of a rapist."

Well. Welcome to the strange world of feminist scholarship.

It used to be that feminists just wanted to open opportunity for women in all fields—a worthy goal. But today there's a new movement of so-called *gender feminists.* They want more than equal opportunity. They want to change the very content of what is taught in every field—to create a feminist music, a feminist art, a feminist science.

For example: In architecture, gender feminists say the development of square-cornered buildings has nothing to do with economy or space; it represents simply "the male take-over of power in architectural shapes." If females were architects, they say, we'd be living in oval mounds and other rounded shapes.

Even science is interpreted as an expression of male dominance. Gender feminists say the scientific method itself is an outgrowth of male bias. They like to quote Francis Bacon, a sixteenth-century scientist, who quaintly described science as a "marriage" between the human mind and nature. He said the mind "penetrates" nature and turns her into his "slave."

Gender feminists pounce on this kind of imagery and insist that *all* science is based on the metaphor of sexual subjugation— of dominance and control. One feminist even suggests that Newton's Mechanics be renamed Newton's Rape Manual.

Those examples are so outrageous they're almost silly. But the underlying theme is far from silly. Gender feminists deny any objective truth. Every theory, they say, is distorted by gender. That ought to be disturbing for people who believe there *is* an objective truth and that the heart of that truth is in the Scriptures.

Christians should stand against the attempt to deny the existence of objective truth, to reduce everything to sexual themes. There's much more to art and science than the battle of the sexes. 🔳

Weekend

ARE WOMEN LOGICAL?

DO WOMEN THINK LOGICALLY? For centuries, it seems, men have had their doubts. But today, amazingly, the old stereotype that women are irrational is being promoted by the feminist movement itself.

Feminist scholar Peggy McIntosh says logical thinking is just a white male construct. In her definition, masculine thought includes "exact thinking or decisiveness"—or even just "being able to make an argument." None of that for women, McIntosh says: Their style of thinking is "spiritual, relational, and inclusive." McIntosh denounces reason as a tool wielded by white males to oppress everyone else.

How did we get to the point where ordinary logic and reason are denounced as means of oppression? In the seventeenth and eighteenth centuries, Enlightenment thinkers defined Reason in terms of a particular world view: It meant classical science—a world-view that sees the entire universe as a vast machine, operating by natural laws. Human beings were just cogs and gears in the world machine.

But people cannot live as though they were cogs in a mechanistic universe—and today we are witnessing a massive revolt. Sandra Harding, a leading feminist scholar, complains that modern science embodies a male-centered view that is "culturally coercive." Feminist Donna Haraway denounces modern science as a product of "White Capitalist Patriarchy." Environmentalists, multiculturalists, and New Agers have all joined in the attack on Reason.

This represents a radical cultural shift. For centuries, the Christian faith has been criticized in the name of Reason—with Reason defined as the belief that the universe is a vast machine. Since Christianity teaches the existence of a spiritual realm *beyond* the machine, it was hauled before the court of Reason and condemned. But today, ironically, Reason itself is being condemned as a tool of oppression.

For Christians this is both good news and bad news. Good news because it means secular reason can no longer be set up as the judge of all truth. But the rejection of reason is also bad news—because Christianity itself is a rational religion. Today Christians must develop a new apologetic for an irrationalist world. ☒

POSTMODERN POWER GRAB

Monday

WHAT IS YOUR DEFINITION OF *discrimination?* These days it may depend on how steady your nerves are.

At George Mason University, a guide for students defines *discrimination* as "jumping when a homosexual touches you on the arm." It also includes "keeping a physical distance from someone because they are a known gay or lesbian." Imagine campus administrators scurrying around with tape measures, unmasking the guilty who jump too high or stand too far away.

Most people chalk up stories like this to overly sensitive campus officials fearful of offending anyone. But political correctness is much more than sensitivity. It is a manifestation of a deep-rooted philosophical struggle over the issue of truth.

College campuses have been overtaken by the philosophy of postmodernism, which denies the existence of *any* universal truth or morality. Postmodernism holds that individuals are merely constructs of social forces—race, gender, and ethnic background. Every cultural group has its own "truth."

But when people stop believing in a transcendent truth, debates about ideas degenerate into power struggles. After all, if there is no truth, then we cannot persuade one another by rational arguments. All that is left is power: Whatever group has the most power imposes its opinions on everyone else.

This is exactly what postmodernists themselves say. Stanley Fish at Duke University wrote a book called *There's No Such Thing As Free Speech, and It's a Good Thing Too,* in which he supports strict campus speech codes. Why not? Fish argues. After all, public discourse is merely a battle to protect our own preferences while restricting everyone else's. He writes: "Someone is always going to be restricted next, and it is your job to make sure that the someone is not you."

This is frightening stuff. It's the perfect philosophy to justify tyranny. As Wheaton College professor Roger Lundin explains in *The Culture of Interpretation,* in postmodernism "all principles are preferences—and only preferences." As a result, "they are nothing but masks for the will to power."

These are ideas that assault the very foundations of social and intellectual life. No society can survive without some shared principles, some shared vision of what moral philosophers call the Good Life.

But if all principles are merely preferences imposed by force, society degenerates into a war of all against all. Campus codes prescribing how high you may jump or what words you may use are harbingers of the coercion we may soon face at all levels of society. ✦

GODDESSES AND GAIA

Tuesday

STEVE MEYER, A PROFESSOR AT WHITWORTH College, tells a story from his student days at Cambridge University. When we studied Isaac Newton, Meyer says, "the professor waggled his finger at the class and said, 'You don't understand Newton . . . unless you understand Newton's theism'"—his belief in God.

This would never have happened in a university classroom a few decades ago. For centuries, historians were embarrassed to admit that many of the founders of modern science were devout Christians. But today historians readily acknowledge the role of religion in science history.

The new openness to religion is part of a movement known as postmodernism. Ever since the Enlightenment, Christianity has been attacked in the name of scientific rationalism. Whatever rationalism did not accept, Christianity was supposed to quietly get rid of.

And many Christians did. Liberal Christians bowed down to the spirit of modernity by stripping Christianity of all its supernatural elements: miracles and prophecy. Liberal theologian Rudolf Bultmann once wrote that "modern man" accepts only events that fit "the rational order of the universe." That excludes miracles, he stated, "because they do not fit into this lawful order."

For Bultmann, whatever "modern man" does not acknowledge, Christians must get rid of.

But today "modern man" has given way to "*post*modern man." Postmodernism cheerfully accepts any brand of spirituality. Just look at all the cults and beliefs that flourish in America today, from goddess worship to Gaia worship to Native American shamanism.

In some ways it's easier to be a Christian in a postmodern world—as Steve Meyer discovered at Cambridge. But we must also develop a new apologetics for this new culture where, spiritually speaking, anything goes. 🔲

CHRISTIAN COLLEGES UNDER FIRE

Wednesday

IT'S "INTOLERANT," SOME PEOPLE said. "Mean-spirited," said others. "Discriminatory." "As bad as South Africa."

What terrible thing are they talking about? Eastern Nazarene College, located just outside Boston, announced that it would hire only Christian teachers.

What's so earth-shattering about that? you may wonder. After all, Eastern Nazarene is a private school established expressly to teach a particular religious view—which is impossible unless its professors *share* that religious view.

But many Americans no longer seem to understand what private institutions are all about. When president Dr. Kent Hill reaffirmed the college's long-standing policy of hiring only "committed Christians," he was pilloried in the local press. He was compared to the Nazis. He was accused of "cleansing" faculty rosters.

Even some of the school's own students denounced the policy as bigoted and discriminatory. A letter to the local newspaper said, "We Christians do not have a monopoly on goodness and ethics."

Well, "we Christians" are not claiming that we do. All we want is to maintain a distinctive identity for our schools. As Dr. Hill argues, the very essence of pluralism is the "right to maintain and nurture distinctive religious communities"—whether Protestant or Catholic, Jewish or Muslim.

We moderns love words like *pluralism* and *diversity*. But we seem to forget it means allowing people freedom to be unique.

History teaches clearly that when Christian schools hire non-Christian teachers, they eventually lose their unique message and ethos.

You see, what goes on in the classroom is far more than the communication of a body of facts. The facts are interpreted within a philosophical framework, a worldview. And that worldview will be either Christian—or it will something else.

And as soon as you allow in that "something else," your message is diluted.

For those who prefer a secular school, there are plenty of options. But unless we allow each institution to maintain its own message, there won't *be* any options. All our schools will give way to a drab sameness, all teaching the same secular outlook.

That isn't diversity, it's uniformity.

Dr. Hill's critics may charge him with religious intolerance. But the truth is that he's a shining beacon of integrity . . . in the face of *secular* intolerance.

THE RULE OF LAW

Thursday

GOVERNMENT ORIGINATED AS AN ORDINANCE of God. While it cannot redeem the world or establish the kingdom of God, civil government does set the boundaries for human behavior. The state is not a *remedy* for sin, but it is a means to restrain it.

When God established ancient Israel as a nation, His first order of business was the propagation of law, not just for religious purposes but also for the ordering of civil life. Even before the giving of the Ten Commandments there was great need for civil adjudication.

The biblical text records that "Moses took his seat to serve as judge for the people and they stood around him from morning till evening" (Exod. 18:13). (Court dockets seemed to have been clogged from the very beginning.) Moses explained that "the people come to me to seek God's will. Whenever they have a dispute, it is brought to me, and I decide between the parties and inform them of God's decrees and laws" (Exod. 18:15-16).

Thus the Israelite involved in a dispute looked not to the whim of a judge or to an arbitrary law but to a ruling based on divine laws. The judicial role was not a mechanism to advance the state's perception of social equilibrium but to discern God's revealed law.

This is the origin of what we call the rule of law; it stands in stark contrast to modern moral relativism. Without transcendent norms, laws are either established by social elites or are merely bargains struck by competing forces in society. In the Judeo-Christian view, law is rooted in moral absolutes that do not vacillate with public taste or the whim of fashion. 🔳

MOLECULES IN A MEANINGLESS COSMOS?

Friday

CHRISTIANITY CAN NEVER BE UTILITARIAN; it holds every human being as precious because human beings are created in the image of God.

To understand the unique nature of this Judeo-Christian view, we need only compare the ancient Hebrew law codes with, say, the Assyrian laws of Hammurabi and other Middle Eastern legal codes from the same period. Historian Paul Johnson has noted that the Assyrian code made the rights of property ultimate, while "the Hebrew [laws] emphasized the essential rights and obligations of man, and their laws were framed with deliberate respect for moral values."

Jesus continued—and expanded—the Old Testament law. He constantly affirmed the dignity and worth of the lowest members of first-century society—women, children, Gentiles, tax-collectors, lepers.

Today's clamor for human rights is ironic. Much of the activism emanates from those who claim no belief in God. But consider what many who have had a major influence on modern thinking believed. Karl Marx thought man a victim of economic forces. Sigmund Freud believed all was lost in the dark web of the psyche. B. F. Skinner insisted that freedom was an illusion and dignity a lost cause.

In this light, human dignity and human rights are tenuous assertions. If man is merely a fortuitous collection of molecules in a meaningless cosmos, why should he have inherent rights?

Spinoza once observed that man builds his kingdoms in accord with his concept of God. The rise of atheism in the twentieth century has provided unlimited license for tyrants. If there is no morally binding standard above the state, it becomes god and human beings mere beasts of bureaucratic burden. A government cannot be truly just without affirming the intrinsic value of human life. ▓

THE 51 PERCENT

Weekend

WE CHRISTIANS FOLLOW THE ONE who says "I am the Truth." What do we mean by truth? It means that there is an ultimate reality. There is ultimate meaning. There is something objectively true, whether or not we understand it or can apprehend it with our senses. There is an absolute. There is a physical order to the universe, and there is also a *moral* order to the universe.

Yet in a 1992 Gallup poll, 69 percent of the people said they believe there are no moral absolutes. In a Barna poll, 71 percent of the American people said there is no such thing as absolute truth. The same poll showed that 40 percent of evangelical Christians responded the same way. They, too, said there is no such thing as absolute truth!

American society is awash in relativism.

What is the basis for law if there is no absolute truth? The basis is whoever has the majority—rule by the 51 percent. Oliver Wendell Holmes once said that "law is the majority vote of that nation that could lick all others." Pure pragmatism.

The inevitable result is tyranny, drawn into the vacuum of moral chaos. If authority cannot be established among people by their shared assumptions, by their agreement about the meaning of life, then it will be imposed on them from the top. As William Penn said, "If we are not governed by God, we will be governed by tyrants."

When truth retreats, tyranny advances. ▓

M IT'S A
NATURAL

Monday

POLITICIANS TYPICALLY PRESENT THEIR own views as the mainstream, while painting their opponents as extremists. Call it the weirdo factor. If you can't undercut someone by rational argument, just make him look weird, out of the mainstream.

We saw that tactic at work in the debate over the nomination of Clarence Thomas to the Supreme Court. Judge Thomas believes in natural law—a belief that human laws must be measured against an objective standard of morality and justice. Opponents were quick to label Thomas's ideas weird. Harvard Professor Lawrence Tribe said that no Supreme Court nominee has held a natural law philosophy in fifty years.

But that's a wild exaggeration.

Natural law has been the dominant legal philosophy throughout Western civilization. Its roots reach back to the ancient Greeks and Romans—to Plato and Aristotle, Cicero and Seneca.

It was the dominant philosophy of law in the Middle Ages as well. The great theologian Thomas Aquinas related the secular concept of natural law to the biblical concept of divine law. Both refer to an objective standard against which human laws are measured.

The Reformers talked about natural law too. John Calvin wrote that God's law is "engraved upon the minds of men" through conscience and natural law. Our modern nations are based on the writings of men such as John Locke and Montesquieu, who offered their own theories of natural law.

Clearly, the idea of natural law has a long and venerable heritage in Western thought. It is hardly novel or unusual. And certainly not weird.

In fact, it is the only basis for human rights. Judge Thomas argued that minority rights depend upon the idea of natural law found in the Declaration of Independence. The Declaration talks about certain rights as unalienable—which means a just government can't take them away.

But rights are not unalienable unless they are based on something beyond the government. As Francis Schaeffer so eloquently put it, Where do unalienable rights come from? From the state? Then they are *not* unalienable. Because what the state gives the state can also take away.

That's why the Declaration of Independence says unalienable rights are endowed "by the Creator." The state doesn't *create* these rights; it merely *recognizes* them as pre-existing by divine creation.

For Jews, for blacks, for all of us, the only sure basis of civil rights is natural law. And there's nothing weird about that. ❦

THE NEW TRIBALISM

Tuesday

ALL ACROSS AFRICA HOPES FOR DEMOCRACY are being shot down by ethnic conflict.

In many emerging nations, violence-prone young males, who were formerly kept at bay by a strong central government, are being dressed in uniforms and formed into militias. It's like putting a spark to the tinder of ethnic hatred. The result is bloody tribal warfare from Burundi to Rwanda.

Christianity offers a unique perspective to understand what is happening in our world today. It all began two hundred years ago with the Enlightenment. Enlightenment philosophers thought they could have all the *benefits* of Christianity without *belief* in God. Without God they hoped for a single, universal truth—uniting everyone in a common vision of reality. Without God they believed in a universal human nature—uniting everyone as brothers and sisters. Without God they held to a universal morality—uniting everyone in bonds of mutual obligation.

But gradually it dawned on people that without God this was all nonsense. No mere human being can possess absolute truth. No mere human being can stand above history to gain a completely objective perspective.

In our own day, the secular ideal of universal truth has collapsed. So have the ideals of a common humanity and a common morality. Today the *modern* era, ushered in by the Enlightenment, has been replaced by the *post*modern era—where the catchword is not unity but diversity.

If there is no universal human nature, then each person finds identity not in our common humanity but as a member of a group. In Africa it's the tribe or ethnic group; in America it's the racial or gender group.

The conflict erupting across the globe is a graphic object lesson that you cannot have absolute truth apart from God. You cannot make universal truth claims unless you believe there is a God who stands above time and space, who has revealed truth from *His* objective perspective. ▨

SOAKING THE RICH

Wednesday

WHY DOES AMERICA NEED 70 PERCENT of the world's lawyers, when it has only 5 percent of the world's population? No wonder America is suffering from a litigation explosion. Lawsuits are even driving some businesses out of the country.

What's behind this staggering increase in lawsuits?

At its root is a change in the concept of law itself. The classical view is that law is based on unchanging principles of justice. The duty of a judge is to apply the law objectively, without being biased by personal feelings or preferences.

But in the 1920s and 1930s a new theory of law appeared: legal realism—so called because it claims to be more realistic than the classical view. The new theory says judges are just ordinary people. They can't help being influenced by their own concerns. They can't be completely objective.

So let's stop asking them to try, legal realism says. Let's stop talking about objective principles of justice and just admit that judges make decisions according to their own personal or political agendas. Law was redefined as social engineering by judges.

Legal realism took hold in the 1960s, when the judiciary turned to the left. Judges came to believe that the rich were rich because they oppressed the poor. They began treating lawsuits as a means of punishing the rich and redistributing wealth to the little guy.

This new theory is at work in many of today's far-fetched lawsuits. Take the case some years ago when angry unionists set fire to a large hotel in Puerto Rico. Lawyers for the victims of the fire didn't sue the individual arsonists. After all, they were union members; they represented the little guy. No, the lawyers went after the companies that made the carpets, the wallpaper, the bar stools—arguing that the companies should have made their products fire-resistant. They even sued the company that made the dice used in the hotel casino.

It was a classic case of using lawsuits to soak the rich.

In the Old Testament law, you won't find this bias against the rich. In Exodus 23:6, Scripture demands justice for the poor. But in the very same context, it warns us not to be *partial* to the poor either. This is the classical view of law—impartial justice for rich and poor alike.

If lawyers were to recover that view, our nation would not be overrun by lawyers whose hidden agenda is to change the social and economic structures of society. ❦

PUTTING THANKS BACK INTO THANKSGIVING

Thursday   THANKSGIVING

A POPULAR MOVIE OF 1989 WAS *Dead Poets' Society*, about a group of school boys who formed a secret society to celebrate American poets.

Well, Christians might do well to adapt their example and form a Dead *Pilgrims'* Society. Why? Because today's kids are being fed a half-baked version of Thanksgiving lore, complete with glazed facts, mashed multiculturalism, and a generous helping of censorship.

As a result, our children are consuming a dumbed-down version of Christian history. They're taught that the Pilgrims risked their lives traversing the ocean for economic gain, not religious freedom. And that first Thanksgiving feast? It's described as nothing more than a three-day binge with the Indians.

Take, for example, a book called *The First Thanksgiving* by Jean Craighead George. As this book tells it, the Pilgrims left Europe "to seek their fortune in the New World." That would have come as news to the Pilgrims themselves. Pilgrim leader William Bradford wrote in his diary that the voyage was motivated by "a great hope . . . for advancing the kingdom of Christ."

When it comes to Thanksgiving itself, in this book the religious dimension finds no place at the table. The author states flat-out, "This was *not* a day of Pilgrim thanksgiving"—thanksgiving to God, that is. Instead, she writes, "This was pure celebration."

Odd. That's not the way the Pilgrims themselves remembered it. Listen again to the account by William Bradford, who was there: "The Lord sent them such seasonable showers," Bradford writes, that "through his blessing [there was] a fruitful and liberal harvest. . . . For which mercy . . . they set apart a day of thanksgiving."

Why aren't we hearing *this* side of the Thanksgiving story?

These people sailed across the dangerous ocean without the benefit of a government grant. They built their own housing in freezing weather without the assistance of a public-works program. And when they fell sick, they didn't look to a government health program to take care of them. Even in the face of death, they nurtured a thankful spirit to God.

Christians need to read the books our children are getting and look for accurate versions of the Pilgrim story. If we can't find them, we may have to start writing our own books. 🔲

LOBBIES AND THE LAW

Friday

THE WHOLE POINT OF LOBBYING IS TO get special privileges for some group or industry. Some lobbyists are looking for handouts, like subsidies. Others lobby for tariffs or quotas to protect their industry from competition. And most government officials are happy to play along with the game. They use the law to dole out pork and privilege to selected groups in exchange for political support.

What a perverted view of law.

A biblical view of law is one that plays no favorites and shows no partiality. In Deuteronomy 16:19, God tells the ancient Israelites: "You shall not pervert justice; you shall not show partiality."

This biblical ideal is what undergirds the rule of law, where the law applies to everyone equally. James Madison wrote that the great aim of government is to be "neutral between different parts of the Society"—so that the law neither privileges nor penalizes any particular group.

To Westerners who have grown up with this ideal it may sound obvious. But, in other parts of the world it is far from obvious. In Communist countries law is a tool to advance the party. In tribal societies, laws are passed to advance the ruling tribe. There is no sense of law as something that stands above all parties, applying to everyone impartially.

What we're seeing in the United States today is a slide toward this pagan view of law. More and more laws are aimed at selected groups—doling out special privileges to those with the most powerful lobbyists. We desperately need to recover what the rule of law really means. ❦

TOO MANY RULES

Weekend

I F THE NUMBER OF FEDERAL REGULATIONS continues to mushroom, overregulation may actually undermine the classic principle of the rule of law. Strange though it may sound, *too many* laws can destroy the rule of law.

Economist Paul Craig Roberts explains: The number of federal regulations is already so large that businesses can't keep up with them. Sometimes the rules are even contradictory—so that compliance with regulation A puts a business *out of* compliance with regulation B.

The effect, says Roberts, is that businesses are being criminalized. They find it increasingly difficult to avoid committing white-collar crime, even without criminal intent. Many businesses would be vulnerable if ever targeted for close scrutiny by government prosecutors.

I'm reminded of a story told by a Polish man: The Communist authorities were obsessed with legality. To guarantee that they would always be able to pin some legal violation on any citizen at will, government officials passed so many laws and regulations that the average citizen couldn't possibly keep track of them all, let alone obey them. As a result, the Polish people knew they could always be charged with some violation, should authorities want to target them for any reason.

The rule of law can be destroyed in many ways. One way is anarchy—the destruction of *all* laws. Another is despotism—rule by the arbitrary decisions of a power elite. But another way is excessive regulation—the creation of so many laws that no one can possibly obey them all. The result is to criminalize every citizen, so that his fate rests on the whim of some government official. If Paul Craig Roberts is right, that is precisely what's happening to many of America's businesses.

The rule of law has biblical roots: Its source is the recognition that the ultimate standard of right and wrong is God's law, not the arbitrary decisions of government. If the rule of law in America is weakened, we will further erode America's biblical heritage.

And put all our freedoms in jeopardy. ▧

OUR ENTITLEMENT MENTALITY

Monday

A WILD EXPLOSION OF NEW RIGHTS IS causing a litigation explosion in America.

The classic conception of rights was simply the freedom to act according to conscience without interference. Take the Bill of Rights. Freedom of religion means Americans can worship without state interference. Freedom of speech means we can express our convictions without fear of a knock on the door.

But in the 1960s, a new concept of rights arose: a right to receive benefits from the government—like a job, medical treatment, a certain standard of living. Where once we spoke of government "aid" programs, we began speaking of "entitlement" programs. Suddenly, it wasn't just an act of compassion to help the poor, the sick, or the elderly. It was a *right* they were entitled to.

How does this fuel the fires of litigation?

Every right I claim imposes an obligation on someone else. If patients have a right to medical treatment, then doctors have an obligation to administer it. If criminals have a right to a lawyer, then the state has an obligation to supply one. If people have a right to financial security, then the government has an obligation to dole out welfare benefits. For each new right that is created, a whole network of laws and regulations is written to enforce the corresponding obligations. And if people feel that's not enough, they can resort to another form of government power—the courts. Private contracts, private conversations, the most intimate details of our lives have become fair game for scrutiny by the courts.

Notice the irony here. The old concept of rights was designed to *limit* state power—to define areas free from government interference. But the new concept of rights *expands* state power. It asks government to regulate all sorts of areas that were once private.

The result: A larger and larger portion of our lives is vulnerable to government control. The entitlement mentality is threatening the fundamental freedoms that were once the whole point of human rights.

What a sad irony: As Americans demand more and more rights, we enjoy fewer and fewer freedoms.

Christians should be calling their neighbors away from a selfish preoccupation with rights—reminding them that they also have responsibilities. It's the only way to save the fundamental freedoms that have made America a light to the world. ▨

KIDS
WHO KILL

Tuesday

THREE MILWAUKEE TEENAGERS WENT ON a robbing spree, but their crime soon escalated to murder. One of the teenagers—a girl named Lisa—pulled out a gun and shot a young girl, then ripped the coat off her body.

In court Lisa's lawyer pleaded insanity. The girl suffered from "urban psychosis," the lawyer said, a psychiatric disorder caused by living in a violent inner-city environment.

It was a novel legal defense, but a dubious one. Evidence showed that Lisa was fully sane and not at all psychotic at the time she committed the crime.

The good news is that the jury didn't buy the urban psychosis defense. The bad news is that other juries have. In one case, a man was charged in a stabbing death. His lawyer applied the urban-psychosis defense, arguing that the man had grown up in a violent family. The charges were reduced from first-degree murder to manslaughter.

This could be the beginning of a troubling trend. As columnist Charles Krauthammer argues, "these newfangled psychiatric syndromes are so elastic that one can always find some expert witness willing . . . to pin an extenuating diagnosis on just about anybody."

And if these "syndromes" are grounds for acquittal, where is justice? "If murder in the ghetto is a failure of stress management rather than a crime," writes Krauthammer, "we might as well give up policing" the inner city and just call in the psychiatrists.

What we're seeing here is the use of psychiatry to trivialize the law. No one can deny that it is traumatic growing up in the ghetto or in a violent home. But that does not excuse criminality.

The Bible teaches that we are morally accountable to God for everything we do. This is not a harsh teaching. Instead, it's a way of giving people hope—hope that they can overcome their backgrounds, no matter how bad; hope that God can give them better lives—that He can cure even newfangled syndromes like urban psychosis. ❧

POOR ENTREPRENEURS

Wednesday

ALFREDO SANTOS IS JUST TRYING TO MAKE an honest buck in the slums of Houston: He wants to drive a jitney. A jitney is a van service that generally runs in crime-ridden neighborhoods where taxis are too expensive and bus service is irregular.

But Santos is facing a tough opponent: his own city government. Houston officials are using an anti-jitney ordinance, passed over half a century ago, to shut down Santos' small business. It's a striking example of the way government regulation can actually hurt the enterprising poor who are trying to pull themselves out of poverty.

This case is being pursued through the courts by the Washington-based Institute for Justice. Its goal is to crack open the doors for poor entrepreneurs whose efforts are being blocked by excessive government regulation.

How ironic that some of the biggest barriers faced by poor entrepreneurs are erected by the government itself. And not only ironic but wrong. In *Poverty and Prosperity*, Cal Beisner argues that excessive regulation violates the eighth commandment: Thou shalt not steal.

The eighth commandment protects property rights—people's right to use their own property for lawful ends. A person's energy and skill are part of his property: his "human capital," as economists say. Laws that restrict the lawful use of that property, Beisner says, are a violation of property rights.

You and I ought to remind our political leaders that economic growth doesn't depend on government programs. Real job creation springs from the entrepreneurial spirit—the urge to create and work—which is part of the image of God. 🔳

MARKETS AND MORALS

Thursday

M ICHAEL NOVAK, RECIPIENT OF THE 1994 Templeton Prize for Progress in Religion, has reconnected markets and morals.

This is a revolutionary accomplishment. Since the last century, it was Communism that claimed to have a moral vision for a just society. Even though actual Communist regimes are always tyrannical, the moral vision of Communism has continued to attract idealists around the world.

Capitalism, on the other hand, has been regarded as a purely pragmatic system. Even Adam Smith, capitalism's founder, did not present it as a means of creating a just society. Instead, he presented it as a practical means of controlling self-interest—of providing a socially useful channel for an anti-social impulse. Hardly a stirring vision to engage the hearts of social reformers.

But Michael Novak has articulated the moral basis of capitalism. A free market expresses a high view of human dignity, Novak argues, because it requires individuals to be creative and responsible. It does not set apparatchiks over everyone telling them what to do.

A free market requires self-sacrifice and delayed gratification, as entrepreneurs invest their time and money into enterprises whose rewards are not immediate.

A free market requires sensitivity and courtesy to others, because if you don't please the customer you're out of business.

Most of all, free markets are an effective tool for helping the poor. Historically, free economies have the best record of empowering the poor to climb out of poverty.

Despite all this, Western intellectual leaders in academia, journalism, and the arts are heavily left-leaning. To be sure, they've been forced to concede that capitalism works better on a *practical* level—that it produces more consumer goods. Yet they still maintain that socialism is superior in its *moral* vision for a just society.

This is why we need to continually defend the moral basis of free-market capitalism. As Michael Novak so brilliantly demonstrates, capitalism rests inescapably on the high view of human creativity and responsibility expressed in the Bible. ▨

FREEDOM
UNDER LAW

Friday

C LASSIC FREE MARKET THEORY IS BUILT on the premise that every institution in society has its own unique role and function. Abraham Kuyper, a Dutch statesman and Christian leader at the turn of the century, argued that societies enjoy the most freedom when each sphere fulfills its own function, without trying to take over the functions of others—when economy and state, church and family, each pursues the role assigned it by God.

The economy is the arena where people exchange goods and services to their mutual benefit. The government, on the other hand, bears the power of the sword. Its role is to protect citizens from crime and lawlessness.

And that includes crime in the marketplace. For example, in the economic realm, government ought to enforce laws against fraud and theft, laws regarding contracts, laws against false advertising and false labeling. Government should also protect society from harmful economic activities: It should prohibit prostitution, pornography, and the recreational use of drugs.

All around the globe, people are turning away from government-controlled economies and seeking to emulate the free market economies of the West. But a free market doesn't mean citizens are free to live by the law of the jungle. It's where the government leaves economic matters to private citizens but vigorously enforces the law.

Freedom thrives only where it is protected by law. ▨

THE BEST
POLICY

Weekend

THOUSANDS OF MILES OF FLORIDA HIGHWAYS have gone dark. The white stripes that are supposed to reflect light aren't doing the job. After months of investigation, state officials have finally uncovered the culprit: business fraud.

In an underhanded scheme to save money, the company that supplied the paint left out an expensive chemical ingredient that makes the stripes glow in the dark. Now the state will have to tear up the stripes and replace them—at taxpayers' expense.

The moral of the story is that economic questions cannot be considered in economic terms alone. An economy is not just a matter of dollars and cents and GNP. Our economy depends on the kind of people we are. And that, in turn, is shaped by our beliefs and values—what we call "culture."

As Cal Beisner argues in *Prosperity and Poverty*, "Culture . . . is the most powerful influence on economic productivity." And "religion," he adds, "is the most powerful influence on culture."

Religion is the major reason the West rose to become the most prosperous civilization in the world. In the Middle Ages, Europe was like a modern Third World country, with little education, widespread poverty, and recurring famine. Medieval Christians thought of holy living as something required only of a spiritual elite—just as the Bible belonged only to an elite, the priests and monks. The common people felt little moral imperative to be honest or industrious.

But the Reformation changed that. The Reformers taught that *all* believers are called to live holy lives—just as all may read the Bible. Every vocation can be a calling, a way to serve God and the human community. As a result, the Reformation stressed an ethic of honesty, diligence, and thrift—what has been called the Protestant work ethic. It had a profound effect economically. Modern business practices became possible, prosperity blossomed.

Today we have nearly forgotten that the foundation of our economy lies in the Christian moral vision. And as a result, we are seeing our economy dragged down by dishonesty and fraud.

Churches across America need to revive the moral teaching of the Reformation. Christian discipleship requires it—and our nation's economy desperately needs it. ※

MIDDLE-CLASS WELFARE

Monday

W HENEVER A POLITICIAN TALKS ABOUT cutting government programs, there's a hue and cry about abandoning the poor.
But did you know that only *two percent* of federal spending goes
to the poor? The rest goes to programs for the middle and upper
classes.

Hard to believe? Consider: Who benefits most from farm
subsidies, Amtrak, and student loans? The middle class. Who
benefits most from art subsidies and public broadcasting? The
middle class. Who benefits most from Social Security, Medicare,
and civil service pensions?

Right. The middle class.

Back when entitlement programs were started, the goal was
to provide a safety net for the needy. But in the 1960s, the Great
Society fostered a new philosophy treating government benefits
as a universal right. Today 80 percent of entitlement programs go
not to the poor but to the middle and upper classes.

The irony is that no one is actually helped by all this. It's all
a game of smoke and mirrors. Think about it: When entitlements
go to the middle class, who foots the bill? There aren't remotely
enough *rich* people to subsidize the middle class. So the bill for
the middle class is paid by . . . the middle class.

It's all a grand illusion. The government picks one man's
pocket and offers it to the next man—while picking *his* pocket for
the next man. And we all enjoy the illusion that the government
is giving us something for free.

The ethical label for this is covetousness, pure and simple.
We're being encouraged to think it's OK to plunder our neighbors
for government benefits.

The whole arrangement is not only wrong but inefficient—
because government *doesn't* just hand the money on to the next
guy. First it takes out a good chunk to pay for its own huge bureaucracy. That means we would save a lot of money if we paid

directly for programs we want, instead of channeling that money through the government.

Politicians are afraid to cut middle-class benefits, and that means it's up to us to decide this is an unethical and inefficient way to run a government.

You and I have to stop demanding something for nothing. ✦

WHEN THE SYSTEM IS SICK

Tuesday

H ANS, A FORMER PHYSICS PROFESSOR in Holland, quit work three years ago. "I was suffering from stress because I was so worried about obtaining research money," Hans says. Well, he isn't worried about money any more: His disability pay is guaranteed until retirement. What's really suffering is the Dutch economy—groaning under the burden of ballooning social welfare programs.

And Holland isn't the only country in trouble. Many European nations are discovering that ample benefit programs can undermine the motivation to work. Disability benefits are easily obtained by vague and subjective complaints, like "stress." There's virtually no penalty for dropping out of the work force. The penalty falls chiefly on those who *stay* in the work force—and pay for all these benefits.

Companies also have to pay out of payroll taxes, which sometimes adds as much as 50 percent to the cost of hiring a new worker. As a result, companies are unable to expand and grow.

No wonder Europe is suffering economic stagnation.

It doesn't take a crystal ball to foresee disaster coming, and many countries are finally setting limits to social benefits. Holland has tightened the rules governing disability benefits. France shortened the length of unemployment benefits. Italy has placed limits on free medical care for people with higher incomes.

Economic well-being starts with the fundamental principle of hard work for all who are able-bodied. The apostle Paul wrote, "He who will not work, neither shall he eat." But a burgeoning welfare state undercuts the biblical rule: It says in effect, "He who will not work can live off the income of those who do."

A policy like this will always backfire: It punishes the diligent and rewards the lazy—those who succumb to vague ailments like "stress."

The Bible outlines the moral principles that undergird a strong economy: diligence, thrift, and hard work—with charity limited to the truly needy. Any government whose policies undermine moral character will surely end in economic ruin.

ETHICS AND THE ECONOMY

Wednesday

THE EDITOR OF A SMALL-TOWN NEWSPAPER wrote, "Family values are important, . . . but people want to hear about the economy right now."

It was a nice way of saying what other commentators say a lot *less* nicely. The major media sneers at the values issue, calling it a smoke screen to take people's mind off the "real" problem: namely the economy.

Okay, let's talk about the economy. What are the factors that make for a thriving economy? Well, for starters people have to be willing to work hard; that's motivation and self-sacrifice. They have to be willing to honor contracts; that's honesty and fidelity. They have to invest time and effort in projects that pay off only in the future; that's self-discipline and delayed gratification. People have to cooperate with coworkers; that's kindness and respect. Lawmakers have to pass bills for industry that are fair and consistent; that's integrity.

The conclusion is obvious. The marketplace depends on people holding high ethical standards. Values aren't peripheral to the economy. They are its very basis.

Columnist Ben Wattenberg puts it this way. Suppose you had a choice of giving your child a gift of $100,000 or instead instilling values like discipline and hard work.

Which one would you choose?

The answer is obvious. A child without self-discipline will soon squander the $100,000. But a child with good values will work diligently and succeed at virtually anything he puts his hand to.

So don't let the pundits tell you values are irrelevant to the economy. The truth is precisely the opposite.

Values are at the very *heart* of the economy. ※

TOO MANY KIDS?

Thursday

DOES RELIGION CAUSE POVERTY? To hear the critics talk, you might think so.

Washington Post columnist Judy Mann wrote that the homeless children dying in Third World countries are the result of the church's "unthinking pro-family polices." Syndicated columnist Georgie Anne Geyer warned darkly that church teachings could "lead to the death of us all."

The premise here is that the more children a nation has, the poorer it will be. But if you look around the globe, the pattern is precisely the opposite. Most rich countries have high population densities: Hong Kong, Singapore, the Netherlands. Famine and poverty are much more common in sparsely populated countries, like Somalia, Ethiopia, Sudan.

The population scare-mongers are operating on a faulty philosophy. They see every child as a mouth to feed—nothing more. In their thinking, every time a child is born, we all end up with a smaller slice of the pie.

But this is incredibly short-sighted. As children grow older they don't just *eat* pies, they can bake *new* ones. They can add to society's pool of labor and creativity. And it is human creativity that determines whether a nation is rich or poor.

Human capital comes up with better ways to grow food—so that today only 3 percent of the American work force grows enough food for the entire nation. Human capital develops new ways to locate natural resources. Since 1950 the known reserves of iron have increased more than 1,000 percent, as we develop better ways to locate and extract it. Human capital finds new ways to be productive with old resources. For example, the silicon in a computer chip is made from ordinary sand.

The real cause of poverty is not people but sin and oppression. The number one cause of hunger in the world today is war, followed closely by political corruption and centralized economic control.

Political leaders don't want to admit that their own misguided policies are holding people down. So they scapegoat families for having more children than the prescribed number. They chastise the church for welcoming children as gifts of God. They call on government to seize control of the economy.

Leaders who respond this way don't seem to realize that what they're doing will only *suppress* human creativity—in the end creating more poverty, and bringing what they fear down on their heads. ▨

THE GREATEST RESOURCE

Friday

A NEW ENERGY CRISIS?" ASKS *Nation's Business*. Is cheap oil "lulling the public into a false sense of security?" asks *National Journal*. Yes, we still hear echoes of the energy crisis of the 1970s.

But are we really facing a resource crisis?

What the doomsayers ignore is that there are two sides to every resource: the physical material itself and the human ability to make use of it—the natural resource and the human resource. In fact, human technology defines what materials qualify as a resource to begin with.

Take oil as an example. Before we had the technology to use it, oil wasn't even considered a resource. If you discovered oil on your land, you threw up your hands in despair.

Perfectly good farm land—ruined.

Then technologies were developed that use oil. And suddenly it became a valuable resource. Black gold, it was called. Discover it on your land, and you throw up your hands in joy.

You've struck it rich!

Of course, the day may come when we do run out of oil. But as that day approaches we will develop alternatives. Our stoves used to burn wood; they now run on gas or electricity.

We used to make things from wood or metal that today we make from plastic.

What all this illustrates is the seminal role of human creativity in the debate over resources. Modern technology isn't limited by the starting materials, it's limited only by what human creativity can make of them. That's what we should expect. After all, we were made in the image of a creative God.

Consider the silicon in a computer chip. It comes from ordinary sand. What makes the chip so fantastically complex is the amount of human engineering and design that goes into it.

And consider all the natural resources that are *saved* by computer technology. A fraction of an ounce of sand in a computer chip holds as much information as a library of books using tons of paper and ink. It performs the work once done by thousands of calculating machines made of tons of metal, using hundreds of reams of paper.

No, the doomsayers notwithstanding, we are not running out of resources.

We are just *beginning* to tap the greatest resource of all: the human mind, made in the image of God. ❧

Weekend

MAKING GOOD TABLES

AMERICA'S WORK ETHIC CAN ONLY be restored by the church. All the characteristics we associate with the work ethic—dedication, excellence, thrift, pride in what we do—find their deepest roots in Scripture and through the centuries have been defined and articulated by the church.

The post-Reformation church believed that one of its primary tasks was to help new converts discover their vocation; that is, to understand how the individual was to use his or her gifts to serve God in the world. Industriousness was an act of obedience. "Make all you can, save all you can, and give away all you can," was John Wesley's credo.

Today the call to recover the traditional virtues of the work ethic should ring forth from our pulpits. But the church, like the culture at large, needs to be re-educated in those virtues. How often have you heard a sermon on the work ethic or on productivity? Or for that matter on the virtues of hard work, thrift, and respect for property? Why aren't churches teaching vocation as an integral part of life?

"In nothing has the church so lost her hold on reality as in her failure to understand and respect the secular vocation," wrote Dorothy Sayers. How would anyone remain interested in a religion "which seems to have no concern with nine tenths of his life," she wondered.

It is all very well to tell a carpenter to stop getting drunk and to come to church, Sayers continued; but we also need to teach him that his vocation as a believer is to make good tables—to the glory of God.

CARPENTERS AND FISHERMEN

Monday

CHRISTIANITY BEGAN AS A WORKING man's faith. As a carpenter in Nazareth, Jesus worked with His hands. The followers He drew were working people who rose before dawn to drag smelly fishing nets through the water of Galilee to earn a living.

The early Christians were working-class folks who, raised in the Judaic tradition, abhorred idleness and made work a requirement of the early church. The apostle Paul, a rabbinical scholar, paid his own way by making tents. He wrote, "If a man will not work, he shall not eat" (2 Thess. 3:10). And those who did work were to share the results of their labor with the needy.

The early Christians did not share the ancient Greeks' two-story distinction between mental and physical work. Plato and Aristotle advocated that the majority of men should do the heavy lifting so that the minority, like themselves, might engage in higher pursuits such as art, philosophy, and politics.

But as historian Kenneth Scott Latourette notes, "Christianity undercut slavery by giving dignity to work, no matter how seemingly menial that might be. Traditionally, labor which might be performed by slaves was despised as degrading to the freeman. But Christian teachers said that all should work and that labor should be done as to God and in the sight of God. Work became a Christian duty."

When the barbarian hordes overran Western civilization, this high view of work was preserved in the monastic communities to which Christianity retreated. Carrying out the commandment to work, the industrious monks built enclaves of industry, learning, scholarship, and beauty. They drained the swamps, built bridges and roads, and invented labor-saving devices. They copied the sacred writings, produced works of art in illuminated manuscripts, and kept faith and scholarship alive. In each of these pursuits they heeded Augustine's exhortation that *laborare est orare*, "to work is to pray."

PREACHING AND
WASHING DISHES

Tuesday

URING THE MIDDLE AGES, THE CHURCH absorbed the Greek dualism that pronounced spiritual and intellectual work superior. Monastic orders divided themselves into lay brothers, who did manual labor, and those who pursued the higher or intellectual tasks.

Then one man, Martin Luther, shook the ethos of the Middle Ages to its very foundations. Most make the mistake of seeing the Reformation strictly in theological terms. But equally profound have been the consequences in the political, social, and economic realms.

The Reformation struck at the dualistic view of work. Just as they saw the church comprised of all the people of God, not just the clergy, so the Reformers saw all work—sacred and secular, intellectual and manual—as a way of serving God.

The work of monks and priests, wrote Luther, "in God's sight are in no way whatever superior to the works of a farmer laboring in the field, or of a woman looking after her home." The view that scrubbing floors held as much dignity as occupying the pulpit democratized the work ethic.

The Reformers encouraged people to abandon the isolation of the cloisters and enter the world of work. What mattered was that each individual understood his or her calling or vocation; in that way they collaborated with God in the grand design of the universe, working for His glory, the common good, and their own fulfillment.

The notion that people should abandon inherited trades and do whatever would maximize their worth to God served to further break down the caste divisions in both the church and society.

The feudal establishment was not amused by these radical doctrines, which spread across Europe. In fact, one of the charges of heresy against English Reformer William Tyndale was that he taught: "If we look externally, there is a difference betwixt the washing of dishes and preaching the Word of God; but as touching to please God, in relation to His call, none at all." Such teachings freed people to do what they did best for God's glory, and a new breed of workers was born.

AMERICA AT WORK

Wednesday

THE MOST PRECIOUS CARGO CARRIED by the Puritans and Quakers who set sail for the New World seeking religious freedom and economic opportunity was their view of work. They came to demonstrate, as William Penn wrote, "What sobriety and industry can do in a wilderness against heat, cold, wants, and dangers."

Contrary to what is often supposed, the Puritans did not regard wealth as a badge of piety. Instead they viewed work as stewardship to God, which made their primary reward spiritual and moral. As Puritan Richard Baxter wrote, "Choose not that [employment] in which you may be most rich or honorable in the world, but that in which you may do most good, and best escape sinning."

This moral understanding of work produced a thriving society—and America became the economic wonder of the world.

But the work ethic inevitably became secularized. The factories of the industrial revolution reduced labor to monotony and repetition, and work lost much of its spiritual significance. But the habits that the work ethic had bred continued: thrift, industry, charity, investment. Labor was still considered worthy; people continued to take pride in their work.

Until, that is, the 1960s. Suddenly a revolution swept America's campuses: God was dead and pleasure was the only purpose in life. This new philosophy profoundly affected our national values, including our view of work. We see the results today: a society where workers work as little as possible, producing second-rate products and looking for any way possible to "get theirs" without giving too much in return.

What will make America work? Nothing less than regaining the robust faith that the Puritans brought to our shores, which produced a commitment to work to God's glory.

Thursday

AMERICA'S CLASS CONFLICT

A MERICA IS BEING TORN BETWEEN TWO basic world views. Soci-ologists call it a class war, but it's a class war of a new kind. Traditional classes were based on economics—the land-owners versus the peasants, or the factory-owners versus the proletariat. But the conflict dividing America today is world views.

On one side is the middle class, which once supplied most of our nation's leaders and officeholders, and shaped America's values. Historically, those values were Christian, emphasizing sac-rifice, responsibility, and moral restraint.

On the other side is what sociologists call the "New Class." In the early part of this century, America's elites began to develop a distinct worldview. It was secular and liberal; it celebrated an ethic of individualism, self-gratification, and rebellion against authority. In the 1960s the elite outlook spread to a large segment of middle-class youth. They broke off from their middle-class roots and formed the New Class.

The New Class is America's intelligentsia. They don't trade in goods and services but in words and ideas. They're the journalists on television news networks. They're the educators who write school curricula. They're the lawyers who work for social causes. They're the public-policy analysts who shape government policy.

Newsweek calls them the nation's "brain workers."

The first empirical studies of the New Class were conducted by Robert and Linda Lichter and Stanley Rothman for their book, *The Media Elite*. Their study found that most leading television journalists and news anchors label themselves politically liberal: 90 percent are pro-choice; 75 percent believe homosexuality is morally acceptable, and only 8 percent attend religious services regularly.

For their next book, *Watching America*, Lichter and Rothman turned to Hollywood and interviewed the writers and producers of prime-time entertainment. They discovered a remarkable sameness in outlook: 75 percent place themselves on the left politi-cally; 97 percent are pro-choice; 80 percent believe homosexuality is morally acceptable; only 7 percent attend any sort of religious service regularly. The same values are held by the New Class everywhere, whether they work in the media, the schools, or the government.

Underlying the political conflicts that blare from the headlines is a deeper conflict: the traditional, middle-class worldview, with its ethic of responsibility and restraint, versus the New Class worldview, exalting individual gratification. ▓

A MOUNTAIN
OF SAND

Friday

DURING WORLD WAR II, IN A HUNGARIAN concentration camp, Jewish prisoners were forced to work producing fuel for the Nazi war machines. One day the prisoners were given a strange task. They were commanded to move a pile of sand from one end of the compound to the other. The next day, they were ordered to move it back again.

Day after day they hauled the mountain of sand back and forth across the compound.

After several weeks of this meaningless drudgery, one old man began sobbing uncontrollably. Another screamed until his captors beat him into silence. A young man threw himself against an electrified fence. There was a blinding flash, followed by the smell of smoldering flesh.

It turns out that the commandant of the camp had ordered this monstrous activity as "an experiment in mental health," to see what would happen when people are given meaningless work. Well, he found out, all right. The prisoners had survived years of back-breaking toil when they at least saw some purpose in it. But given work with no purpose, dozens went mad or electrocuted themselves against the fence.

People need meaningful and creative work in order to be whole. Human beings were made in the image of the God who created the heavens and the earth. When we work, we express God's image in us. ▓

BUILDING
CATHEDRALS

Weekend

T HE STORY IS TOLD OF A MAN WHO visited a stone quarry and asked three of the workers what they were doing.

"Can't you see?" said the first one irritably. "I'm cutting a stone."

The second replied, "I'm earning a hundred pounds a week."

But the third put down his pick and thrust out his chest proudly. "I'm building a cathedral," he said.

People view work in many ways: as a necessary evil to keep bread on the table; as a means to a sizable bank account; as self-fulfillment and identity; as an economic obligation within society; as a means to a life of leisure.

Yet none of these represents an adequate view of work that provides ongoing or complete satisfaction for our labors. We are more than material beings, more than social beings, and more than cogs in the machinery of work.

We are, above all, spiritual beings, and as such we need to rediscover the moral and spiritual significance for every area and aspect of our lives, including our work.

Whether we are digging ditches, managing a bank, or cleaning houses, the important thing to remember is that we are building a cathedral. 🔲

EUPHEMISTICALLY SPEAKING

Monday

W HEN GENERAL MOTORS CLOSED ONE of its plants, the company called it a "volume-related production schedule adjustment." It didn't mention all the people who were adjusted right *out* of the production schedule.

When Chrysler closed a plant, it announced that it was initiating "a career alternative enhancement program." Bet those workers out pounding the pavements were grateful for the opportunity to enhance their career alternatives.

What we're seeing here is a rash of euphemisms—misleading verbiage designed to paper over life's harsher realities.

Educators are some of the worst offenders. Students don't fail anymore. They "achieve a deficiency"—which sounds like something to be proud of. Tests are called "evaluation instruments." And they're not used to find out whether students can read but whether they can "construct meaning from the text."

Supporters of Prison Fellowship will be interested to learn that solitary confinement is now called "involuntary administrative segregation." And some states have renamed Death Row the "capital sentences unit." Sounds so much more benign, doesn't it?

The Department of Defense is another fertile source of euphemisms. Today's soldiers are never surrounded or ambushed. Instead, they "engage the enemy on all sides." They're never outnumbered either. They simply "operate in a target-rich environment."

At some hospitals patients don't die, they just experience a "negative patient-care outcome." And governments don't raise taxes, they "enhance revenues." I wonder if Benjamin Franklin's proverbs would be remembered today if he had said "There's nothing certain in life but negative patient-care outcomes and revenue enhancement."

The examples I've listed are all genuine, documented in *The Quarterly Review of Doublespeak*. Some are just silly, but the overall trend reveals something profoundly disturbing. People invent euphemisms when there's something they don't want to face: a risk or a responsibility or a painful experience. The explosion of euphemisms in our language today indicates an unwillingness to be honest and straightforward.

We refuse to face reality.

And so we clutter up our language with post-consumer secondary materials—excuse me, I mean with garbage. And hope in that way to hide the negative net worth—I mean the bankruptcy—of our ideas. 🐚

DIVERSITY
FOR DOLLARS

Tuesday

DIVERSITY CONSULTANTS COMMAND huge fees by promising to enhance sensitivity in the workplace. But the workshops themselves are often highly confrontational, encouraging people to dredge up stereotypes and air their gripes against one another.

One reporter dubs them "blame and shame" sessions.

The outcome is often the opposite from what is intended: Instead of eliminating group prejudice, these sessions often spark interoffice politicking by race and gender. Diversity trainers often encourage women and minorities to blame all their workplace woes on a white male corporate culture. For example, if you're not advancing as fast as you think you should, trainers say it's because performance standards are biased to favor white males.

Some diversity experts even recommend tossing out standard business qualifications, like basic literacy and math skills. They insist that people who lack these skills are not *under*qualified; they're just "*differently* qualified."

This is "sensitivity" to the point of insanity.

A Christian CEO in Seattle has a better way of dealing with minorities who lack traditional business skills. He works through his church to teach English to newly arrived immigrants from around the world. The church helps them enroll in job-training programs, and the CEO helps them find work.

This is diversity training that doesn't look for a scapegoat; it treats everyone with dignity. It's an approach that doesn't set groups against each other; instead it sets them helping one another. It's an approach that refuses to patronize people by lowering standards for them; instead it lifts them up to the high standards America requires to stay competitive.

Most of all, it shows that Christians don't have to copy the culture in its diversity fad; instead we can create something better. Christians have a real basis for treating all people with dignity because we all came from the hand of a loving God. ▓

LET US ADORE HIM

Wednesday   CHRISTMAS

THIS MONTH, AS AMERICANS BUSTLE to shopping centers and holiday parties, the strains of a familiar hymn fill the air. "O come let us adore Him," we sing heartily, "Christ the Lord."

But do we realize what we're singing? Or are the words so familiar they've lost their real meaning?

"Jesus is Lord." This confession is one of the oldest Christian creeds. By it, New Testament believers submitted themselves to Christ and proclaimed Him ruler of the world. And in doing so they put their lives on the line, the earthly "lords" of their day being anxious to feed them to the lions.

Down through the centuries, the Christian assertion by word and deed that Christ is Lord has been the chief cause of hostility to the gospel. Today a secular society seeks to neutralize Christianity by reducing it to a private affair.

The greatest challenge facing the church today is to reassert the lordship of Christ. The Scriptures make clear the totality of Christ's claims upon us: "If anyone would come after me, he must deny himself and take up his cross and follow" (Matt. 16:24). Paul describes Jesus as the "only sovereign, the King of kings and Lord of lords." The Word tells us that Jesus became God incarnate—the One before whom all peoples must one day stand for judgment and whose lordship every tongue will confess.

If we really understand what being Christian means—that this Christ, the living God, actually comes in to rule one's life—then everything must change: Values, goals, desires, habits. If

Christ's lordship does not disrupt our own lordship, then we must question the reality of our conversion. ▨

THE REINDEER RULE

Thursday   CHRISTMAS

CHRISTMAS IS COMING, AND FOR towns and municipalities across the nation 'tis the season to be worried—worried about lawsuits, that is.

One year local officials in Vienna, Virginia, were so worried that they banned religious carols at their annual Christmas celebration. "Frosty the Snowman" and "Jingle Bells" were permissible, but not "Joy to the World."

What made officials so skittish is that the previous year Vienna had been the target of a lawsuit by the American Civil Liberties Union (ACLU) for allowing a local group to set up a Nativity scene in front of a community center. The town was careful to add plastic reindeers, Santas, and snowmen, in accord with a 1985 Supreme Court ruling known as the "reindeer rule," which requires any religious display on public property to be balanced by secular displays.

But the careful balancing act was all for naught. The ACLU charged that, in spite of the Santas and reindeer, the crèche was still the primary focus of the display and hence violated the separation of church and state. Now, the Supreme Court hadn't said anything about primary focuses, but no matter. A federal judge sided with the ACLU, and the crèche was taken down.

The following year, the controversy in Vienna was about Christmas carols. At the advice of nervous lawyers, city officials banned all religious songs at the annual town celebration.

On the day of the festivities, two hundred people massed in the parking lot across the street to hold a counter-celebration. They erected a creche and sang religious carols. A few protesters brought banners. One read: "A baby in a manger or a fat guy in a red suit? The choice is yours."

I will never forget the pathos of the image on the evening news. The protesters were huddled behind barricades—carefully keeping their feet off public property—praying and singing their carols. Instead of Christmas joy, the atmosphere was one of confrontation and protest.

Have we really come to this? Here in the shadow of the nation's capitol, Christians are having to fight for the right to sing traditional religious carols. If we don't speak out against the secularization of society—if we stand by quietly while the ACLU takes away our rights one by one—then America will lose what our forefathers called the First Liberty: the freedom of religion.

And then the message on the banners in Vienna will no longer apply. Instead of being able to choose the baby in a manger, we will be left with only a fat man in a red suit. ❧

SEEING MOM FOR CHRISTMAS

Friday   CHRISTMAS

"WHAT DID *YOU* GET FOR CHRISTMAS?" Ida asked. Ida was an elementary school teacher and she was following the tradition of teachers everywhere, asking her pupils about their Christmas vacation.

Each child stood up and rattled off a list of toys and gifts. But one little girl stood up, her chin quivering, and whispered, "I didn't get anything this year. But we went to Tutweiler to see my Mama."

Tutweiler—it was the name of a women's prison in the area. Suddenly Ida realized how cruel the classroom activity was that exposed this little girl to such humiliation. How could she undo the damage she had done?

Ida decided she would participate in Angel Tree®. Sponsored by Prison Fellowship, Angel Tree mobilizes volunteers to distribute Christmas gifts to children on behalf of a parent behind bars. Churches and other Christian groups in all fifty states participate. No child should ever have to say, *I didn't get anything for Christmas because my mom or my dad is in prison.*

Angel Tree can even be a factor in diverting a child from a life of crime. Studies have shown that "children of inmates are more likely to land in prison than the general population," says Mark Morgan, national Angel Tree coordinator. But Angel Tree—

especially when church contacts with children are maintained year-round—provides a positive experience that can help reduce the likelihood that children of inmates will follow in their parents' footsteps.

Angel Tree is a way to care for "the least of these" victims of crime. For Christmas—and for the whole year. 🕸

CHRISTMAS
IN JAIL

Weekend   CHRISTMAS

B ESSIE SHIPP WAS SPENDING CHRISTMAS in jail. She had not been sentenced to death by the state, but she was under a different death sentence: Bessie had AIDS.

I met Bessie when I came to give a Christmas message to the inmates. After the service, we walked down a narrow corridor, and a heavy door was opened to reveal a small, dark cell. There sat Bessie Shipp, wrapped in a bathrobe, shivering in the cold, with an open Bible on her lap.

After chatting a few minutes, I came right to the point. "Bessie," I said. "Do you know the Lord?" "I want to," she replied softly. "But I don't always feel like He's there." Her voice trailed off.

"Would you like to pray with me to know Christ as your Savior?" I asked. Bessie looked down, twisted a Kleenex in her thin hands, and finally whispered, "Yes, I would."

So we prayed together in that cold, concrete cell. And Bessie made a decision that would change the rest of her short life: She gave it to Jesus Christ.

Going home as a new Christian, Bessie was immediately drawn into a church and a Bible study where her new-found faith could be nurtured. Just three weeks after her release, Bessie contracted pneumonia and had to be hospitalized. A Prison Fellowship area director visited her and found her spirit strong to the end. "These are the happiest days of my life," she whispered. "I know Jesus loves me, and that you do too."

Two days later Bessie died. She went to meet the Savior she had accepted only a short time before, on Christmas Day, in a cold prison cell.

When Jesus came to earth, He wasn't born in a grand palace. He was born in a dirty stable that reeked of animals, with mice scurrying underfoot. And He still comes to us wherever we are. Not only to warm, well-lit homes, but also to run-down tenement buildings and gray prison cells. ▩

A BABY VERSUS THE WORLD

Monday   CHRISTMAS

A CHRISTMAS MESSAGE CAME TO MY mind as I stood shivering in the autumn chill at the side of a grave—the grave of Father Jerzy Popieluszko. Jerzy was a young pastor who once delivered the dynamic messages that stirred the Polish people to overthrow their Communist oppressors. His theme was always the same: The Christian is called to overcome evil with good.

It was a passion that dominated Jerzy's own life as well. In 1980 martial law was declared in Poland. Tanks and troops clogged the streets until the entire country was one vast prison. Jerzy hated the occupation as much as his countrymen, but he fought it using God's weapons—overcoming evil with good. On Christmas Eve Jerzy slogged through the snow handing out Christmas cookies to soldiers in the streets.

Even in his death, Jerzy was victorious. In 1984 he was kidnapped by the secret police. The nation was electrified. In churches across Poland, people gathered to pray. Steelworkers demanded his release, threatening a national strike. Fifty thousand people gathered to hear a tape of his final sermon.

Then the blow fell: Jerzy's body had been found in the river. He had been brutally tortured, his eyes and tongue cut out, his bones smashed. Yet the gentle pastor had taught his people well: After his funeral, hundreds of thousands of Polish people marched through the streets of Warsaw—right past secret police headquarters—carrying banners reading, "We forgive."

They were assaulting evil with good. And under the impact, the Communist regime crumbled.

The message Jerzy preached has always been God's strategy for overcoming evil. The supreme example is the Incarnation itself—when God Himself entered human history to overcome the evil of sin.

America is not in the grip of a Communist regime as Poland was, yet Christians *are* battling a hostile secular culture. And we often wonder how we can fight more effectively. The answer is that God's people are to fight evil using God's strategy and weapons.

When God wanted to defeat sin, His ultimate weapon was the sacrifice of His own Son. On Christmas Day two thousand years ago, the birth of a tiny baby in an obscure village in the Middle East was God's supreme triumph of good over evil. ☒

A CANDLE IN THE DARKNESS

Tuesday

CHRISTMAS

WHEN LASZLO TOKES BECAME PASTOR of Timisoara's small Hungarian Reformed Church, he preached the gospel boldly, and within two years membership had swelled to five thousand.

But success can be dangerous in a Communist country. Authorities stationed police officers in front of the church on Sundays, cradling machine guns. They hired thugs to attack Pastor Tokes. They confiscated his ration book so he couldn't buy food or fuel. Finally, in December 1989, they decided to send him into exile.

But when police arrived to hustle Pastor Tokes away, they were stopped cold. Around the entrance to the church stood a wall of humanity. Members of other churches—Baptist, Adventist, Pentecostal, Orthodox, Catholic—had joined together to protest.

Though police tried to disperse the crowd, the people held their posts all day and into the night. Then, just after midnight, a young man pulled out a packet of candles. He lit one and passed it to his neighbor. Then he lit another. One by one the burning candles were passed out among the crowd. Soon the darkness of the December night was pierced by the light of hundreds of candles.

When Tokes peered out the window, he was struck by the warm glow reflecting off hundreds of faces. That moment, he said later, was the "turning point in my life." His religious prejudices evaporated. Here were members of the body of Christ, completely disregarding denominational divisions, joining hands in his defense.

What a powerful image for us as we celebrate Christmas this year in the United States—the picture of a black December night when the darkness was lit up by a glowing testimony to Christian unity. 🕮

ANGEL SIGHTINGS

Wednesday   CHRISTMAS

CHRISTMAS IS THE SEASON FOR ANGELS: angels hovering over nativity scenes, angels crowning Christmas trees. But it doesn't stop with Christmas anymore. Angels are becoming a new fad.

It started in 1975 when Billy Graham penned a book called *Angels: God's Secret Agents*. Then Joan Wester Anderson wrote *Where Angels Walk* which includes a dramatic story told by a woman who was walking alone in a rough section of Brooklyn when she saw a man loitering on the sidewalk ahead. She whispered a quick prayer, then hurried past safely. Afterward she discovered that minutes later, on the same spot, another woman had been brutally attacked.

Stunned, she went to the police station and identified the assailant as the very man she had passed. The man recognized her too. So why hadn't he attacked her? a police officer asked. The man shook his head. "Why would I have bothered with her? She was walking down the street with two big guys, one on each side of her."

The woman felt a little like Elisha's servant when his eyes were opened to the surrounding invisible hosts.

But while Christians are exploring a biblical view of angels, counterfeits are multiplying just as fast. These angels don't sound very much like the ones in Scripture: Stories tell of angels that appear on command, like genies, to change a tire on a deserted road or to make a bus slow down and pick someone up. And these angels never, ever confront or challenge anyone. They make no demands on your behavior or character.

These sound more like the "imaginary guides" of the New Age movement than real angels.

In biblical accounts, the first thing an angel says is, "Don't be afraid." In other words, real angels are a fearsome sight. They are mighty warriors in the great cosmic battle between good and evil.

The Bible calls them ministering spirits, but they are definitely *not* our personal genies.

As angels become a fad lasting beyond Christmas, let's redouble our efforts to make sure people are getting biblical truth, not New Age counterfeits. ▨

HOLIDAY
DREAR

Thursday   CHRISTMAS

T HE HOLIDAY SEASON SEEMS TO BRING out the theologian in everyone. One Christmas, *USA Today* ran an article called "Who Was Jesus?" which portrayed the gospel as a collection of myths and legends. *Newsday* ran an article with a similar theme. So did the *Toronto Star* and *U. S. News and World Report.*

Yet the media virtually ignored a much more interesting story that broke at the same time—and one that *supports* the Bible.

Archaeologists have uncovered two cities within a few miles of Nazareth, where Jesus grew up, which reveal a surprisingly advanced level of culture. Gently scraping away the dust of centuries, archaeologists uncovered jewelry, stoneware dishes, industrial olive presses, and a Roman amphitheater big enough to seat four thousand spectators. Scholars were amazed. Obviously, Nazareth was no backwater village. It was situated in the middle of a cosmopolitan center of culture and commerce.

Nor were Jesus's disciples ragged, rustic wanderers. They were small-business owners with considerable economic savvy, engaged in trade with far-off cities. Galilee, it turns out, was as sophisticated as any other part of the Roman empire.

This is not the first time archaeologists have added to our historical understanding of the Bible. There was a time when critics said Moses could not have written the Pentateuch, because writing hadn't been invented yet in his day. Then archaeologists discovered that writing was well developed not only in Moses' day but even before *Abraham.* Centuries before Abraham was born, Egypt and Babylonia were filled with schools and libraries. Dictionaries have been dug up written in four languages, compiled for translators.

There was a time when critics cast doubt on the geography of the Bible. For example, the *Encyclopedia Britannica* once referred to the Hittites as "a mythological people mentioned only in the Bible." But today museums overflow with the massive stone statues characteristic of Hittite culture.

Critics once reserved their sharpest skepticism for the early chapters of Genesis, reducing the patriarchs to sheer legend. But today archaeology has shown that Genesis gives a highly accurate description of names, places, trade routes, and customs of patriarchal times.

Of course, there will always be critics. But every time the Bible has been put to the test of history, it has passed with high marks. Like a witness on the stand, it has been cross-examined—and found reliable. ▩

SINK-OR-SWIM FAITH

Friday

MATURING FAITH—FAITH WHICH deepens and grows as we live our Christian life—is not just knowledge, but knowledge acted upon. It is not just belief, but belief lived out—practiced. James said we are to be doers of the Word, not just hearers.

Dietrick Bonhoeffer, the German pastor martyred in a Nazi concentration camp, succinctly stated this crucial interrelationship: "Only he who believes is obedient; only he who is obedient believes."

This may sound like a circular proposition, but many things in life are. Think of learning how to swim. We are told what to do. We gingerly enter the water, launch out, and promptly forget everything we've been told. We flail about, splashing frantically, gasping and sinking. Finally, usually at the point of utter despair, we capture for a moment the sensation of staying afloat. Realizing it is possible, we remember our instructions and begin to follow them. They work.

Like learning to balance a bicycle or mastering a foreign language, faith is a state of mind that *grows out of* our actions, just as it also *governs* them. Obedience is the key to real faith. ▩

TRIED AND
TESTED

Weekend

CRITICS OFTEN DISMISS SCRIPTURE, saying, "It's out of date." The events described there took place thousands of years ago when shepherds tended flocks and primitive tribal customs prevailed. Times change, says the modern relativist; ancient ritual is irrelevant to today's morality.

How semantics influence our values! Words like "progressive" can reverse the rules of logic. This is, the longer historical evidence persists, the less reliable it becomes; the newer the conclusion, the less proven by history, the more "progressive" and—presumably—more appealing it is.

Yes, the biblical account does deal with ancient times, for ancient Israel was the particular place God chose to covenant with His people some twelve hundred years later to enter time and space through Jesus Christ. But God's truth is eternal.

Time passes. Customs change. But truth remains. Absolute, objective truth can never depend on custom, common perceptions, or changing trends. It remains true whether believed or not. 🔅

NOTES

WEEK ONE

1. *Born Again,* (Old Tappan, NJ: Fleming H. Revell Company, by arrangement with Chosen Books, Inc., 1976), pp. 125-126.
2. Ibid., pp. 114-117.
3. Ibid., pp.
4. *Loving God,* (Grand Rapids, MI: Zondervan Publishing House, 1983), pp. 94-95.
5. *Born Again,* pp. 206-207.
6. Ibid., pp. 271-274.

WEEK TWO

1. *The Body,* (Dallas, TX: Word Publishing, 1992), pp. 83-84.
2. *Who Speaks for God?,* (Westchester, IL: Crossway Books, 1985), from the Introduction.
3. *Kingdoms in Conflict,* (Grand Rapids, MI: Zondervan Publishing House, 1987), p. 85.
4. Ibid., p. 69.
5. *Loving God,* pp. 58-59.
6. Ibid., pp. 57-58.

WEEK THREE

1. *Against the Night,* (Ann Arbor, MI: Servant Publications, 1989), pp. 152-153.
2. *Kingdoms in Conflict,* pp. 68-70.
3. *A Dance with Deception,* (Dallas, TX: Word Publishing, 1993), pp. 277-279.
4. *Against the Night,* pp. 149-150.
5. *BreakPoint,* September 20, 1993.
6. *BreakPoint,* January 4, 1994.

WEEK FOUR

1. *Loving God,* pp. 55-56.
2. *BreakPoint,* August 9, 1993.
3. *Born Again,* pp. 122-123.
4. *A Dance with Deception,* pp. 281-283.
5. *BreakPoint,* October 10, 1993.
6. *A Dance with Deception,* pp. 265-266.

WEEK FIVE

1. *BreakPoint,* February 16, 1994.
2. Ibid., August 7, 1993.
3. Ibid., July 15, 1994.
4. Ibid., August 15, 1993.
5. Ibid., February 13, 1994.
6. *A Dance with Deception,* pp. 263-265.

WEEK SIX

1. *The Body,* pp. 275-276.
2. *Against the Night,* pp. 140-141, 147.
3. *Loving God,* pp. 128-129.
4. *A Dance with Deception,* pp. 274-275.
5. *The Body,* pp. 195-196.
6. *BreakPoint,* October 29, 1992.

WEEK SEVEN

1. *The Body,* pp. 99-100.
2. Ibid., pp. 107-108.
3. Ibid., pp. 93-94.
4. Ibid., p. 105.
5. Ibid., pp. 123-124.
6. *Jubilee,* October 1992.

WEEK EIGHT

1. *Against the Night,* pp. 140-142.
2. Ibid., pp. 132-134.
3. Ibid., pp. 139, 159-160.
4. Ibid., pp. 156-157.
5. *Who Speaks for God?,* pp. 73-75.
6. *Jubilee,* June 1991.

WEEK NINE

1. *BreakPoint,* January 19, 1994.
2. *Loving God,* p. 36.
3. *Who Speaks for God?,* pp.30-33.
4. *Christianity Today,* March 3, 1989.
5. *Loving God,* pp. 126-127.
6. Ibid., pp. 131-132.

WEEK TEN

1. Ibid., pp. 133-134.

2. *BreakPoint,* May 15, 1993.
3. *The Body,* pp. 296-299.
4. *Christianity Today,* February 5, 1990.
5. *Who Speaks for God?,* pp. 28-29.
6. *The Body,* pp. 276-278.

WEEK ELEVEN

1. *BreakPoint,* November 17, 1992.
2. *The Body,* pp. 181-182.
3. Ibid., pp. 184-185.
4. *Jubilee International.*
5. *BreakPoint,* February 14, 1993.
6. Ibid., March 16, 1993.

WEEK TWELVE

1. *Life Sentence,* (Tarrytown, NY: Fleming H. Revell Company, 1979; originally published by Chosen Books), pp. 195-197.
2. *Loving God,* p. 192.
3. *The God of Stones and Spiders,* (Ann Arbor, MI: Crossway Books, 1990), pp. 17-19.
4. *Loving God,* p. 172.
5. *The God of Stones and Spiders,* pp. 121-123.
6. *The Body,* pp. 333-334.

WEEK THIRTEEN

1. *BreakPoint,* June 23, 1993.
2. Ibid., February 14, 1994.
3. *Christianity Today,* October 25, 1993.
4. *BreakPoint,* June 2, 1994.
5. *A Dance with Deception,* pp. 153-154.
6. *Christianity Today,* November 9, 1992.

WEEK FOURTEEN

1. *The Body,* p. 225.
2. *The God of Stones and Spiders,* pp. 128-13
3. *BreakPoint,* June 18, 1992.
4. *Loving God,* pp. 121-122.
5. Ibid., pp. 119-120.
6. Ibid., pp. 24-25.

WEEK FIFTEEN

1. *BreakPoint,* June 1, 1994.
2. *A Dance with Deception,* pp. 209-210.
3. *BreakPoint,* September 5, 1993.
4. Ibid., March 18, 1993.

5. Ibid., April 10, 1994.
6. Ibid., March 19, 1993.

WEEK SIXTEEN

1. *BreakPoint,* March 22, 1993.
2. Ibid., March 23, 1993.
3. Ibid., November 3, 1993.
4. Ibid., January 31, 1994.
5. Ibid., March 24, 1993.
6. Ibid., April 14, 1994.

WEEK SEVENTEEN

1. *BreakPoint,* March 31, 1993.
2. Ibid., April 6, 1993.
3. Ibid., March 29, 1993.
4. Ibid., March 30, 1993.
5. Ibid., October 19, 1993.
6. Ibid., June 9, 1993.

WEEK EIGHTEEN

1. *A Dance with Deception,* pp. 224-226.
2. *BreakPoint,* April 7, 1994.
3. Ibid., July 24, 1994.
4. *Kingdoms in Conflict,* pp. 89-90.
5. Ibid., p. 272.
6. Ibid., pp. 274-275.

WEEK NINETEEN

1. Ibid., pp. 270-272.
2. Ibid., pp. 303-305.
3. Ibid., pp. 265-273.
4. Ibid., pp. 109-110, 113.
5. Ibid., pp. 113-114.
6. *BreakPoint,* June 4, 1994.

WEEK TWENTY

1. *Born Again,* pp. 128-129.
2. *Kingdoms in Conflict,* pp. 246-247.
3. Ibid., p. 237.
4. Ibid., pp. 92-93.
5. Ibid., pp. 115-117.
6. Ibid., pp. 84-85.

WEEK TWENTY-ONE

1. *Who Speaks for God?,* pp. 24-25.
2. *Jubilee,* July 1990.
3. *A Dance with Deception,* pp. 135-136.
4. *Jubilee,* April 1994.
5. *A Dance with Deception,* pp. 136-138.
6. *BreakPoint,* December 9, 1993.

WEEK TWENTY-TWO

1. *A Dance with Deception,* pp. 127-128.
2. *Kingdoms in Conflict,* pp. 118-120.
3. Ibid., pp. 120-12
4. *Who Speaks for God?,* pp. 39-4
5. *BreakPoint,* January 14, 1993.
6. Ibid., July 11, 1994.

WEEK TWENTY-THREE

1. *A Dance with Deception,* pp. 62-64.
2. *BreakPoint,* December 4, 1993.
3. Ibid., July 13, 1993.
4. Ibid., June 9, 1994.
5. *Kingdoms in Conflict,* p. 94.
6. Ibid., pp. 47-48.

WEEK TWENTY-FOUR

1. Ibid., pp. 240-24
2. *Jubilee International,* November/ December 1994.
3. *Kingdoms in Conflict,* pp. 279, 29
4. Ibid., pp. 220-222.
5. Ibid., p. 240.
6. *BreakPoint,* May 2, 1993.

WEEK TWENTY-FIVE

1. *A Dance with Deception,* pp. 19-20.
2. "Enduring Revolution," 1993 Templeton Address.
3. *A Dance with Deception,* pp. 145-147.
4. Ibid., pp. 15-16.
5. *BreakPoint,* May 10, 1993.
6. Ibid., May 17, 1994.

WEEK TWENTY-SIX

1. *A Dance with Deception,* pp. 99-10
2. *BreakPoint,* January 22, 1993.
3. *A Dance with Deception,* pp. 240-242.
4. *BreakPoint,* July 7, 1994.
5. *Christianity Today,* December 15, 1989.
6. *BreakPoint,* February 5, 1994.

WEEK TWENTY-SEVEN

1. *BreakPoint,* July 18, 1993.
2. *A Dance with Deception,* pp. 140-14
3. *BreakPoint,* June 10, 1994.
4. *A Dance with Deception,* pp. 250-252.
5. *BreakPoint,* July 7, 1993.
6. Ibid., September 5, 1993.

WEEK TWENTY-EIGHT

1. *A Dance with Deception,* pp. 259-26
2. *BreakPoint,* June 20, 1994.
3. Ibid., June 21, 1994.
4. Ibid., June 22, 1994.
5. Ibid., June 23, 1994.
6. Ibid.

WEEK TWENTY-NINE

1. *BreakPoint,* June 28, 1994.
2. *Convicted* with Dan Van Ness, (Westchester, IL: Crossway Books, 1989), pp. 58-59.
3. *Christianity Today,* April 9, 1990.
4. "Christians and the Media Elite," address to the National Press Club, *Sources* No. 3, given in Washington D. C. on March 11, 1993. pp. 9-10.
5. Ibid., pp. 10-1
6. *BreakPoint,* July 10, 1993.

WEEK THIRTY

1. *BreakPoint,* January 21, 1994.
2. *The Washington Times,* October 1993, winner of the 1993 Amy Foundation Award.
3. *BreakPoint,* March 14, 1994.
4. "Christians and the Media Elite," address to the National Press Club, *Sources* No. 3, given in Washington D. C. on March 11, 1993, pp. 16-17.
5. *BreakPoint,* June 5, 1993.
6. *The Body,* pp. 182-183.

WEEK THIRTY-ONE

1. *BreakPoint,* June 24, 1994.
2. Ibid., March 21, 1994.
3. Ibid., March 17, 1994.
4. Ibid., November 6, 1993.
5. *Justice Report,* Winter 1994.
6. *Christianity Today,* November 22, 1993.

WEEK THIRTY-TWO

1. *Jubilee,* May 1994.
2. *A Dance with Deception,* pp. 177-179.
3. Ibid., pp. 9-10.
4. Ibid., pp. 184-186.
5. Ibid., pp. 173-175.
6. Ibid., pp. 167-168.

WEEK THIRTY-THREE

1. *BreakPoint,* June 17, 1994.
2. Ibid., November 14, 1993.
3. Ibid., November 15, 1993.
4. Ibid., November 16, 1993.
5. Ibid., November 17, 1993.
6. Ibid., November 19, 1993.

WEEK THIRTY-FOUR

1. *BreakPoint,* February 5, 1993.
2. Ibid., April 2, 1994.
3. *Why America Doesn't Work,* (Dallas, TX: Word Publishing, 1991), pp. 91-92.
4. *BreakPoint,* June 4, 1993.
5. *A Dance with Deception,* pp. 44-46.
6. *BreakPoint,* February 2, 1993.

WEEK THIRTY-FIVE

1. *BreakPoint,* August 13, 1993.
2. Ibid., February 25 1993.
3. *Born Again,* pp. 282-284.
4. *Jubilee International,* September/October 1984.
5. *Loving God,* pp. 40-4
6. *Christianity Today,* December 11, 1987.

WEEK THIRTY-SIX

1. *BreakPoint,* October 24, 1993.
2. *Convicted,* pp. 49-50.
3. *The God of Stones and Spiders,* pp. 193-194.
4. *BreakPoint,* March 11, 1994.
5. Ibid., May 23, 1993.
6. *Justice Report,* Summer 1991.

WEEK THIRTY-SEVEN

1. *BreakPoint,* July 15, 1993.
2. Ibid., December 16, 1993.
3. Ibid., June 21, 1994.
4. Ibid., August 3, 1993.
5. *The God of Stones and Spiders,* pp. 209-21
6. *BreakPoint,* March 23, 1994.

WEEK THIRTY-EIGHT

1. *The God of Stones and Spiders,* p. 186.
2. Ibid., pp. 178-180.

3. "Enduring Revolution," 1993 Templeton Address.
4. *The Body,* pp. 192-194.
5. *Against the Night,* p. 165.
6. *The Body,* pp. 191-192.

WEEK THIRTY-NINE

1. Ibid., pp. 360-36
2. *Life Sentence,* pp. 147-149.
3. *Kingdoms in Conflict,* pp. 87-88.
4. *Jubilee International,* September/October 1984.
5. *BreakPoint,* July 13, 1994.
6. *BreakPoint,* July 21, 1993.

WEEK FORTY

1. *BreakPoint,* February 7, 1994.
2. Ibid., February 3, 1994.
3. *Christianity Today,* January 10, 1994.
4. *BreakPoint,* August 22, 1993.
5. *A Dance with Deception,* pp. 92-93.
6. *BreakPoint*

WEEK FORTY-ONE

1. *Against the Night,* pp. 170-174.
2. *A Dance with Deception,* p. 40.
3. *BreakPoint,* January 28, 1993.
4. Ibid., August 10, 1993.
5. *A Dance with Deception,* pp. 43-44.
6. *BreakPoint,* June 14, 1993.

WEEK FORTY-TWO

1. *BreakPoint,* June 15, 1993.
2. Ibid., July 3, 1994.
3. *Jubilee,* February 199
4. *A Dance with Deception,* pp. 103-104.
5. *BreakPoint,* June 6, 1994.
6. *Against the Night,* pp. 79-82.

WEEK FORTY-THREE

1. *A Dance with Deception,* pp. 30-32.
2. *BreakPoint,* February 17, 1993.
3. Ibid., February 9, 1993.
4. Ibid., February 12, 1993.
5. Ibid., September 17, 1993.
6. *A Dance with Deception,* pp. 39-4

WEEK FORTY-FOUR

1. Ibid., pp. 27-29.

2. Ibid., pp. 36-37.
3. *The Body,* p. 367.
4. *Jubilee,* April 1988.
5. *A Dance with Deception,* pp. 48-50.
6. *BreakPoint,* July 11, 1993.

WEEK FORTY-FIVE

1. *A Dance with Deception,* pp. 55-57.
2. *BreakPoint,* May 11, 1994.
3. Ibid., June 11, 1993.
4. *A Dance with Deception,* pp. 149-15
5. Ibid., pp. 53-55.
6. *BreakPoint,* March 17, 1994

WEEK FORTY-SIX

1. *Christianity Today,* June 20, 1994.
2. *BreakPoint,* May 19, 1994.
3. Ibid., July 8, 1993.
4. *Kingdoms in Conflict,* pp. 91-92.
5. Ibid., pp. 74-85.
6. "The Crisis of Truth," January 29, 1994, Speech to the National Religious Broadcasters.

WEEK FORTY-SEVEN

1. *A Dance with Deception,* pp. 75-76.
2. *BreakPoint,* March 22, 1993.
3. *A Dance with Deception,* pp. 73-74.
4. Ibid., January 20, 1994.
5. Ibid., January 12, 1993.
6. Ibid., March 4, 1993.

WEEK FORTY-EIGHT

1. *A Dance with Deception,* pp. 71-73.
2. *BreakPoint,* December 12, 1993.
3. Ibid., July 23, 1993.

4. Ibid., June 1, 1994.
5. Ibid., December 21, 1993.
6. Ibid., December 20, 1993.

WEEK FORTY-NINE

1. *A Dance with Deception,* pp. 111-112.
2. *BreakPoint,* December 19, 1993.
3. *A Dance with Deception,* pp. 123-125.
4. *BreakPoint,* January 29, 1993.
5. *A Dance with Deception,* pp. 121-123.
6. *Why America Doesn't Work,* pp. 93-94.

WEEK FIFTY

1. *Why America Doesn't Work,* pp. 34-35.
2. Ibid., pp. 35-37.
3. Ibid., pp. 38-39.
4. *A Dance with Deception,* pp. 17-18.
5. *BreakPoint,* December 6, 199
6. *Why America Doesn't Work,* pp. 177-178.

WEEK FIFTY-ONE

1. *A Dance with Deception,* pp. 125-127.
2. *BreakPoint,* July 22, 1994.
3. *Who Speaks for God?,* pp. 58-60.
4. *A Dance with Deception,* pp. 61-64.
5. *BreakPoint,* September 19, 1993.
6. Ibid., December 25, 1991.

WEEK FIFTY-TWO

1. *BreakPoint,* February 21, 1994.
2. *Jubilee,* December 1992.
3. *BreakPoint,* February 20, 1994.
4. Ibid., January 14, 1993.
5. *Loving God,* p. 37.
6. Ibid., pp. 72-73.

INDEX